CONCEIVED in Liberty

CONCEIVED in Liberty

Volume V
The New Republic, 1784–1791

Murray N. Rothbard

Edited by
Patrick Newman

Foreword by
Judge Andrew P. Napolitano

Preface by
Thomas E. Woods, Jr.

MISES INSTITUTE
AUBURN, ALABAMA

Published 2019 by the Mises Institute. This work is licensed under a Creative Commons Attribution-NonCommercial-NoDerivs 4.0 International License.
http://creativecommons.org/licenses/by-nc-nd/4.0/

Mises Institute
518 West Magnolia Ave.
Auburn, Ala. 36832
mises.org

ISBN: 978-1-61016-719-2

Liberty, the greatest of all earthly blessings—give us that precious jewel, and you may take every thing else! But I am fearful I have lived long enough to become an old-fashioned fellow. ... Twenty-three years ago was I supposed a traitor to my country? I was then said to be the bane of sedition, because I supported the rights of my country. I may be thought suspicious when I say our privileges and rights are in danger. ... Guard with jealous attention the public liberty. Suspect every one who approaches that jewel. Unfortunately, nothing will preserve it but downright force. Whenever you give up that force, you are inevitably ruined. ... Consider what you are about to do before you part with the government. Take longer time in reckoning things; revolutions like this have happened in almost every country in Europe; similar examples are to be found in ancient Greece and ancient Rome—instances of the people losing their liberty by their own carelessness and the ambition of a few.

~ Patrick Henry, 1788

The meeting at Philadelphia in 1787 for the sole and express purpose of revising the Articles of Confederation, got the name of a Convention (I believe before long that of a Conspiracy would have been more Significant), [and] paid no more regard to their orders and credentials than Caesar when he passed the Rubicon. Under an Injunction of Secrecy they carried on their works of Darkness until the Constitution passed their usurping hands.

~ Abraham Yates, 1789

Contents

Foreword

When Professor Patrick Newman first asked me to write the Foreword to his painstakingly and brilliantly crafted fifth volume of Murray N. Rothbard's iconic *Conceived in Liberty*, I had two initial reactions. The first was "What fifth volume?" By now, the reader knows that Rothbard wrote the guts of volume five by hand and Professor Newman—who, in addition to his economic expertise, is now an expert in Rothbard's unique handwriting—"translated" it all for us.

My second reaction was my perceived need to re-read the first four volumes in order to do justice to a foreword to the fifth. This was a happy task and one that refreshed my memory from having read the first four volumes shortly after my graduation from law school. I wish they had been available to me when I was studying colonial American history under the late Professor Wesley Frank Craven at Princeton University. Just as Rothbard's work on the Progressive Era was not appreciated by my Princeton professors, his work on the colonial era would have been treated similarly.

Yet the *Conceived in Liberty* that we all have known is quite simply the most thorough recitation and analysis of the events, forces, and personalities leading up to and triumphing in the American Revolution that has ever been written in the English language. The research is so prodigious that it eclipses even academia's favorite versions of these events, Lawrence Henry Gipson's *The British Empire Before the*

American Revolution (1936) and Gordon S. Wood's *The Creation of the American Republic* (1969).

Professor Craven, a white southern liberal, with commendable disdain for his slave-owning forbearers, gave all the credit for all the good in American society not to personal liberty but to the post-Civil War federal government. He instilled that awe—or attempted to—in his students. Rothbard, of course, saw the battle for secession from Great Britain as a classic one of Liberty versus Power. It is through that lens that he created in 1,600 pages the four-volume masterpiece with which all who love the early history of American liberty should generally be familiar.

The fourth volume ends with the adoption of the Articles of Confederation, and numerous descriptions of the chicanery that brought about this "halfway house to central government," as only Rothbard could have called it. Yet, the pages of volumes one through four recount basically a happy story: A story that ends with the unambiguous triumph of Liberty over Power; and, but for that halfway house which followed, a story of the most just war in the history of the western world.

There is little joy in volume five.

Volume five recounts the counterrevolution that culminates in the halfway house becoming a jail for Liberty, and a triumph for Power. It shows that some of the heroes of the first four volumes became conservative corporatists, power hungry politicians, and even central bankers yearning for big government to enrich them, and utilizing the Constitution as their instrument for that enrichment.

Rothbard's incredible ability to absorb information is as apparent in volume five just as it was in his first four. He read everything. He will tell you, for example, not only the views of the major delegates to the Constitutional Convention—and how victory over Great Britain altered those views—but the opinions of the principal participants to all the state ratification conventions as well. Rothbard's powers of analysis and synthesis account for the book's freshness. As Tom Woods points out in his fascinating and insightful preface to this volume, Rothbard often was able to anticipate historiography, owing to the depth of his learning and the powers of his analysis.

Rothbard sets the stage for the secret drafting and unscrupulous ratification of the Constitution by analyzing the economic impact and legacy of the immediate aftermath of the American Revolution—a time when Americans finally became freed from the shackles of British mercantilism and, for the first time, could trade freely with the rest of the world. Any economist or historian will appreciate the backdrop Rothbard provides of the postwar period, as he sheds light on the boom-bust cycle of bank credit expansion and contraction that occurred, which eventually brought about a depression in mid-1784 and 1785. Such conditions set the stage for state protective tariffs and monopolies, which by 1786, Rothbard explains, virtually every state had enacted.

In fascinating detail, Rothbard then describes the early struggle between the states to determine whether a strong central government was an attractive goal or a future disaster. Rothbard lays out the inner negotiations within each state and between the states on important issues such as congressional taxing power versus state control of proposed imposts. He moves on to the burdens of state debt, the issuance of paper money, as well as an analysis of the banking difficulties in the early post-Revolutionary Era. Interestingly, Rothbard dispels the common myth that identified proponents of inflation with "farmer-debtors" and hard-money men as "merchant-creditors" by explaining that merchants were even more likely than farmers to be heavily in debt since they had better credit ratings and could borrow more.

He discusses Congress' difficulties in paying its bills and its inability to enact any impost; it was even unable to pay the interest on its debts to its American and foreign creditors. As a result, by the end of 1786, the nationalist push for a new central government was in full swing. Congress had failed to aggrandize itself into the dominant power. It could not achieve a federal navigation act or more importantly a federal impost for its own source of tax revenue.

At the same time, Rothbard unpacks the expansion of the new country into western lands as well as the foreign policy accompanying that expansion. Starting with the passage of its Ordinance of 1784, and later of 1785, Congress had nationalized the public domains and pledged itself to allow full self-government to any settlers of new territory whenever the territory should amass a population of 20,000 or more. In those settled areas with fewer than 20,000, there was no central government reach! Rothbard contrasts Thomas Jefferson's highly liberal Ordinance with the disdain felt by greatly inconvenienced land speculation companies, which lobbied and paved the way for the Northwest Ordinance, replacing settler self-government with territorial government in the hands of Congress and corporatists.

Meanwhile, in the Southwest, the Spanish claim, by conquest and occupation, was in fact far more tenable and moral than that of America, which had sent no settlers there. Nevertheless, Rothbard describes the flood of migration westward, and in turn, the drive by persons of these regions—this is how Kentucky seceded from Virginia—for independence and statehood. He details reasons for the sharp North-South sectional split on the western issue, and of course on slavery, rapidly disappearing in the northern states but still rampant in the South.

Rothbard rejects the commonly held view that America needed a stronger national government than the Articles of Confederation allowed. To the contrary, he maintains that the Articles gave too much power to the central government. In particular, he stresses the dangers of a standing army. This is a lesson lovers of liberty should bear in mind today: "The Continental Army had disbanded with the advent of peace, and the states would not stand for such a gross assumption of central power as a peacetime standing army. But Congress evaded this clear policy by creating a temporary western force, made up of militia from several states [under congressional control] interested in grabbing the Northwest."[1]

What aroused the fears of those who sought through the Constitution to establish a strong national government? In part, the nationalists were afraid of tax resistance. Rothbard details the key libertarian uprising in Massachusetts, Shays' Rebellion, a revolt against excessive burdens on the taxpayer for the benefit of public creditors, mainly eastern merchant-speculators who had purchased the state's debt at a great discount. Oppressed by taxes and frustrated by the imprisonment of those who could not pay them, mobs throughout western Massachusetts and their supporters seized courthouses and closed the courts until a redress of the people's grievances were achieved. Why the courthouses? Because that's where creditors went to find friendly judges and secure orders to seize debtors' properties and imprison the debtors themselves;

---

[1]See below, p. 90.

and that's where the state government pursued those who could not pay their taxes.

But this outburst of anarchist freedom had a counter-reaction. Shays' Rebellion conservatized many state leaders who felt that the state governments and the Confederation were too weak to prevent such tax uprisings from recurring. Rothbard expertly demonstrates that such events served to spur nationalist sentiment by providing fuel for demagogic attacks about the dangers of weak government under the Confederation.

> True, democracy may be turbulent, as presumably in the Shays episode, "But weigh this against the oppression of monarchy, and it becomes nothing ... [and] even this evil is productive of good. It prevents the degeneracy of government and nourishes a general attention to the public affairs. ... It is a medicine necessary for the sound health of government."[2]

Urban merchants and artisans, as well as many slaveholding planters, came together in support of a strong nation-state that would use the coercive power of a distant central government to grant them privileges and subsidies. With such a backing, nationalist forces were able to execute a political *coup d'état* which illegally liquidated the Articles of Confederation and replaced it with the Constitution.

James Madison of all people—the scrivener of the Constitution and, later, the author of the Bill of Rights, the Federalist Framer who would become an Antifederalist president—began this *coup* when he pushed through the Virginia legislature a "proposal for a convention of commissioners from *all* states to provide for uniform commercial regulations and for 'the requisite augmentation of the power of Congress over trade.'"[3] Madison was so cautious about what he was really planning for Philadelphia in the summer of 1787 that he revealed his true objectives only to his close personal friends. What were those plans? Not enhanced commercial arrangements, but instead the beginning of radical political reform. Rothbard explains that Madison called for an all-state convention in Philadelphia, to propose a comprehensive

---

[2]See below, pp. 125–26.
[3]See below, p. 131.

revision of the Articles of Confederation so as "to render the Constitution of the Federal Government adequate to the exigencies of the Union."[4] He sounded here more like his successor Woodrow Wilson than his one day predecessor Thomas Jefferson.

The Constitutional Convention opened on May 25, 1787 in Philadelphia, and Rothbard methodically traces each topic of discussion and breaks down the debates between the major players, recounting their impassioned speeches and fascinating back-and-forth. He focuses on the recommendations from each of the state delegations regarding all the basic attributes of the Constitution that would form the basis of the nascent central government.

In particular, Madison and the Virginians meant political revolution rather than reform of the Articles of Confederation. They had wanted "not a 'merely federal' union, but a *national* government … consisting of a *supreme* judicial, legislative, and executive.'"[5] We learn that these revelations, to many, like Charles Cotesworth Pinckney of South Carolina and Elbridge Gerry of Massachusetts, were "illegal, revolutionary, and violated the express instructions of Congress."[6] But nevertheless, eventually, those delegates who attended the Convention agreed on certain broad objectives, crucial for a new government, and designed to remodel the United States into a country with the British political structure; albeit, contrary to Alexander Hamilton's wishes, without a monarchy.

Yet another crucially important point to settle was the procedure for ratification of the Constitution—submit the new Constitution to the state legislatures or to *ad hoc* popular state conventions? Not only does Rothbard detail the debate over the procedure, he then goes into detail about the negotiations and compromises that occurred behind the scenes to get the deal done—by bypassing the state legislatures.

Ultimately, we see that the nationalists, though forced to make a few concessions, carried the substance of their program: The creation of a supreme national government, supreme national judiciary with inferior courts established by Congress and appointed by the president all for

---

[4]See below, p. 132.
[5]See below, p. 147.
[6]See below, p. 147.

life terms, and a bicameral Congress, with the lower house elected by those people who were permitted to vote.

The process was not, however, without its flaws. Rothbard identifies two deep failures of the Constitution from the standpoint of liberty. First, of course, "slavery was ... driven into the heart of the Constitution: in the three-fifths clause, in the protection of slave importation for twenty years, in the fugitive slave clause, and even in the congressional power to suppress insurrections within the states."[7] Citing Luther Martin, Rothbard notes that:

> the American Constitution was a grave betrayal of the idea of natural rights set forth in the Declaration of Independence. The Revolution, Martin strikingly declared, was grounded in defense of the natural, God-given rights possessed by all mankind, but the Constitution was an "*insult to that God ...* who views with equal eye the poor *African slave* and his *American master.*"[8]

Second, the Constitution sent to the states for ratification failed to include a bill of rights—a prohibition against governmental interference with personal liberty. Although "libertarian restraints were placed on state powers, no bill of rights existed to check the federal government."[9]

In the meantime, beyond the Convention, Rothbard takes us behind the scenes of the ratifications by recounting the paper battles between the Federalists and Antifederalists in the streets. He focuses on the dissemination of information, the control of the newspapers and the monopoly over the post office, and in doing so, provides intriguing insight into the massive propaganda campaigns, such as the fact that "letters between nationalists of Virginia and New York regularly took six to fourteen days to arrive, [while] mail between Antifederalist leaders in the two states often took six to ten weeks to get through."[10] All in all, Federalist control of the press meant not only the spreading of

---

[7]See below, p 197.

[8]See below, pp. 197–98.

[9]See below, pp. 211–12.

[10]See below, p. 216.

their own propaganda and the suppression of opposition articles, but that they were free to dictate the news at will—and this they did as they sought to drum up support for the Constitution.

Rothbard takes us through the ratifications, state by state, county by county, with a who's who of the different factions for and against the proposed Constitution. From the initial setback in New Hampshire, to the battle for states like Massachusetts, New York, and Virginia, and even the hold out of tiny Rhode Island, Rothbard lays out the inner dialogue between citizens of each state (from seaboard merchants to backcountry farmers), as well as detailing the influence of bribery and back room dark dealing amongst politicians who had weaknesses that were exploited by their opponents. As the debate proceeded around the country, even the reluctant Madison finally realized that the Federalists would have to agree to a bill of rights, not as a condition of ratification, but as a corollary recommendation.

In my work, I have emphasized that we do not get our rights from the government; our rights come from our humanity. The Constitution limits what government can do, not what the people can do. Our rights are just that—inalienable claims to personal liberty—not favors that the government doles out to us.

Rothbard defends this position with great force. He notes that Madison would become the reluctant author of the Bill of Rights. He was a strong nationalist and didn't want the government to be limited. But he thought that a bill of rights would head off the call of the Antifederalists for a second constitutional convention by offering concessions.

Madison's deft maneuvering succeeded in securing the ratification of the Constitution in Virginia, a matter Rothbard obviously regrets. Nevertheless, he praises the Bill of Rights:

> Of the twelve amendments submitted to the states, the first two were not ratified; these were minor provisions dealing with the organization of Congress. The remaining ten amendments composed nine highly significant articles guaranteeing various personal liberties against the federal government, as well as one complementary structural amendment. None of the political and economic liberties desired by the Antifederalists (prohibition of direct taxes, standing army, two-thirds requirement for laws regulating commerce, etc.) were included, but

the adopted bill of rights was significant enough, and all of their provisions were intensely libertarian.[11]

Rothbard goes on to summarize the Bill of Rights, but he does more than this. He makes insightful remarks about each of the amendments. For example, he comments on the Second Amendment:

> The Second Amendment guaranteed that "the right of the people to keep and bear Arms, shall not be infringed." While the courts have enumerated the clause to apply only to Congress, leaving the states free to invade this right, the wording makes it clear that the right "shall not be infringed," period. Since states are mentioned in the body of the Constitution and restrictions placed upon them there as well, this clause evidently also applies to the states. Indeed, the subsequent amendments (three to nine) apply to the states as well as to the federal government; only the First Amendment specifically restricts Congress alone. And yet the courts have emasculated the amendments in the same way, counting them as not applying to the invasions of personal liberty by the states.[12]

No reader of *Conceived in Liberty* could miss the fact that Rothbard usually supported the states over the central government and personal liberty over all government. To me, the highlight of the entire volume was what Rothbard says about the Ninth Amendment. He first recognizes how nationalist judges derailed the Tenth Amendment's limits on the power of the central government:

> This amendment did in truth transform the Constitution from one of supreme national power to a partially mixed polity where the liberal anti-nationalists had a constitutional argument with at least a fighting chance of acceptance. However, Madison had cunningly left out the word "expressly" before the word "delegated," so the nationalist judges were able to claim that because the word "expressly" was not there, the "delegated" can vaguely accrue through judges' elastic interpretation of the Constitution. This loophole for vague "delegated"

---

[11]See below, p. 301.
[12]See below, pp. 301–02.

power allowed the national courts to use such open-ended claims as general welfare, commerce, national supremacy, and necessary and proper to argue for almost any delegation of power that is not specifically prohibited to the federal government—in short, to return the Constitution basically to what it was before the Tenth Amendment was passed. The Tenth Amendment has been intensely reduced, by conventional judiciary construction, to a meaningless tautology.[13]

Rothbard goes on to highlight what I regard as the decisive point in the entire Bill of Rights:

Ironically, the most potentially explosive weapon of the anti-nationalists was ignored then and for the next 175 years by the public and the courts. This was the Ninth Amendment, which states: "The enumeration in the Constitution, of certain rights, shall not be construed to deny or disparage others retained by the people." With its stress on the *rights* of the people, rather than on state or federal *power* as in the Tenth Amendment, the Ninth Amendment is even more acutely the answer to the [James] Wilson argument than the Tenth. The *enumeration* of rights may not be so construed as to *deny* other unenumerated rights retained by the people.

The Ninth Amendment has unfortunately (a) erroneously been held to apply *only* to the federal government and not also to the states, and (b) has been reduced to a simple paraphrase of the Tenth Amendment by the courts. But then why have a Ninth Amendment that simply repeats the Tenth? In truth, the Ninth Amendment is very different, and no construction can reduce it to a tautology; unlike the formulaic Tenth Amendment, the Ninth emphatically *asserts* that there *are* rights which are retained by the people and *therefore* may not be infringed upon by *any* area of government. But if there *are* unenumerated rights, this means that it is the constitutional *obligation* of the courts to find, proclaim, and protect them. Moreover, it means that it is *unconstitutional* for the courts to allow a government infringement on *any* right of the

---

[13]See below, pp. 302–03.

individual on the grounds that no express prohibition of that act can be found in the Constitution.[14]

In response to the famous dictum of Justice Holmes dissenting in *Lochner v. New York* (1905) that "The Fourteenth Amendment does not enact Mr. Herbert Spencer's *Social Statics*," Rothbard says:

> The Ninth Amendment is an open invitation—nay, a command—to the people to discover and protect the unenumerated rights and never to allow governmental invasion of rights on the ground that no express prohibition can be found. ...
>
> Moreover, if it is asked what "other rights" were intended, the context of the time dictates but one answer: they meant the "natural rights" held by every human being. But a commandment that the courts are duty-bound to protect all of man's natural rights, enumerated or retained, would reduce the powerful scope of government action to such a degree as to give the last laugh to Herbert Spencer over Justice Oliver Wendell Holmes.[15]

Toward the end of this work, Murray Rothbard wrote that the spirit of "the American Revolution was liberal, democratic, and quasi-anarchistic; for decentralization, free markets, and individual liberty; for natural rights of life, liberty, and property; against monarchy, mercantilism, and especially against strong central government."[16]

In a myriad of ways, many seemingly irreversible without bloodshed, and all in the name of the Constitution, that spirit has been negated.

Andrew P. Napolitano
New York City
June 2019

---

[14]See below, p. 303.

[15]See below, pp. 303–04.

[16]See below, pp. 307–08.

Preface

I have lost track of how many volumes of new material by Murray N. Rothbard have been released since his death in the early days of 1995. Rothbard has achieved in death more scholarly output than many scholars can hope for in a lifetime.

The reader can learn about the background to this volume and the *Conceived in Liberty* series as a whole in Patrick Newman's capable introduction. How this book finally came to light after its recovery had seemed hopeless—Rothbard's indecipherable handwriting an apparently insuperable stumbling block—makes for a delightful story.

When I got my hands on the manuscript for volume five of *Conceived in Liberty*, I did something unusual: I skipped ahead immediately to Rothbard's treatment of Shays' Rebellion. Historians got this one wrong for a very long time. The correct understanding had to wait for 2002, with the release of *Shays' Rebellion: The American Revolution's Final Battle*, by Leonard Richards.

For obvious reasons, most people who participate in political rebellions do not go out of their way to keep records of their involvement. It turns out that Shays' Rebellion was a rare exception: participants were required to sign loyalty oaths, which were kept on record. Richards found these records, and used them to learn about the people involved: their towns, their families, their debt level (if any), and so on.

What he found: historians' standard morality play of Shays' Rebellion—that it was a revolt of desperate debtors against their creditor tormentors—was false. More than anything else, the Rebellion had been a tax revolt.

So I had to know: what was Rothbard's interpretation of this event?

Answer: Rothbard managed to intuit the true nature of Shays' Rebellion even without the benefit of this later research. It was not a revolt of debtors, he declared, but rather a tax revolt—precisely what everyone else had to wait until 2002 to discover.

I was astonished—though, having read Rothbard for decades now, not altogether surprised.

Rothbard found that the program of the rebels was, for the most part, a libertarian one. He likewise observed that a great many wealthy people, not in debt, took part in the rebellion, which further undermined the cartoon version that was to be found in school textbooks.

So when readers encounter in these pages Rothbard's treatment of this episode, I hope this historiographical background will enhance their appreciation of the author's cogency and insight.

This was hardly unusual for Rothbard, I might add, who had a knack for seeing through the cartoonish narratives that dominate the standard tale of American history. In his work on nineteenth-century monetary history, for example, he was aghast at scholars who thought the fight over money and banking could be reduced to agrarians who hated banking *per se* versus wise industrialists who understood and appreciated it, or that it was "capitalists" who favored national banks that enjoyed government privilege.

A glance at the treatises of the great opponents of national banks made clear that they were supporters of hard money who favored as little government involvement in money and banking as possible. It wasn't that they opposed banking *per se*. They opposed inflationist banking, which they (correctly) believed led to the boom-bust cycle. *These*, and not the cronies who wanted privileged, inflationist banks, were the genuine capitalists. Hence it was the hard-money, sound-banking Jeffersonians, and not the special-privilege, often inflationist Hamiltonians, with whom supporters of *laissez-faire* should sympathize —the very opposite of how the uncomprehending textbook treatment (which portrays Hamilton as the very embodiment of "capitalism") would have it.

In the present volume, therefore, we should not be surprised to find Rothbard berating historian Bray Hammond for falling precisely into this error in his coverage of the Bank of North America, and failing even to consider the economic arguments of the bank's opponents. For Hammond, it is enough to describe them as "agrarians," and leave the impression that their complaints about the bank were merely political rather than economic.

Of course, a substantial portion of this book involves the drafting and ratification of the Constitution, which the eminent Judge Napolitano, in his foreword, commented on. Instead, allow me simply to point out how rare it is to encounter a volume in which the ratification of the Constitution is treated as something other than a great triumph, with the events leading up to it carrying a glorious inevitability.

Schoolchildren are duly informed that the situation under the Articles of Confederation was untenable, and that the Constitution established a superior system in its place. This is obviously a matter of opinion, but it is presented essentially as fact in every textbook and classroom in America.

Of course, even if every accusation against the Articles were true, someone might still note that the Constitution has had its own share of problems. It has allowed (as in, been unable to prevent) such overwhelming enormities in the ensuing two and a half centuries, as government has grown to levels unimaginable to everyone at the ratification debates and positively unthinkable under the Articles, that perhaps by comparison the Articles may not have been so bad after all.

No such arguments are to be heard, except from the occasional libertarian gadfly.

I once heard Rothbard say he never earned much money from his books. Unlike the right-wing radio hosts who earn small fortunes year after year churning out volumes of no significance at all, Rothbard wrote for the ages. He was building an intellectually fulfilled libertarian movement. For Rothbard that meant foundational works of economics, history, and philosophy.

The release of volume five of *Conceived in Liberty*, assumed to be lost to the world forever, is an occasion for rejoicing, if somewhat surreal:

Rothbard's familiar voice here returns to us from beyond the grave. May it not only inform us, but also inspire us, especially our rising young people, to carry on the libertarian project Rothbard began.

Thomas E. Woods, Jr.
Orlando, Florida
April 2019

Introduction

The prolific Murray Rothbard (1926–1995) worked on four major treatises during his life. The first, *Man, Economy, and State with Power and Market*, was a three-volume work on economic theory written in the 1950s and published in 1962 and 1970. The second, *Conceived in Liberty*, was a four-volume series on early American history largely written in the 1960s and published throughout the 1970s (1975, 1976, and 1979). The third, *The Ethics of Liberty*, was a single volume on the political philosophy of natural rights libertarianism written mainly in the 1970s and published in 1982. The final treatise, *An Austrian Perspective on the History of Economic Thought*, was a projected three-volume work (only two were completed) on the history of economics written in the 1980s and published posthumously in 1995.[1] Each project covered a massive amount of material and was influential in the Austrian and libertarian movement of the mid-to-late twentieth century and cemented Rothbard's status as a legitimate scholar in

---

[1]Murray Rothbard, *Man, Economy, and State: A Treatise on Economic Principles*, 2 vols. (Princeton, NJ: D. Van Nostrand, 1962, 1962) and *Power and Market: Government and the Economy* (Menlo Park, CA: Institute for Humane Studies, 1970); *Conceived in Liberty*, 4 vols. (New Rochelle, NY: Arlington House Publishers, 1975, 1975, 1976, 1979); *The Ethics of Liberty* (Atlantic Highlands, NJ: Humanities Press, 1982); *An Austrian Perspective on the History of Economic Thought*, 2 vols. (Brookfield, VT: Edward Elgar, 1995, 1995).

the respective field of research. However, the project that had the least impact in both the aforementioned community as well as the broader academy was undoubtedly *Conceived in Liberty*.

Conceived in Liberty analyzed early American history up to the end of the American Revolutionary War from a libertarian perspective. *Volume I—A New Land, A New People: The American Colonies in the Seventeenth Century* covered everything from the discovery of the New World up to the early 1700s. *Volume II—"Salutary Neglect": The American Colonies in the First Half of the Eighteenth Century* carried the narrative of the thirteen colonies through the French and Indian War (1754–1763). *Volume III—Advance to Revolution, 1760–1775* described the tumultuous events that brought about the American Revolution (1775–1783), and *Volume IV—The Revolutionary War, 1774–1784* engaged in a military, political, and economic analysis of that secession from Great Britain. The project grew out of a research grant awarded in the 1960s to write a text on American history. The four volumes totaled over 1,600 pages in length and remarkably covered only a fraction of Rothbard's output and research interests. What makes it even more astonishing is that Rothbard not only wrote the four published volumes, but also an unpublished fifth volume that finished the series. While the fourth volume ended with the American Revolution and the unshackling of the thirteen colonies from British mercantilism, *Volume V—The New Republic, 1784–1791* carried the narrative through the adoption of the U.S. Constitution when the thirteen states were shackled with a new domestic mercantilism.

To paraphrase a statement from Rothbard's preface to each of his four volumes: "What! Another Rothbard book? The reader may be pardoned for wondering about the possibility of another addition to the seemingly inexhaustible flow of books and texts from Murray Rothbard."[2] Rothbard was an enormously productive writer and

---

[2] Rothbard's statement was "What! Another American history book? The reader may be pardoned for wondering about the point of another addition to the seemingly inexhaustible flow of books and texts on American history." Murray Rothbard, *Conceived in Liberty*, 4 vols. (Auburn, AL: Mises Institute, 2011), p. xv; vols. 1 and 2, p. 9; vols. 3 and 4, p. 11. The original *Conceived in Liberty* volumes were published in individual editions. Page numbers to the earlier individual editions will follow page numbers to the 2011 all-in-one edition.

published extensively during his life, but since his sudden death in 1995 there has been a stream of new Rothbard books and papers, the most recent being an unpublished and unfinished work from the late 1970s on late-nineteenth- and early-twentieth-century American history titled *The Progressive Era*.[3] Unlike that book, Rothbard actually finished the fifth volume of *Conceived in Liberty*. However, also unlike that book, Rothbard largely handwrote the fifth volume, and since his handwriting is largely indecipherable for most people, it remained dormant. At long last, it is published here for the first time to complete the series.

This editor's introduction provides the important background and context for *Volume V—The New Republic, 1784–1791*. It describes Rothbard's historical approach and the themes he emphasized, and a brief narrative of the *Conceived in Liberty* series. This is done in order to explain why Rothbard's history is unique and what is important in the fifth volume as well as *Conceived in Liberty* as a whole.

1. The Rothbardian Approach to History

Murray Rothbard was an expert American historian who often constructed an overarching narrative that not only presented the important facts but also analyzed the motivations and ideologies of relevant individuals. This was because Rothbard was both a formal student of the noted institutional economist Joseph Dorfman and heavily steeped in the works of Ludwig von Mises. Rothbard adhered to Mises's economic analysis (praxeology) and his historical analysis (thymology). Whereas praxeology refers to the logical implications of human action, thymology refers to understanding human motivations behind individual actions. In the science of history, or the study of past human actions, understanding motivations is crucial. The good historian needs to not only unearth unknown and neglected facts and use them to craft a narrative, but also to understand why humans behaved the way they did. This is especially relevant when it comes to investigating the history of government policy where a serious understanding of the motives of the relevant actors (e.g., policymakers and politicians) is often neglected by

---

[3]Murray Rothbard, *The Progressive Era*, ed. Patrick Newman (Auburn, AL: Mises Institute, 2017).

assuming that they act in the public interest.[4] Rothbard went beyond Mises by applying the thymological approach to a wide range of empirical topics, particularly in American history. In fact, Rothbard's vast theoretical writings were actually a smaller fraction of his output than his historical work.[5]

There are two common characteristics that underlie Rothbard's American history, which, when combined together, make it unlike any other. They are his rich detail and his libertarian perspective. Regarding the first, Rothbard never shied away from presenting a vast array of unknown facts about individuals, organizations, and events that are significant for understanding motivations and consequences of important human actions. Anyone who has read a Rothbard history can attest to the sheer mass of information presented and how Rothbard always had some important and underappreciated detail for the topic at hand. Rothbard always wanted these oft-neglected facts—such as an individual's familial and business history, unknown and obscure libertarian thinkers, or new

---

[4]Motivations are also neglected and underappreciated in economic history to the extent that they are derived from the empirical outcomes of an action or policy, which in the modern era is almost always a statistical and heavily quantitative approach. This procedure of deriving motivations from results assumes that people never err and that the outcome is always the intended result. Historical analysis needs appropriate psychologizing from relevant private remarks, personal relationships, public speeches, and so on in order to discover why individuals acted the way they did.

For more on the thymological approach and Rothbard's application of it, see Patrick Newman, "Introduction," in Murray Rothbard, *The Progressive Era,* ed. Patrick Newman (Auburn, AL: Mises Institute, 2017), pp. 19–24. In addition, see Joseph Salerno, "Introduction," in Murray Rothbard, *A History of Money and Banking in the United States: The Colonial Era to World War II,* ed. Joseph Salerno (Auburn, AL: Mises Institute, 2005), pp. 7–43. These works discuss other aspects of Rothbard's historical method that space constraints preclude from discussing here, such as Power Elite analysis, the Iron Law of Oligarchy, and the Alliance of Throne and Altar.

[5]When discussing history, Mises mainly wrote on the methodological approach, particularly in his *Theory and History: An Interpretation of Social and Economic Evolution* (New Haven, CT: Yale University Press, 1957). Rothbard paid his debts to Mises and considered him one of his three major influences as a historian. The others were the libertarian political philosopher Albert Jay Nock and the English historian Lord Acton (John Emerich Edward Dalberg Acton). Rothbard, *Conceived in Liberty,* p. xviii; vols. 1 and 2, p. 11; vols. 3 and 4, p. 13.

information on an overrated historical figure—to be known and speak for themselves. "Unearthing" these details was an important motivation for Rothbard when it came to writing history, as explained in the prefaces to *Conceived in Liberty*:

> ... the survey studies of American history have squeezed out the actual stuff of history, the narrative facts of the important events of the past. With the true data of history squeezed out, what we have left are compressed summaries and the historian's interpretations and judgements of the data. There is nothing wrong with the historian's having such judgements; indeed, without them, history would be a meaningless and giant almanac listing dates and events with no causal links. But, without the narrative facts, the reader is deprived of the data from which he can himself judge the historian's interpretations and evolve interpretations of his own. A major point of this and the other volumes is to put the historical narrative back into American history.

At the end of the first volume of *Conceived in Liberty* Rothbard continued:

> It is rare these days to find a general work on American history that retains the richness of narrative and the vital factual record. Instead, while historians have written excellent monographs on specific areas, the more comprehensive works have either been brief essays presenting the author's point of view, or textbooks remarkable for the increasing skimpiness of their material. Perhaps college students these days are expected to know less and less actual history in their courses. The result is a series of unproven, *ad hoc* dicta by the historian; such a product fails to present the student or the reader with the factual data that support the historian's conclusions or that allow the reader to make up his own mind about the material.[6]

Rothbard's selection, collation, and synthesizing of facts directly relates to the second characteristic common in his historical writings: his overarching libertarian perspective. Rothbard's five-volume history of early America is unique in that it is from such a perspective, as

---

[6]Rothbard, *Conceived in Liberty*, pp. xv, 502; vol. 1, pp. 9, 512.

opposed to most historians who are either of a conservative or (more likely) liberal point of view. The central theme underlying his narrative, which Rothbard emphasizes more than any other historian, is the eternal battle waged between Liberty and Power. Rothbard argues that Liberty, or consensual agreements between individuals regarding their private property rights, is a moral good responsible for all human flourishing and modern civilization. On the other hand, Power refers to invasive actions of one individual over another that interferes with those aforementioned private property rights and is a moral evil responsible for mankind's setbacks. Liberty comes from the decentralized actions of individuals freely and peacefully interacting with each other, while Power generally resides in the centralized engine of coercion known as the State. Throughout human history these two forces have always clashed in a titanic struggle, with the forces of government coercion generally in a dominant position over the forces of the voluntary society. To make matters worse, all too often when the individuals of Liberty succeed and take the reins of a government with a goal to dismantle it, they become corrupted and start to soften their radical stance and even use government intervention for their own policy goals. This was especially prominent in early American history, from colonial America to the Antifederalists, and from the Jeffersonian Democrat-Republicans to the Jacksonian Democrats.[7] As will be shown below, while Rothbard attributed the founding, growth, and desire for independence of the American colonies to Liberty, he considered the adoption of the U.S. Constitution as a triumph for Power.

Rothbard's iconoclastic desire to present a wide range of underappreciated facts and interpret them from a libertarian perspective explains why many of his history projects grew in length, such as *Conceived in Liberty* and *The Progressive Era*. In fact, in a neglected public interview in 1981, Rothbard explicitly linked the growth and development of both projects together. When asked by an audience member about the status of *The Progressive Era*, Rothbard replied:

---

[7]Rothbard was especially influenced by Nock's dichotomy of social (voluntary) power versus state (coercive) power, and Lord Acton's famous dictum that "Power tends to corrupt and absolute power corrupts absolutely." Ibid., pp. xvi, xviii; vols. 1 and 2, pp. 10–11; vols. 3 and 4, pp. 12–13.

The status is I'm in the middle of it. … What happened with [it], as [what] happens with all my books, [is that] they get longer as I get into it. The way I got started with my history book was that I got a small grant to write a two-volume history of the United States. Somebody came to me and said "Murray, we want you to write a two-volume history of the United States. Take the usual facts that everybody agrees on, like Lincoln was elected president, something like that, and write the libertarian interpretation of it, right? It should be a lead-pipe cinch." Okay, great, [I] could get it done in a year and a half. What happened was, unfortunately, I found out that two-volume textbooks leave everything out. You can't just take the facts and put a new interpretation on them, because the facts were all left out. So I started bringing in the facts. I'd find tax rebellions in colonial New Jersey. I can't leave that out, right? So the thing starts getting longer and longer, and I wind up with a five-volume book on the colonial period and the rest of it dropping out.[8]

It is now time to turn from Rothbard's unique historical approach to his equally unique history of early America.

2. The Rothbardian Perspective on Early American History: From Jamestown to the Constitution

It is an extremely tall order to publish the fifth volume of a five-volume series on early American history forty years after the fourth was published in 1979 and expect the reader to be able to start right where the previous volume ended. Although the latest volume can be read as a stand-alone book for someone well-versed in Revolutionary War history, the book was meant as a continuation of previously published material and should be treated as such. With that being said, it is an even taller order to expect the reader to first plow through over 1,600 pages of early American history in order to be able to properly read and understand the fifth volume. It is for this reason that the remainder of the introduction will provide an overview of all five volumes of

---

[8]Murray Rothbard, "Transcript: How Murray Rothbard Became a Libertarian," *Mises.org* (April 2014).

Conceived in Liberty. Space will naturally be devoted to later volumes and especially to *Volume V.*[9]

Volume I—A New Land, A New People: The American Colonies in the Seventeenth Century describes the founding and initial development of all the original thirteen colonies except for Georgia, beginning with Jamestown in Virginia (1607) and Plymouth in Massachusetts (1620). English settlements soon spread throughout New England and the South, and by the middle of the seventeenth century, the Mid-Atlantic region was conquered from the Dutch and brought under English control. Although many settlers made the difficult journey across the Atlantic in search of greater freedom and escape from European statism, it was only a happy accident that the colonies were allowed to grow and prosper. This was due to several reasons. First, the sheer abundance of unsettled land and distance from the mother country made it extremely hard to establish feudalism (although it was certainly not for lack of trying). Colonists recognized that they were the true appropriators, and thus owners, of the land, and this fueled them with a rudimentary libertarian understanding of private property. Second, while the English did impose many mercantilist restrictions called Navigation Acts (e.g., subsidies and monopolistic privileges to English shipbuilders and manufacturers intended to enrich England at the expense of her colonies and other nations), they were generally not enforced due to internal strife in England and English wars with other European countries, such as France, the Netherlands, and Spain. In the mid-seventeenth century England experienced its own Civil War (1642–1651) between supporters of the monarchy and those in favor of a limited representative democracy, and in 1688 underwent the bloodless Glorious Revolution whose effects were in many respects similar to the American Revolution nearly one hundred years later.[10] The third was that whenever elements of mercantilism and feudalism were coercively imposed on the colonies, a revolt soon followed, such

---

[9]This is certainly not to discourage reading the original four volumes but only to note that with this introduction it is not a requirement in order to understand volume five.

[10]The Glorious Revolution led to the establishment of the English Bill of Rights in 1689, which stated that the King could not suspend laws, Parliament had supreme taxing and martial powers, and subjects could not be unlawfully arrested and detained. In the same year John Locke published his libertarian politico-philosophy tract grounded in natural rights called *Two Treatises of Government*.

as Bacon's Rebellion in Virginia (1676), Leisler's Rebellion in New York (1689), and Morris' Rebellion in New Jersey (1699). While sometimes partially inspired and motivated by anti-libertarian goals, Rothbard considered all of these revolts manifestations of Liberty:

> All of these revolutions may be classified as "liberal" and popular; in short, as essentially mass movements in behalf of libertarian objectives and in opposition to the tyranny, high taxes, monopolies, and restrictions imposed by the various governments. ... Through subsidies, taxes, privileges, monopolies, land grants, etc., the royal or proprietary governor and his Council *formed* an allied oligarchy, against which the people and their representatives in the lower house rebelled. ... But when these colonies rebelled, they did so not against England *per se*, but against the oppressions of the state, dominated by the English government.[11]

These rebellions mainly failed because their leaders too often succumbed to Power and became tyrannical, and as a result the English crown could successfully dismantle them and prop up the existing government institutions.

Volume II—"Salutary Neglect": The American Colonies in the First Half of the Eighteenth Century carries the narrative through the middle of the eighteenth century and describes the continuing libertarian progression of the colonies. Here Rothbard engages in a sectional analysis of the colonies and how they each individually and uniquely progressed. There are, however, several important common themes that bear emphasizing. The first is the enormous religious liberalization that emerged as a new rationalist Enlightenment fought back against the dominant Calvinist tradition. The Enlightenment's emphasis on man's reason and ability to discover natural law and the inner workings of the world around him led to a desire to obtain greater freedom and improve one's condition. Second, libertarian ideology spread and prospered in the colonies, with the formal theories of John Locke presented to popular audiences through the Englishmen John Trenchard and Thomas Gordon's *Cato's Letters*. It was through these writers that the bulk of the colonists learned of natural rights,

---

[11]Rothbard, *Conceived in Liberty,* p. 500; vol. 1, p. 510.

the social contract, state tyranny, and the battle between Liberty and Power. Third, the political system of the colonies developed into a constant battle between the royally appointed governor and Council (the upper house) on one side and the democratically elected Assembly (the lower house) on the other. This friction made the colonists suspicious of entrenched oligarchy and inclined toward democracy and greater political representation. Thus, on the contemporary political spectrum, while the Right represented conservative oligarchs who wished to maintain the traditions of mercantilism and feudalism, the Left represented the radical forces who desired greater freedom and independence from state depredations.

In addition, while Great Britain—formed out of the 1707 union between England and Scotland—was beginning to establish herself as a European superpower and enjoyed stable government at home, she still did not adequately enforce the Navigation Acts in the growing colonies. This was due to the conscious policy of "Salutary Neglect" practiced by the liberal Whig leaders, the Prime Minister Robert Walpole and the Secretary of State for the Southern Department the Duke of Newcastle (Thomas Pelham). Against a recalcitrant and easily corruptible Whig Party, Walpole and Newcastle realized that the best way for the colonies to grow and prosper (which in turn would benefit Great Britain) was to practice a hands-off approach and let the colonies spontaneously develop. This extremely beneficial policy ended, however, with the French and Indian War (1754–1763). "New France," in the present-day Midwest and Canada, was always (and still is, by many historians) portrayed as an aggressive power that could not peacefully coexist with the English colonies. In reality, with its far greater population and alliances with the hostile Iroquois, the English were the true aggressors and imperialists. When Walpole died in the early 1740s and Newcastle's power gradually eroded, the aggressive War Party in England and their colonial agents were able to force a costly war and impose conscription and the quartering of soldiers on a reluctant and resistant public. By the end of the war Great Britain was the undisputed superpower in both North America and Europe and was all too eager to foist upon their hapless colonial subjects the previously unenforced Navigation Acts along with new taxes.

Volume III—Advance to Revolution, 1760–1775 furthers the study through the tumultuous years after the French and Indian War. Great

Britain, unchallenged in its hegemony and covetous of funds to maintain its imperial dominion and "protect" its ungrateful colonists, could finally enact its "Grand Design." With the liberal Whigs out of power and the warmongering Tories in control, Great Britain, supported by the new King George III, would station its troops in the colonies during peacetime, enforce the Navigation Acts, restrict western settlement to stunt growth, and institute new Parliamentary taxation. While many historians view Great Britain's demands as reasonable tributes to pay for the eradication of the French "menace," Rothbard dismisses such arguments and recognizes the Grand Design for what it was: a statist attempt to suffocate and control the increasingly liberty-minded and independent colonies. Great Britain proceeded in rapid fashion: the Proclamation Line of 1763 restricted western settlement, the 1764 American Revenue Act enacted taxes on sugar and increased customs enforcement, and the 1765 Stamp Act raised new taxes on paper products. The Stamp Act was especially hated and produced a storm of protest. While Rothbard cheered mass movements in support of Liberty, he never lost sight of the importance of radical intellectuals to teach and motivate the people in a revolution:

> Ultimately, revolutions are mass phenomena, and cannot succeed without the support—indeed the active and enthusiastic support—of the great majority of the population. ... Otherwise it will not even make a respectable showing, much less take and keep the reins of government. But the masses will not move, will not erupt, if they lack aggressive leaders to articulate their grievances and to point the path for them to follow. The leaders supply the necessary theoretical justification and analysis of the revolution's short- and long-term goals. Unaided by leaders, the masses tend to accept each act of tyranny, not out of willing agreement, but from failure to realize that successful opposition can be mounted against the status quo. The articulation by the leaders is the final necessary spark that ignites the tinderbox of revolution.[12]

Who were these libertarian leaders who rose to the cause in early 1765 upon hearing the news of the Stamp Act? They included Patrick

---

[12]Ibid., p. 861; vol. 3, p. 97.

Henry and Samuel Adams, who respectively wrote the Virginia Resolves and Massachusetts Resolves. Sam Adams also established a resistance group known as the Loyal Nine, which soon expanded into the colony-wide Sons of Liberty. A Stamp Act Congress was called for late 1765 to unify resistance, and colonists across North America participated in mass civil disobedience by not recognizing the taxes. Great Britain, realizing that open rebellion was imminent, quickly repealed the measure in 1766.

While this seemingly resolved the crisis, problems still continued, particularly in Massachusetts after the passage of the tax-increasing Townshend Acts in 1767. British troops soon occupied Boston and colonial assemblies were dissolved. The colonies responded to this increasing coercion with mass nonimportation protests that severely hurt British commerce. The result was that the Townshend Acts were partially repealed in 1770. But despite the uneasy lull, matters reached a fever pitch with the Tea Act of 1773 that extended the British East India Company's tea monopoly to American shores. Colonists were fearful that this would soon extend to other imported goods, and they responded accordingly with the famous Boston Tea Party of December 1773. Great Britain responded with the Coercive, or "Intolerable" Acts of 1774, which provoked the assembly of the First Continental Congress in late 1774. Here the radicals, led by Massachusetts' Sam and John Adams and Virginia's Patrick Henry and Richard Henry Lee, battled the conservatives and decided upon a colony-wide boycott of all British products. In the spring of 1775, the British responded by trying to arrest Massachusetts radicals John Hancock and Sam Adams, who were currently near military supplies in Concord. Paul Revere traveled to nearby Lexington to warn of the impending British, and colonial minutemen confronted the approaching British troops. The showdown led to the famous "Shot Heard Round the World," and the American Revolution began.

Volume IV—The Revolutionary War, 1775–1784 brought the original series to a climax with the American Revolutionary War (1775–1783) and the founding of the United States of America. In this volume, Rothbard engages in a military, economic, and political history of the nation's most important conflict. It was with managing the war that the forces of Liberty faced their most difficult challenge, since war is naturally a coercive event that leads to death and destruction. A problem immediately presented itself: how to conduct the war effort? The solution to this question would prove momentous and led to the emergence of the U.S. Constitution more than a decade later. In contrast to contemporary wisdom, Rothbard utilized the insights of new historians who showed that the Patriots' greatest military strength lay in their guerrilla warfare tactics (ambushing armies, sneaking behind enemy lines, disrupting supply chains, etc.) and he argued that the only libertarian method of fighting a war is through such guerrilla warfare. This is because it is relatively inexpensive since there is no standing army, soldiers are better motivated because they are close to home, and there is far less need for a stifling and oppressive military bureaucracy. On the other hand, the traditional way of fighting a war, with professionally conscripted and trained armies that are sent across a territory to fight other standing armies in costly and often pointless pitched battles, requires extensive government intervention to plan, coordinate, and finance the war machine.

The Second Continental Congress, which met in mid-1775, faced the two options and chose the conventional and conservative military commander George Washington of Virginia over the guerrilla strategist and liberal military commander Charles Lee of Great Britain. Rothbard, much like he did earlier with Benjamin Franklin in *Volume II*, criticized Washington's importance and also his capabilities as a military leader and argued that the Patriots' military successes were due to their idiosyncratic guerrilla warfare strategies and commanders. To make matters worse, Rothbard also realized that the decision to fight the war conventionally led to enormous government intervention in the economy through paper-money inflation, debt financing, price controls, and confiscation of goods (it would also require the foreign aid of France and Spain, who were still smarting over their earlier defeats to Great Britain).

Despite this, the emergence of the conflict pushed the Patriots to a highly radical and libertarian goal: secession and independence from Great Britain. During the war new highly liberal and democratic governments were formed to replace the old colonial systems, and liberals on the Left fought with conservatives on the Right over a problem that would plague the new nation in its infancy: the problem of "home rule." Whereas many colonists wanted to reduce British mercantilism, they were fine with domestic mercantilism so long as it was controlled by Americans, and many even opposed independence so long as Americans had representation in Parliament. It was due to the radical Thomas Paine and his explosive pamphlet *Common Sense* (1776) that many colonists were persuaded to abandon the conservative cause and break off their former relations with Great Britain. In July 1776 many of the esteemed "Founding Fathers" signed the most libertarian document of the nation: the Declaration of Independence. Drafted by the radical Thomas Jefferson, the Declaration was grounded in a fiery Lockean, natural-rights philosophy and proclaimed American independence. But shortly thereafter, conservatives drafted the Articles of Confederation and Perpetual Union, which would ultimately be unnecessary to win the war and whose long-term effects would be highly conservative:

> The myth abounded that formal confederation was necessary to win the war, although the war would be virtually won by the time confederation was finally achieved. The war was fought and won by the states informally but effectively united in a Continental Congress; fundamental decisions, such as independence, had to be ratified by every state. There was no particular need for the formal trappings and permanent investing of a centralized government, even for victory in war. Ironically, the radicals were reluctantly pulled into an arrangement which they believed would wither away at the end of the war, and thereby helped to forge an instrument which would be riveted upon the people only in time of peace, an instrument that proved to be a halfway house to that archenemy of the radical cause, the Constitution of the United States.[13]

Finished in late 1777, the Articles were sent to the states and only ratified unanimously in 1781. Its centralizing provisions included the prohibition of state armies, requirements that states supply Congress revenues in proportion to land values (though it could only request funds), and provisions that made Congress the final court of appeal with the sole power to establish post offices and appoint high-ranking military officials. The Articles also assumed all of Congress' old debts and paper money. Important benefits, however, were that it established a unicameral legislature whose representatives were annually elected by

---

[13] Ibid., p. 1357; vol. 4, p. 243.

state legislatures on a rotating basis, and that unanimity was needed to enact the Articles and to make amendments (most other policy matters required the approval of nine states).

After conservatives in New York and Pennsylvania were thrown out of power during the war, they switched to supporting a strong national government. These conservatives wanted to enact a national tariff to pay off the war debt and a central bank to better reap the personal benefits of an expanding money supply. Conservatives took over the state governments of Massachusetts and Virginia and proceeded to enact their nationalist desires. In 1781, the Continental Congress created numerous executive departments, the most important being the Department of Finance headed by Robert Morris of Pennsylvania. Aided by his allies Gouverneur Morris (no relation) of Pennsylvania and Alexander Hamilton of New York, Morris quickly proceeded to institute the nationalist dream: the Bank of North America, plans to assume state debts, and a federal impost to finance the new government. By this time most of the radicals (such as the Adamses and Thomas Paine) had shifted rightward and were in no position to stop the new leviathan. It was only with the heroic resistance of Rhode Island that the impost plan was defeated and Morris and his allies consequently lost their influence.

Although the Revolution was enormously costly and resulted in the near destruction of the economy (through hyperinflation, military confiscation of goods, British pillaging of infrastructure and supplies, and the flight of British loyalists), the war was worth it since it led to the achievement of highly libertarian goals of inestimable value. Rothbard explains that the American Revolution was radical and led to the restriction of slavery in many areas, the end of feudalism, the emergence of religious freedom, democratic constitutions with increased suffrage, and revolutions in European nations. It was only in America, however, with its relatively limited feudalism and adherence to British liberalism that the revolutionaries succeeded in implementing a libertarian program.

Volume V—The New Republic, 1784–1791 takes the *Conceived in Liberty* series to its climactic conclusion: the triumph of Power in the adoption of the U.S. Constitution. Rothbard picks up right where the fourth volume ended, in 1784, and it is in this book that his radical analysis contrasts the most with conventional historians of the era. For many, including libertarians, the U.S. Constitution is a holy document that deserves to be respected and revered. Whenever any political party is against the actions of its opponents, they wear the mantle of a noted "constitutionalist" (only to conveniently forget constitutionalism when they are in control). Every student in school learns its fundamental and inviolable importance, and historians and legal scholars wax eloquently about its wisdom and how it was essential and saved the nation from the brink of total and utter destruction. They learn that it was only with "The Wise Men," or the Founding Fathers, that the country managed to rise above the chaos of the decentralized and limited Articles of Confederation and institute a far stronger central government that could properly control the states and its subjects. Rothbard shares none of these scruples and no cherished myths are left unturned.

"Part I—The Economic Legacy of the American Revolution" explains how many of the new nation's difficulties were not caused by too little, but rather by too much government during the 1780s. Trading patterns were altered because of changes in the American economy and retaliatory legislation by other countries. In the 1780s trade disruptions and bank credit expansion led to a depression that hit an already weakened and war-ravaged economy. Unfortunately, the states and the Confederation Congress did not repudiate their debt, but instead had an almost irrational desire to service it. This was despite the fact that the debt passed out of the original hands of soldiers and farmers and into mostly wealthy northern speculators who bought it at severely depreciated prices. Repudiation would have removed the need for most taxes, including a federal tax, and would have permanently weakened the states and federal government. States tried to partially fund the debt by raising taxes and printing money, both of which caused problems of their own and delayed economic recovery. Attempts by both the state and federal governments to impose tariffs and navigation laws failed due to interstate competition and the ironclad unanimity requirement of the Articles.

"Part II—The Western Lands and Foreign Policy" goes through America's relationship with its neighbors. Unlike many historians, Rothbard sees no fundamental and urgent need to drive the British out of their forts in the Northwest and the Spanish from the Southwest Mississippi River, and even supports secession of the western territories and a fracturing of the Confederation. For the nationalists—

proponents of big government who wanted a unified empire, a strong standing army, and federal taxation and regulation—this was simply too much.

"Part III—The Nationalists Triumph: The Constitutional Convention" describes the conspiratorial drive toward the bloodless *coup d'état*. Capitalizing on the 1786–1787 tax revolt in Massachusetts known as Shays' Rebellion, largely through the impetus of James Madison and Alexander Hamilton were the nationalists able to secure a convention in Philadelphia in the spring of 1787 for the sole and express purpose of revising the Articles of Confederation. By this time since the libertarian Left was so conservatized, the radical leaders who remained declined to attend, and the famous Constitutional Convention was able to scrap the Articles and devise a new system of government.

In "Part IV—The Nationalists Triumph: The Constitution," Rothbard shows his skill as a constitutional scholar and breaks down the fateful arguments made at the convention, which was dominated by conservatives who largely quibbled over details but agreed on the basic goal. Although there was some notable resistance, particularly by Luther Martin of Maryland, the nationalists succeeded in establishing a strong central government with the power to tax and regulate, maintain a standing army, and weaken the states. Far from creating a limited government with "enumerated" powers, Rothbard shows that the Constitution was designed to be broad and was filled with enough loopholes to not actually be restrictive.

The narrative escalates with "Part V—The Nationalists Triumph: The Constitution Ratified," where Rothbard goes through a fascinating and informative state-by-state analysis of the ratification of the Constitution. For many political theorists, States originate through a "social contract" where the people unanimously agree to restrict their liberties and place some power in a coercive government. For Rothbard, States historically originate through conquest and were imposed on a recalcitrant public, who only grudgingly acquiesced to the new dispensation after years of propaganda and patriotism. Rothbard shows that although the U.S. Constitution did not emerge through a bloody war, it was still coercively imposed on the majority of the public. The nationalists, who by now cleverly called themselves Federalists, allowed no compromise and said the Constitution would have to be accepted as it stood. They also castigated their opponents as Antifederalists, who were the true radical liberals and torchbearers of the American Revolution and supporters of real decentralized federalism. The Federalists managed to win the majority of delegates in each state convention through newspaper propaganda, bribery, malapportionment of delegates, threats of secession, hostile retaliatory trade legislation on resistant states, and the broken promise of restrictive amendments. Patrick Henry led a valiant stand against the Constitution in Virginia, and in New York the Clintonians, led by Governor George Clinton, proved to be formidable opponents. But one by one the bulk of the Antifederalists in each state cracked under the pressure until only little Rhode Island was left, who begrudgingly joined the new Union in 1790 when part of the state seceded and the U.S. government threatened a draconian trade act against it.

"Part VI—The Nationalists Triumph: The Constitution's Legacy" brings the epic series to a close. The Federalists had managed to secure the adoption of the Constitution only with the promise of amendments and even calls for a second constitutional convention, and the shrewd James Madison realized that this would inevitably lead to the destruction of the nascent national government. He therefore decided to nip the movement in the bud. As a congressman he pushed for a bill of rights which included only lukewarm protections of individual liberty and were not actually the restrictive amendments Federalists promised. It is no coincidence that Antifederalists realized that they had been tricked and the promised amendments were a sham. For Rothbard, unlike the American Revolution, which was a radical event on the side of Liberty, the adoption of the U.S. Constitution was a conservative event on the side of Power. The demoralized and broken Antifederalists scattered and became strict constitutionalists who hoped to destroy the Constitution from within. They and their followers were absorbed largely by the Jeffersonian Democrat-Republicans of the early nineteenth century and the Jacksonian Democrats of the mid-nineteenth century. In some sense, the late-nineteenth-century Bourbon Democrats of the Northeast, who Rothbard describes so expertly in *The Progressive Era,* could also claim a lineage to the Antifederalists.

3. Conclusion

The 2019 publication of the fifth volume marks the forty-year anniversary of the fourth volume. Although Murray Rothbard and many fans of the original series are no longer alive to see its release, it will hopefully encourage new and younger readers to start the series and become well versed in early American history. Rothbard's writings are timeless, and this book, so near to the point of being lost forever, is no exception. *Volume V—The New Republic, 1784–1791* is Rothbard, the master of political economy, at his finest: insightful, forceful, engaging, and enjoyable to read. Anyone who is interested in understanding the U.S. Constitution and how the modern federal government is able to assume such broad powers must read this book.

———— ~ ————

Rothbard typed out only a small fraction of the manuscript and left the rest of it handwritten in rough-draft form. His cursive, scrawling longhand almost reminds one of the Founding Fathers and is *very* hard, if not impossible, for most people to read. I am indebted to Barbara Pickard, Archivist of the Mises Institute, and Judy Thommesen, Managing Editor of the Mises Institute, for helping me in the initial stages of this project. Were it not for their encouragement and assistance, I would have given up long ago. As editor, I have, albeit imperfectly, done my best to read the handwritten pages, edit the entire manuscript, and track down and cite all of the material.

To keep its format similar to the original *Conceived in Liberty* series, I added the opening quotes to the book, divided it into parts, and added sectional titles. I have not written a bibliographical essay but instead continued to footnote citations Rothbard had included in the manuscript, and provided a simple bibliography of all the material cited. I have also added select [Editor's remarks], my additions to existing footnotes, and [Editor's footnote], my entirely new footnotes.

I would like to thank the Mises Institute, and Academic Vice-President Joseph Salerno in particular, for offering me the once-in-a-lifetime opportunity to work on this project. I would also like to thank Chris Calton and Joseph Salerno for reading the manuscript and providing helpful comments, and Judy Thommesen for finalizing the book and correcting typographical errors. All errors are entirely my own. Most importantly of all, I am grateful to Murray Rothbard for writing such an incredible book, for never giving up or getting discouraged, and for inspiring libertarians around the world.

Patrick Newman
Tampa, Florida
March 2019

PART I

The Economic Legacy
of the American Revolution

1

Changes in Foreign Trade

After peace came in 1783, the new republic faced a two-fold economic adjustment: to peacetime from the artificial production and trade patterns during the war, and to a far different trading picture than had existed before the war. The largest change between the two eras of peace was the shift in trading patterns resulting from independence. Most importantly, while Americans were freed from the shackles of British mercantilism and could trade freely with the rest of the world, the United States was now a foreign country that could no longer freely enjoy a market *within* the British Empire.

While the bulk of America's trade remained with the British Empire, the pressure of New World opportunities and tightened British restrictions greatly changed the structure of American trade. American exports to Great Britain fell almost in half during the 1780s, the bulk of the drop being in rice and especially in tobacco. Before the war, tobacco was compelled to go to Britain and was re-exported from there by British merchants. Now American tobacco found other markets abroad, especially in France, where tobacco formed 70 percent of the imports from the United States. Part of this shift was impelled by a heavy English tax on foreign tobacco and rice, which lowered the British demand for American staples. Tobacco grew and prospered immediately after the Revolutionary War, particularly in the new frontier areas: Kentucky, Tennessee, and up-country South Carolina and Georgia. Virginia and other southern tobacco-growing states were initially buoyed by the high price of the crop, but by 1785 the great postwar tobacco boom was over and tobacco prices began a sharp fall.

The American naval stores—largely pitch and tar—and indigo industries had been artificially stimulated in the colonial period by British bounties; now, shorn of these subsidies, the indigo and the naval stores industries—concentrated particularly in North Carolina—declined, and their shipments were made to the northern states rather than to Great Britain. The decline of indigo, however, was offset by the rapid growth of a new southern crop: cotton, particularly in backcountry Georgia and South Carolina. Also expanding in the South was the production of grain, previously confined largely to the middle provinces. Corn, wheat, and flour production expanded greatly in the South, and Alexandria became a leading center for the export of grain.

With American-built ships now excluded from British ports, the New England shipbuilding industry, previously used by British owners and then prosperous from profiteering during the war, declined during the postwar period. The Massachusetts whaling industry, crushed during the war from loss of access to the fisheries, never really recovered due to an American shift from spermaceti to tallow candles and to prohibitory British import duties on American whale oil. The continued British military occupation of the Northwest also deprived Americans of fur trade with the Indians of that region.

While severe British restrictions diminished the British West India trade, and the Spanish West India trade was similarly cut off, smuggling helped to evade these regulations. Furthermore, American commerce expanded with the French West Indies, which furnished a ready market for American fish and wood products. Holland also greatly expanded its imports of tobacco and rice, as well as its entire trade with America. American imports of British manufactures, however, barely declined, reflecting the American consumers' (especially the New Englanders) overwhelming preference for British goods. An additional development was America's launching trade with Canton in China in 1784–85, in which ginseng and furs were traded for tea and calicoes. The China traders tried to get the Confederation Congress, as well as the state of Connecticut, to intervene heavily to encourage the trade, but these governments refused; one important interpenetration of politics and economics, however, was the appointment of two leading China traders, Samuel Shaw and Thomas Randall, as consuls to China—this at the instigation of John Jay, the Secretary for Foreign Affairs.

Thus, the Revolution heavily altered American foreign trade. In response, merchants expanded their partnerships to cover every major marketing center. New England shipping had been hurt by blockaded fisheries during the war but were even more stimulated by extensive profiteering. After the war, shipping declined, however, even though many Tory Boston merchants were replaced by enterprising new men moving in from smaller seaport towns in Massachusetts. The fisheries continued to be crippled since access to Newfoundland was cut off by Britain. Hence, the New England ports were not as prosperous as ports elsewhere. Newport was permanently damaged by the war and was replaced by Providence as the commercial hub of Rhode Island. The severe cutback of West India markets, moreover, crippled New England agriculture and played a large role in the chronic postwar depression of the New England farmers. In general, many coastal areas experienced consolidation of the large seaports at the expense of the smaller, e.g., Boston at the expense of smaller ports in New England, Providence replacing war-torn Newport, Hartford winning over war-ravaged New Haven, and Baltimore gaining rapidly at the expense of Annapolis. Virginia, which had never had or needed a leading port (its trade taking place on coastal rivers and wharves) created an artificial port by granting Alexandria, in 1784, a monopoly for the official entry of foreign ships. New York, devastated by occupation and war, recovered remarkably and moved to catch up to Philadelphia as the nation's largest port.

The Revolution also produced a great (but as yet unstudied by historians) stimulus to foreign investment of capital from France and Holland that had previously been shut out by British mercantilism. French and Dutch investments were placed in American securities, currency, and commercial houses.

The slave trade, cut off during the war, resumed with the arrival of peace, especially in slave-depleted South Carolina, which imported 7,000 slaves during 1783–85. But all the states except the Carolinas and Georgia had prohibited slave imports by the end of the war, and the Carolinas followed suit in the late 1780s. Rhode Island's gradual abolition of slavery, passed in 1784, had the effect of breaking up the large plantations of its Narragansett County, for the economic viability of these plantations had rested on slave labor. The end of slavery led to the breaking up of these quasi-feudal slave-maintained large estates and their dissolution into independent farms. The American Revolution, indeed, had an intangible—and hence neglected—but highly significant economic impact in freeing land for the market and business enterprise. The abolition of entail and primogeniture throughout the country, and especially in the South, the elimination of British proprietary estates and quitrents, the confiscation of royal forests, the redistribution of large Tory estates—all of this served to free land for flexible economic use by private enterprise. And, as Professor Ver Steeg has emphasized, the almost unnoticed abolition of Crown sovereignty over minerals and other subsoil natural resources moved these resources into the realm of free private discovery, property, and use—an event of incalculable importance for the future.[1]

American manufacturing in that era took place almost exclusively in homes and in small local shops; it was undertaken by self-employed artisans, or "mechanics." It is important to realize that these mechanics were *not* modern proletarians, but self-employed small businessmen. The drastic reduction of imports during the war, especially from Britain, the great source of manufactured goods, stimulated an expansion of such manufacturing as textiles, salt, and iron products in the United States. It was inevitable that the end of the war should bring about a flood of British imports of which Americans had been deprived, especially textiles and all manner of specialized manufactured goods, and that much of the artificial wartime expansion would prove to be uneconomic in peacetime conditions. A readjustment of production and commerce to the new peacetime conditions had to be made, and the faster, the better. Some of the war manufacturing, notably the new iron furnaces and forges in Pennsylvania, proved to be viable, as did much of the household textile manufacturing in the South. But wartime domestic salt production was far too uneconomic to continue, and many of the manufacturers and artisans were forced to cut back

---

[1]Clarence L. Ver Steeg, "The American Revolution Considered as an Economic Movement," *Huntington Library Quarterly* (August 1957), pp. 361–72.

in the face of the renewed competition of British and other imported goods.[2]

---

[2][Editor's footnote] Merrill Jensen, *The New Nation* (New York: Knopf, 1950), pp. 177–257; Curtis P. Nettels, *The Emergence of a National Economy, 1775–1815* (New York: Holt, Rinehart and Winston, 1962), pp. 45–64.

2

The Depression of the 1780s
and the Banking Struggle

It has been alleged—from that day to this—that the depression which hit the United States, especially the commercial cities, was caused by "excessive" imports by Americans beginning in 1783. But this kind of pseudo-explanation merely betrays ignorance of economics: a boom in imports *reflects* voluntary choices and economic improvement by consumers, and this expression of choice can scarcely be the cause of general depression. In short, an improved standard of living for the bulk of consumers reflects improvement and not depression. It is impossible for consumers to buy "too many" imports, for they must pay for them with something, and this payment is financed from exports or from previously accumulated specie. Specie, indeed, had been accumulated in the colonies by the end of the war from British and French war expenditures. In either case, the payments reflected affluence rather than destitution, and these purchases were an enormous help after the ravages of the war. A specie drain is also the result of consumer desires and obviously cannot continue indefinitely. Clearly, Americans could not merely buy from abroad and not sell; indeed, if they could have done so they would have found a utopian cornucopia in which one need only consume without having to produce or sell in exchange.

There was, however, an excess of imports, but this was not caused by the free choices of American consumers. In the first place, as we have seen above, many manufacturers were artificially expanded during the war and with the resumption of peace these businesses now had to compete with the more efficient British, who at the same time restricted American exports. In addition, there was inflationary credit expansion by the Bank of North America, headed by wealthy Philadelphia merchant and former economic czar Robert Morris, and by two new banks which sprang up in 1784 to take advantage of the large profits of this new-found occupation: the Bank of Massachusetts in Boston and the Bank of New York in New York City, the latter organized mainly by large public creditors. Each institution enjoyed a monopoly on banking in its region. Inflationary expansion of bank credit leads bank clients to believe that they have more *real* money than they actually possess, and this leads to an artificial expansion of imports, which must be paid for in specie. The consequent drain of specie from the expanding banks, and increased calls for payment of their notes and deposits in specie, inevitably creates difficulties for the banks and forces them into hasty contraction, which in turn leads to deflation and depression. It is this boom-bust cycle of bank credit expansion and contraction that occurred in the immediate postwar period and brought a depression in mid-1784 and 1785. This trade cycle was superimposed on and aggravated the inevitable postwar distress of over-expanded wartime manufactures by increasing imports more than would have otherwise been the case.

Excessive importation continued into the 1780s. At the end of the Revolutionary War, the contraction of the swollen mass of paper money, combined with the resumption of imports from Great Britain, cut prices by more than half in a few years.[3] As we shall see below, vain attempts by seven state governments, beginning in 1785, to cure the "shortage of money" and re-inflate prices were a complete failure. Part of the reason for the state paper issues was a frantic attempt to pay the wartime public debt, state and pro rata federal, without resorting to crippling burdens of taxation. The increased paper issues merely added

---

[3] [Editor's footnote] For more on Revolutionary War finance, see Murray Rothbard, *Conceived in Liberty*, vol. 4: *The Revolutionary War, 1775–1784* (Auburn, AL: Mises Institute, 1999), pp. 1487–97, 1508–13; pp. 373–83, 394–99. The original *Conceived in Liberty* volumes were published in individual editions. Page numbers to the earlier individual editions will follow page numbers to the 2011 all-in-one edition.

to the "shortage" by stimulating the export of specie and aggravated the importation of commodities from abroad.

By the end of 1783, Robert Morris had succeeded in divorcing his Bank of North America—which had begun the year before as a virtual central bank—from the federal government.[4] Its growing profitability—it had paid a dividend of 14.5 percent in 1783—stimulated its own expansion as well as new bank projects. The bank increased its subscription by $500,000 in January 1784 and soon a new group, disgruntled by the loans of the Bank of North America going to favored insiders, asked for the chartering of a Bank of Pennsylvania. The Bank of North America was furious at the threat of competition at home (it worried not at all about the new banks in Boston and New York), and Pelatiah Webster, a bank stockholder, argued presumptuously in the Pennsylvania Assembly that the two banks "might act in opposition to each other and of course destroy each other," i.e., compete. When this argument unsurprisingly failed to impress the legislators, the Bank of North America in March used the ancient device of cooptation: it expanded its new shares to $1.6 million and cut in the promoters of the new bank. Thus the Bank of North America's expansion ended the threat of another bank in Pennsylvania. But the bank was scarcely out of trouble. Soon it was forced by liabilities accrued from its previous expansion to contract sharply during 1784 and precipitate a financial crisis.[5]

After the victory of the radicals in the fall 1784 elections, the victors, led by Assemblymen William Findley of Westmoreland, Robert Whitehill of Cumberland, and John Smilie of Fayette counties, moved to repeal the charter of the Bank of North America. While the radical Constitutionalists acceded to the depression-born demand of artisan-manufacturers and passed a protective tariff, their push against the bank in the spring of 1785 precipitated a notable debate over the bank's activities. A pamphlet war, as well as a legislative debate and mass petitions, raged over the Bank of North America. While much of

---

[4][Editor's footnote] For more on the Bank of North America, see ibid., pp. 1506–07, 1523–24; pp. 388–93, 409–10.

[5]The Bank of Massachusetts, having expanded from its inception in 1784, was also forced to contract as losses hit its mercantile customers in the spring of 1785; this contraction aggravated the depression during that year.

the anti-bank argument was political—attacking its special privileges, its favoritism, in general its negation of the liberal ideal of equality before the law—the radicals also emerged with some sophisticated economic arguments against the bank. The Assembly committee that recommended repeal, as well as the anti-bank men in subsequent debates, stressed the crucial economic point that, as one legislator phrased it, the bank was "an engine of trade that enabled the merchants to import more goods than were necessary, or than there was money to pay for, [and that] by means of a bank the European merchants were enabled to procure and carry off money for their goods." Then, after the temporary expansion of this fictitious credit, the bank "overtraded" and was later forced to contract and precipitate an economic crisis. In short, the radicals in the anti-bank debate of 1785, led by Findley and Smilie, adumbrated the later Ricardian theory of banking and international trade which was also in essence a monetary theory of the trade cycle. The following year, the eminent Reverend John Witherspoon, in his *Essay on Money* (1786), though favoring the bank, explained in greater detail how inflation of bank paper raises prices and drives specie out of the country. Indeed, in the course of the controversy an anonymous pamphleteer, "Nestor," first proposed in America the "currency principle" of 100 percent specie backing for bank liabilities and argued that a bank "should not emit a single note beyond the sum of specie in its possession."

In accordance with his general theory of the history of American banking struggles, the historian Bray Hammond persists in labeling the radical hard-money opposition to the bank "agrarian," even though he inconsistently admits that wealthy Philadelphia capitalists like George Emlen also stood for hard money and against the bank. This view, furthermore, is hard to square with the fact that the Philadelphia delegates (at this point radicals) voted overwhelmingly for repeal of the bank charter.[6]

---

[6]Bray Hammond, in his eagerness to denigrate the radicals, discusses only their political arguments and completely omits their economic reasoning. Bray Hammond, *Banks and Politics in America* (Princeton: Princeton University Press, 1957), pp. 53–62. In addition, see ibid., pp. 87–88. Contrast Hammond's analysis with the thorough and judicious treatment in Joseph Dorfman, *The Economic Mind in American Civilization, 1606–1865*, vol. 1 (New York: The Viking Press, 1946), pp. 260–68. See also

To defend its existence, the Bank of North America brought out heavy guns indeed, all its supporters being either stockholders, in pay of, or in debt to, the bank. Leading the defenses was the noted James Wilson, the bank's counselor and heavily in the bank's debt. Wilson not only advanced the specious legal argument that the bank's charter, though granted as a privilege by the state, was now somehow its "property right"; he also insisted that the cause of the depression was *only* excessive importation *per se*. Other prominent defenders were Robert Morris, Gouverneur Morris, and Pelatiah Webster, who opined that "a good bank may increase the circulating medium of a State to double or treble the quantity of real cash, without increasing the real money, or incurring the least danger of a depreciation."

The Pennsylvania Assembly overwhelmingly repealed the charter of the Bank of North America in September 1785, but the debate continued to rage. Finally, the conservatives' political victory in the 1786 elections, in which they carried Philadelphia and eastern Pennsylvania, led to the re-charter of the bank in the following year, though with considerably restricted powers.

The most inglorious role in the continuing debate was played by Thomas Paine, author of the fiery libertarian pamphlet *Common Sense* (1776), who was reportedly hired by the bank to lend his formidable pen to its cause. In a 1786 pamphlet, Paine not only defended bank inflation and advanced the flimsy "property right" argument, he had the presumption to urge that the state privilege the bank by making it a kind of central bank to the commonwealth, with the state borrowing from the bank instead of issuing state paper to meet its expenses. Understandably denounced by his old radical comrades as a mercenary renegade, Paine not only mendaciously denied any vested interest in defending the bank, but he also lashed out at the opposition as an unholy alliance of irresponsible frontiersmen and urban capitalists and usurers. So far had Paine advanced down the right-wing road that he now advocated a return to a bicameral legislature.

Harry E. Miller, *Banking Theories in the United States Before 1860* (Cambridge, MA: Harvard University Press, 1927), pp. 23, 30, 49–51, 139; Robert L. Brunhouse, *The Counter Revolution in Pennsylvania, 1776–1790* (Harrisburg, PA: Pennsylvania Historical Commission, 1942), pp. 172–75. [Editor's remarks] Nettels, *The Emergence of a National Economy,* pp. 61–62, 77–81.

3

The Drive for State
and Federal Protective Tariffs

Every depression generates a clamor among many groups for special privileges at the expense of the rest of society—and the American depression that struck in 1784–1785 was no exception. If excess imports were the culprit, then voluntary economizing could help matters, and the press was filled with silly fulminations against ladies wearing imported finery. Less foolish and more pernicious was a drive by the beleaguered and often sub-marginal artisans and manufacturers for the special privilege of protective tariffs.

As early as July 1783, a group of manufacturers from Philadelphia met to petition the Assembly for protection against foreign imports. The following year, a group of Boston manufacturers submitted a similar plea. During the depression year of 1785, the urban artisans banded together in earnest. The Boston manufacturers in twenty-six trades formed The Association of Tradesmen and Manufacturers of the Town of Boston in the spring of 1785 to agitate for a protective tariff in their state, and they were followed by the formation of a General Committee of Mechanics in New York, which soon merged with the Manufacturers Society of New York to fight for protection. Mechanics from Philadelphia, Baltimore, Providence, and Charleston were also active though not formally organized. In particularly hard-hit New England, the town of Nantucket actually asked the state legislature in 1785 for permission to secede and rejoin Great Britain in order to try and regain prosperity. In Philadelphia, the master cordwainers, the shoemakers of the city, decided in March 1785 to engage in concerted economic pressure to try and block further imports of boots and shoes. They agreed not to buy, sell, or mend any imported shoes, and they obtained the support of their employees, the journeymen cordwainers.

Since the bulk of the country's imports came from Great Britain, it was easy for the protectionists to employ anti-British demagogy and denounce American economic troubles as a British plot. For their part, the urban merchants were of course happy to ban British *importers* or British *ships*, but did not want any restrictions on British *goods*; in short, each group sought its own special privileges. Thus, when the Boston merchants agreed to boycott all British merchants, the Boston manufacturers bluntly pointed out that *they* didn't care whether British goods were imported by British or American merchants, and they petitioned for a comprehensive protective tariff in Massachusetts. Finally, in the summer of 1785 the Massachusetts General Court passed a protective tariff for artisans and a navigation act for the merchants. The navigation act banned any exports from Massachusetts in a British vessel, and goods imported in all foreign vessels were to pay double duties as well as a special levy. Import duties, for their part, were raised to a new high and were levied on almost every type of manufactured good; excise taxes were also levied on the consumption of luxuries. While the merchants chafed at the protective tariff, the Boston artisans maintained their organization as a pressure group and a vigilance committee to check upon local merchants. In August 1785, the Boston artisans wrote to "tradesmen and manufacturers" of the other large towns, urging them to put equivalent pressure for a protective tariff upon their legislature. Massachusetts raised the tariff rates again the following year. However, because its navigation law had also injured French shipping while all French ports were open to American vessels, Massachusetts was pressured into repealing her navigation act in 1786.

Rhode Island levied a schedule of protective tariffs in 1785; New Hampshire levied import duties in 1784, forbade exports of goods on British ships the following year, and added a protective tariff schedule in 1786. Much lower tariff duties were levied by Virginia, the Carolinas, and Georgia.

Most important was the drive for a protective tariff in the most industrialized and populous city in the United States, Philadelphia. Under artisan pressure the radical-dominated legislature passed a protective tariff in the autumn of 1785, as well as an anti-British navigation law. The conservatives, it may be noted, were far more enthusiastically in favor of a tariff than were the radicals. By 1786, indeed, virtually every state had passed a navigation law against British shipping. However, there were sharp differences in degree, with Connecticut, New Jersey, Delaware, South Carolina, and Georgia only discriminating against British shipping to a slight extent.

It soon dawned upon the manufacturers and the merchants, however, that state tariffs and state navigation laws were not as effective a grant of privilege as they desired. For while most of the manufacturing states of the North imposed high protective tariffs for the benefit of their manufacturers, the South, with less manufacturing, understandably imposed lower tariffs upon themselves. The growing manufacturing of Pennsylvania and the rest of the North now wanted to secure the large southern market for themselves. Even enjoying the mild tariffs of the South, they could not successfully compete with the more efficiently produced and lower-cost English goods, or with English shipping. Hence, the northern manufacturers concluded that a nationalist system in which only the federal government could set a uniform tariff was important for monopolizing the southern market—at the expense, of course, of the southern consumers and any of the consumers of the low tariff states. Hence, the urban artisans in the North began to look with favor on the old nationalist idea of a strong, overriding central government and began to ally their important mass support with the longstanding schemes of the northern financial oligarchy.

Merchants, too, began to long for a uniform national navigation law. For those states which taxed or restricted foreign vessels very heavily (e.g., New Hampshire, Massachusetts, and Rhode Island) soon found that they lost substantial trade to those that retaliated very lightly against British shipping (e.g., Connecticut, New Jersey, Delaware, South Carolina, and Georgia) and they even had to abandon their much stronger laws. Hence, the merchant's drive for a nationally imposed privilege to close the "loophole" of relative freedom and consumer choice in the other states. Again, a strong central government began to loom as a particularly attractive goal.[7]

In April 1785, merchants and traders (retailers) of Boston turned to Congress for depression remedies, and Boston, a few months later, urged Congress to repel foreign merchants and shipping. In fact, James Bowdoin, the ultra-conservative governor of Massachusetts, urged that state to call a constitutional convention to endow Congress with greater powers, a plan endorsed by the Massachusetts legislature and by John Adams, then Minister to England. New Hampshire quickly followed suit. Also early in 1785, the New York merchants in the New York Chamber of Commerce urged congressional action against foreign traders, and the manufacturers and traders of the city joined in calling for greater power to Congress. Citizens of Philadelphia, in June 1785, asserted that only full powers to Congress over the commerce in the United States could bring relief from the economic depression; the Council of Pennsylvania followed with a plea for stronger congressional power. The Virginia and Maryland legislatures, as early as 1783, urged authorization for a congressional navigation act, and they were followed by the merchants of Philadelphia.

On April 30, 1784, Congress responded by asking the states for the authority to enact a navigation law for fifteen years, prohibiting British vessels from engaging in the United States coastal trade or from importing any goods not produced in Britain. In order to be ratified, nine states had to agree to this measure. Virginia agreed at once, but other states balked at the centralized control and the domination of the carrying trade that the law would grant to New England merchants. Delaware, South Carolina, and Georgia particularly balked at the restrictions of the law, and the attempt to gain agreement by the states failed.

No sooner was the Congress rebuffed than its power-seeking nationalist forces began anew. Early in 1785, the young Virginia lawyer James Monroe headed a congressional committee that urged an amendment to the Articles for perpetual congressional power to regulate interstate

---

[7]While Connecticut taxed imports from Massachusetts, and New York in 1787 moved to tax foreign goods imported from neighboring states, the specter of disunity and disrupting interstate tariffs was more of a bogey to sell the idea of a powerful national government than a real factor in the economy of the day.

and international trade, and to levy duties on imports and exports. State powers were to be safeguarded, for all duties were to be collected by state authority and the funds were to accrue to the states where they were collected. The proposal, however, was defeated in the Congress, largely by southerners understandably reluctant to place a monopoly of the carrying trade in the hands of American merchants, a monopoly that at the same time would raise the price of imported goods and lower the prices of southern exports. The redoubtable Richard Henry Lee, back in Congress as its president, led the libertarian forces in staunchly opposing any sweeping powers for federal regulation of trade and managed to defeat the Monroe amendment in August 1785. A year later, a similar amendment again failed to pass the Congress.

A determined movement for national power was also welling up in Massachusetts. Governor Bowdoin's scheme, propounded during mid-1785, for a new centralizing constitutional convention was stopped in its tracks by the refusal of the Massachusetts delegates to Congress to press for the plan. Writing sternly to Bowdoin in early September 1785, the delegates, headed by the redoubtable liberal Elbridge Gerry, blasted the schemes of the centralizers: "plans have been artfully laid, and vigorously pursued, which had they been successful, We think would inevitably have changed our republican Governments, into baleful Aristocracies. Those plans are frustrated, but the same Spirit remains in their abettors."[8] The Massachusetts legislature was forced by this rebuff to rescind its resolutions for a new centralizing convention.

Even more important to the nationalists than regulation of commerce was the acquisition of the taxing power. In the last gasp of nationalist dominance, Congress in April 1783 had accordingly proposed a new impost after the last one failed in 1782.[9] This time, the impost power was only to be granted for twenty-five years and the states were to administer the collection of duties. The accompanying message sent by Congress to the states on behalf of the impost was drawn up by Virginia's nationalist congressman James Madison.

---

[8]Edmund Cody Burnett, *The Continental Congress* (New York: W.W. Norton and Co., 1964), p. 637.

[9][Editor's footnote] For more on the failed imposts of 1781 and 1783, see Rothbard, *Conceived in Liberty,* vol. 4, pp. 1514–17, 1521; pp. 400–03, 407.

Around this proposed federal impost of 1783, there raged the most important political controversy of the postwar Confederation period. Here was the rallying ground for both the nationalist and the radical-liberal forces. In Congress, Jonathan Arnold and John Collins of Rhode Island had led the opposition to the impost. Now, first to raise public voice in opposition among the citizenry was the great George Mason. Drafting the Fairfax County (Virginia) resolutions, Mason found both in the impost plan and in Madison's plea "strong proofs of the lust for power." Trenchantly, Mason likened the plan to the arbitrary measures of the Stuart monarchs in England. Any congressional taxing power spelled disaster: "Congress should not have even the appearance of such a power. Forms generally imply substance, and such a precedent may be applied to dangerous purposes hereafter. When the same men or set of men, holds both the sword and the purse, there is an end of liberty." To the nationalists' plea for taxing power to pay the public debt, the liberals proposed that the debt be divided up and paid by the several states, according to their realistic depreciated value. Thus, there would be no amassing of centralized power.

Unanimity of agreement by the states was again required to adopt the impost of 1783. New Jersey, North Carolina, and Delaware, with little direct import trade, were willing enough to have national revenue derived from tariffs, and consented readily. New Jerseyites, furthermore, had invested large sums in federal securities. One of the few opponents in North Carolina was the old Regulator leader, Thomas Person.[10] South Carolina followed suit in support of the impost, and Pennsylvania, still under the iron control of the right-wing, soon followed also, over weak objections by the Constitutionalists.

Massachusetts ratified the impost in the fall of 1783, but only after a tight struggle. Old radicals like James Warren and liberal merchants like Stephen Higginson led the opposition, but in general the commercial eastern and the Connecticut River towns favored the impost

---

[10][Editor's footnote] Thomas Person was a North Carolina assemblyman and later a prominent Antifederalist. The Regulators of North Carolina was a movement in the late 1760s and early 1770s upset over the colony's arbitrary land grants, corrupt tax officials, and high taxes and quitrents. Murray Rothbard, *Conceived in Liberty*, vol. 3: *Advance to Revolution, 1760–1775* (Auburn, AL: Mises Institute, 1999), pp. 997–1009; pp. 233–45.

by a large majority while interior and especially western Massachusetts was bitterly opposed. Despite Massachusetts' narrow approval in 1783, the urban towns continued to be restive, and the towns of western Suffolk County urged a county convention in 1784 against the impost, a request that was angrily turned down by Boston. As late as 1786, the country town of Rochester, in southern Plymouth County, attacked Congress' half pay for army officers, and attacked the impost as eliminating "the Constitutional Check which the General Court had on Congress."

The struggle was also intense in Connecticut, where agricultural opinion brought the impost to defeat, while Tory Fairfield County voted for it. The intense rural opposition to the impost in these states was not surprising since these were precisely the people who would have to suffer the burden. But after insisting that the revenue be paid only for public debts and not for any pensions, to which New England was bitterly opposed, the impost finally passed the Connecticut legislature in 1784.

Debate was more heated in Virginia, following that state's crucial role in blocking the previous impost plan of 1781. Such powerful figures in Virginia as Thomas Jefferson lobbied for the plan, and Patrick Henry came out in its support. The opposition was led by George Mason and Richard Henry Lee; Lee, too, denounced the thirst for power and aristocracy exhibited by the plan, as well as the breakdown of the limits which the Confederation had hedged around federal encroachment on the liberties of the states. Patrick Henry's sudden shift into opposition seemed to doom the impost, but open pressure by George Washington, combined with the surrender of Mason, secured Virginia's approval of the impost at the end of 1783.

The story was similar in South Carolina. The state had first turned down the congressional request but, after pressure by George Washington, was finally persuaded to approve the impost. In Georgia, the opposition was so great as to delay approval until 1786. One by one, however, the states fell into line; even Rhode Island, over the bitter opposition of David Howell, who led the resistance against the 1781 impost, approved the impost in early 1786. Rhode Island's shift was propelled by the change of heart of Nicholas Brown of Providence, one of the leading merchants of the state, and previously one of Howell's major backers. Owner of $50,000 of federal securities, Brown decided that these securities were being "neglected," so he swung over to the impost. As in Massachusetts, the opposition to the impost rested with the inland towns, while the urban interests, merchants, and mechanics favored the tax.

By August of 1786, every state but New York had approved the impost. While the oligarchs and the urban artisans united to favor the impost, the opposition was led by Abraham Yates, the Albany lawyer and cobbler who had risen to leadership of the radical forces in New York State. Yates stressed the thirst-for-power theme and, along with other opponents of the impost, cited the English theorist James Burgh in warning of the inner tendency toward the expansion of government power.[11] Unerringly, Yates centered on the central importance of the taxing power and warned that it "is the first, nay, I may say the only object of tyrants. ... This power is the center of gravity, for it will eventually draw into its vortex all other powers."[12] Yates also warned that true republicanism can only be preserved in small states, and keenly pointed out that in the successful republics of Switzerland and the Netherlands the local provinces retained full control over their finances. A taxing power in Congress would demolish state sovereignty and reduce the states, where the people could keep watch on their representatives, to mere adjuncts of congressional power, and liberty would be gone.

In New York the struggle was over congressional versus state control of collecting the proposed impost. In the critical vote in the spring of 1786, and again the following year, the New York legislature refused to grant Congress any control over collection, and insisted that New York's paper money be accepted in payment of duties. Congress refused to accept these conditions, and the impost of 1783 was defeated. Thus,

---

[11][Editor's footnote] James Burgh was a Scotsman known in the colonies for his *Political Disquisitions* (1774). He wrote in the tradition of John Trenchard and Thomas Gordon of *Cato's Letters* and criticized taxation without representation and Britain's stern actions against her colonies. Rothbard, *Conceived in Liberty*, vol. 4, pp. 1262–63; pp. 148–49.

[12]Jackson Turner Main, *The Antifederalists: Critics of the Constitution, 1781–1788* (Chapel Hill: University of North Carolina Press, [2004] 1961), p. 79. [Editor's remarks] For more on Abraham Yates and the liberals in New York, see Rothbard, *Conceived in Liberty*, vol. 4, pp. 1389–90; pp. 275–76.

the unanimity principle under the Articles of Confederation had made all attempts to impose a congressional taxing power impotent.

The votes of the New York legislature aligned with the merchants of New York City and Albany, led by Alexander Hamilton and Philip Schuyler, and the bulk of urban mechanics, in favor of the impost, while the followers of Governor George Clinton from the other upstate counties, led by Abraham Yates, were overwhelmingly opposed. Similar lines would be drawn in the ratification debates over the Constitution.[13]

---

[13] [Editor's footnote] Merrill Jensen, *The New Nation*, pp. 225–27, 282–301, 400–13; Main, *The Antifederalists*, pp. 72–102; Nettels, *The Emergence of a National Economy*, pp. 69–75; Burnett, *The Continental Congress*, pp. 633–53.

4

The Burdens
of State Public Debt

A key to the politico-economic problems of the Confederation period, as well as one of the leading arguments for centralized power, was the swollen *corpus* of war-born public debt. The mass of federal and state debt could have depreciated and passed out of existence by the end of the war, but the process was stopped by Robert Morris. Morris and the nationalists moved to make the depreciated federal debt ultimately redeemable at par, and also agitated for federal assumption of the states' debts. This was done to benefit speculators who purchased the public debt at depreciated values and to force a drive for a national taxing power. As a result of the nationalists' efforts to assume the public debt, the value of the public debt, in specie, increased from $11 million in 1780 to $27 million in 1783, the vast bulk of which was held in the northern states. While scrambling to assume some of the debt themselves, the states had also amassed a huge burden of their own debt. Thus, by the end of the war, Massachusetts' total debt was nearly £1.5 million; Rhode Island, about $0.5 million; Connecticut, over $3.75 million; Pennsylvania, over £4.6 million; Virginia's over £4.25 million. As a result, payment of interest on the debt amounted to an overwhelming proportion of the state budget, and one estimate is that 50–90 percent of state expenditures went for this purpose: out of South Carolina's total budget of roughly £104,000 in 1786, over £83,000 went to pay interest on the debt; of Virginia's budget of roughly £256,000 in 1784, over £207,000 went to payment of interest.[14]

One problem that bitterly divided the states during the Confederation period was the settlement of common accounts. Under the Articles, expenses made by the several states for causes common to them all would be lumped together as "common charges" and the charges paid proportionately by the various states. In short, "debtor" states would pay their share to claimant "creditor" states through Congress and thus settle their accounts. Wartime expenses were clearly a common charge for the general welfare, and therefore those states which had expended more in the war effort (notably the southern states, because of the nature of the last few years of the war) were entitled to payment from the others. Logically, the public debt incurred by Congress should also have been assumed pro rata by the separate states, but the nationalists' fierce determination to amass and retain a federal debt was able to keep that debt a federal rather than a "common" charge.

Throughout the 1780s the southern states tried to obtain their just settlements, but the northern states faithlessly fell back on technicalities, lack of official vouchers and authorization, etc., to keep the southern states from their just due. Also the South in particular had gone

---

[14][Editor's footnote] The continual use of both pounds and dollars may be confusing to the reader. The states generally used English units (pounds, sterling, and pence) as their unit of account, which they began while they were still British colonies. During the colonial era, since Britain used mercantilist restrictions to prevent English specie from leaving the country, the colonists imported specie from other regions, in particular the Spanish silver dollar. The colonies also heavily issued paper money, which was indirectly linked to the specie unit of account through taxes and legal tender laws. In the early 1790s the new government put the country on a dollar accounting system that defined the American dollar in terms of both gold and silver (at a 15 to 1 ratio). Murray Rothbard, *Conceived in Liberty*, vol. 2: *"Salutary Neglect": The American Colonies in the First Half of the Eighteenth Century* (Auburn, AL: Mises Institute, 1999), pp. 621–38; pp. 123–40; Murray Rothbard, "A History of Money and Banking Before the Twentieth Century," in *A History of Money and Banking in the United States: The Colonial Era to World War II*, ed. Joseph Salerno (Auburn, AL: Mises Institute, 2005), pp. 65–68.

much further than other states in assuming unliquidated federal debt during the war (e.g., Quartermaster and Commissary certificates) and had exchanged them for state debts, only to find Congress (i.e., the North) balking about accepting these federal certificates as evidence for expenditures in the common welfare. Again, the North was depriving the South of their just due. As the dispute dragged on during the decade with the southern states unable to redeem their claims, Robert Morris' wily "solution" proposed in 1783 began to look better to all concerned. An ultra-nationalist's dream, the proposal was to accept *all* southern claims without cavil, but *not* to be paid by the debtor states: to be assumed by the federal government, which would issue federal securities for all claims. In short, the federal government would assume all war-born state debts.

The tax-and-debt burdens of the states were, of course, aggravated when the depression of 1784 hit the country, for now a fixed sum of taxes and debt payments had to be exacted from a depressed economy in which prices were generally lower and therefore the *real* tax burden greater. One critical problem was whether the debt would be paid at its depreciated market value, which at least reflected current economic realities, or whether the state would insist on paying them at their far greater face value, and thus impose an enormously greater tax burden upon the people. The anger of people at paying debt charges was considerably aggravated by the fact that the bulk of this debt had passed from its original owners at highly depreciated amounts into the hands of speculators. Payment of face value, then, would not even benefit the original public creditors; in fact, they too would suffer from being taxed for the benefit of a windfall to a comparative handful of speculators in the public debt.

Virginia was sensible enough to pay much of the debt at its depreciated market value, and make its taxes to pay the debt payable in depreciated certificates. Hence, Virginia was able to reduce its debt rapidly and without imposing enormous burdens on its taxpayers. Massachusetts, on the other hand, so handled its debt during the war as to benefit its debt holders and speculators, consolidating its debt by 1784 at twice its market value. To pay this particularly large debt, Massachusetts levied enormous taxes and insisted on collecting them in specie. This is not surprising, since the Massachusetts government was basically run by the very groups that owned the great mass of state debt. The debt burden was borne particularly by the poor, since roughly 33 to 40 percent of Massachusetts' state revenue was raised by poll taxes, which were equal for each citizen. As a result, it is estimated that at least a third of a Massachusetts farmer's income after 1780 was extracted from him in taxes, and in specie at that. Farmers and the poor demanded that the state debt at least be scaled down to market value, but the conservative ruling groups angrily refused.

Typical of the eastern mercantile oppression over the mass of citizens and farmers was the imposition of excise taxes, which harmed the bulk of consumers. Thus, the tax on spirits (e.g., cider brandy) distilled from one's own apple orchard was twice the level of the tax on New England rum: a clear privilege to the Boston and other eastern merchants over the western farmers. Tax oppression upon the Massachusetts people was enormous, and the courts ruthlessly threw those who could not pay into jail. Tax defaulters' property was seized, but in the time-honored way of neighborhood solidarity, local mobs prevented anyone but the owner from bidding for the property.

To the distressed people of Hampshire and Berkshire counties in western Massachusetts, it became increasingly clear that salvation must lie in their own hands alone: specifically by taking direct action to close the hated tax-enforcing courts. On February 11, 1782, a convention of Hampshire County at Hadley urged the suspension of civil suits; leading a call at the convention for direct action was the Reverend Samuel Ely of the town of Conway. The convention also prioritized the discriminatory excise taxes: "We esteem it as a matter of great grievance that Excize should be paid on any articles of Consumption in a free Republick." Throughout January, Ely had stirred up the northern towns of the county, attacking the Massachusetts government and the constitution, and denouncing the highly excessive salaries of the governor and the superior court judges. Now, his views appeared so radical that one Northampton divine feared that the government itself was in danger, and none other than Joseph Hawley, the former leader of the western Massachusetts Left, accused Ely of treason. It was clear that the hard-pressed masses of western Massachusetts had found a new leader.[15]

---

[15][Editor's footnote] During the Revolutionary War there was a crisis of leadership among the Massachusetts radicals. Since John Hancock and John and Sam Adams began to move rightward, new radical leaders had to be found in 1775 and 1776.

Samuel Ely was a Yale graduate and former preacher in Connecticut, and a volunteer fighter at the Battle of Bennington in August 1777. On April 4, Ely addressed the mob in front of the common pleas court of Northampton and called for the people to rise up and close the court. The Hampshire moderates tried to take the play away from Ely with a county convention at Hatfield on April 9, which opposed the holding of county courts and suits for debt, but also opposed all radical measures to close them; particularly staunch in their conservatism on this issue were the older commercial Connecticut River towns—Northampton, Springfield, Hatfield and Hadley—with Joseph Hawley the leading delegate from Northampton. Samuel Ely scorned the schemes of the moderates, designed to quell his movement, and again raised a mob in front of the Northampton courts on April 12, calling for armed uprising. His plan was blocked by people standing to defend the courts. For his leadership in the Northampton riots, in mid-May Samuel Ely was arrested, convicted, and imprisoned in a Springfield jail. On June 13, a mob of 120 Hampshire men marched from Northampton to Springfield to free their leader from prison. Ely was freed, and, after an armed clash with a sheriff's posse, the insurgents yielded three hostages for their return of Ely. But on the eighteenth, 600 rebels marched on Northampton to demand release of the hostages, but withdrew upon pleas of the hostages themselves. The situation eased only when the hostages were freed; Ely eventually fled to the free air of Vermont.

The General Court suspended the right of *habeas corpus*, and sent a grievance committee headed by Sam Adams, which called a Hampshire County convention for August. While doing nothing to allay grievances, Adams and Hawley were able to use their former radical reputations to grant amnesties and quiet the county; people's conventions continued in the following year but without further major riots. The following August, one of Ely's men, Justus Wright, led a rescue mob in Northampton on behalf of another Ely follower and tried to close the courts in Westfield. After Wright's arrest in 1784, petitions of amnesty on his behalf were made by the towns of Goshen and Chesterfield. Wright himself, from prison, denounced the Massachusetts

---

One of them was Joseph Hawley, who later criticized the new Massachusetts constitution in 1780 as overly conservative and infringing on religious liberty. Rothbard, *Conceived in Liberty*, vol. 4, pp. 1258–63, 1500; pp. 141–49, 386.

government as an "aristocracy" of "tyrants." A small rump convention at Hatfield, in March 1783, also voted to pay no more taxes to the state of Massachusetts.

Disturbances had also occurred further west in Berkshire County. At the end of February 1782, a mob of 300 in Pittsfield succeeded in closing the common pleas court, but a month later, a large county convention in Pittsfield repudiated such radical methods. The leader of the successful Pittsfield uprising had himself been a justice of the peace, James Harris of Lanesborough. Harris had refused to pay taxes to the town, resisted the sheriff in serving court writs, rescued a neighbor's cow from the sheriff, and declared that the courts must be "ripped up" to make the General Court listen to the people's grievances. The following autumn, the mob rescued a pair of oxen from the hands of the sheriff; the mob, led by Major Thomas Lusk, had formally agreed to set themselves against the government. The General Court resorted here to continuing its suspension of *habeas corpus*.

At the beginning of the depression, Massachusetts managed to quiet Hampshire and Berkshire temporarily by lightening the tax burdens on the towns; however, it compensated for this by imposing a harsh stamp tax on all documents and papers, hitting at all state transactions and distressing the newspapers of the state; the newspaper tax, however, was soon repealed.

While the tax burden was most severe in Massachusetts (other New England states levied taxes at one-fourth the rate), all the states groaned from the postwar tax and debt burden, which undoubtedly aggravated the postwar depression. Much of the revenue, especially in importing states like New York, was derived from the state imposts. A particularly burdensome tax was the fixed tax *per acre* of land prevalent in the South. Thus Virginia levied a tax of one shilling per 100 acres and North Carolina five times that amount—these taxes greatly discriminated against the owners of the poorest land. Mass pressure from the backcountry forced Virginia, the Carolinas, and Georgia to abandon this tax and to moderately graduate the land tax. South Carolina, indeed, established a uniform land tax by value.

When the depression came, Connecticut, in contrast to the unyielding Massachusetts, agreed to abate taxes and grant time for their payment. Virginia sheriffs in the western country ran into similar trouble as in western Massachusetts. Any property they seized was rescued, many taxpayers refused to pay taxes and threatened to resist seizure of their property by force, and other delinquent taxpayers went into hiding. Numerous county petitions in Virginia pleaded the impossibility of paying taxes, a condition aggravated by the low price of tobacco in the mid-1780s. The Virginia legislature reacted sagely to the protests—again in contrast to Massachusetts—and agreed to lower or suspend taxes, and to allow hemp-growing western farmers to pay their taxes in hemp or flour. Indeed, Virginia agreed, in the spring of 1784, to suspend all tax collections for six months, and then agreed to cut taxes in half for the year 1785.[16]

---

[16][Editor's footnote] Jensen, *The New Nation*, pp. 302–12; Robert J. Taylor, *Western Massachusetts in the Revolution* (Providence, RI: Brown University Press, 1954), pp. 103–27; E. James Ferguson, *The Power of the Purse* (Chapel Hill: University of North Carolina Press, 1961), pp. 203–19.

5

The Issuance
of State Paper Money

A severe depression, bank contraction, a heavy burden of taxes to pay state debts, all this turned men's thoughts to issuing paper money to finance government. Historians influenced by the Populist struggles of the late nineteenth century have always identified proponents of inflation with "farmer-debtors" and hard-money men as "merchant-creditors." Actually, while it is true that debtors, especially during hard times, tend to favor inflation, merchants are even more likely than farmers to be heavily in debt since they have higher credit ratings and can borrow more. The result was that most of the economic groups in the 1780s favored inflation: the main problem was in determining which groups would obtain the enjoyment of the newly created money. Those wealthy cliques of merchants who already enjoyed the favors of the existing monopoly-chartered banks naturally opposed competition of state paper money; others tended to favor the new emissions. The exceptions were largely the sober-minded who remembered the rapid depreciation and dislocation during the war.

The first state to push through paper money during the postwar period was Pennsylvania, in March 1785. The Constitutionalists drove the measure through, but this "radical" act was essentially an alliance of farmers and wealthy public creditors who were anxious to have the state supply itself with money to pay their interest claims. Thus, of the emission of £150,000 of paper bills of credit, £100,000 went to pay the interest on the public debt, and £50,000 to be loaned on the security of land. The money could be used for payment of taxes; it was not, however, legal tender for private debts. Indeed, it was the provision of legal tender, not the paper money itself, at which the conservatives balked. Thus, as during the Revolutionary War, the conservative Pelatiah Webster balked not at banks nor at paper money, but at legal tender legislation. The main opposition to the state paper cause came, naturally enough, from the Bank of North America clique, these being the two major competing methods for supplying new money in the states. The Bank of North America refused to accept the already depreciated state notes at par, a major factor in impelling the legislature to repeal its charter. Despite frenzied attacks on all denigrators of the state paper, it had depreciated by 7.5 percent by the summer of 1786, and in the following year the conservative-dominated Pennsylvania legislature began to destroy and contract the outstanding notes.

In South Carolina, the "farmer-debtors" who led the state to adopt paper money were the great planters heavily in debt to British traders for the purchase of slaves to replace the thousands lost during the war. They were joined by Charleston merchants also in debt to the British. In October 1785, South Carolina authorized the emission of £100,000 of interest-bearing notes to be loaned on the security of land. The bills were receivable in payment of taxes, but again were not legal tender. Opponents managed to scale down the issue from the originally proposed £400,000. Extraordinary efforts, including boycotts, organized and individual, were made by merchants and planters of South Carolina to keep up the value of the notes, but they fell nevertheless to a 10 percent discount by the spring of 1787.

North Carolina issued £100,000 of paper in 1786, and these *were* legal tender. Over a third of the issue was used by the state to buy one million pounds of tobacco at twice the market price, and thus to provide a windfall subsidy to the state's tobacco planters. The rest of the money went to pay some of the claims of the veterans of the Revolutionary War. Since the money was legal tender, Gresham's Law (that money overvalued by the State will drive out undervalued money) came quickly into operation. Specie disappeared from North Carolina, and the paper depreciated by over 50 percent by the end of 1787. And since out-of-state creditors would not accept the depreciating paper, the merchants found it difficult to pay their creditors. Thus, the merchants suffered greatly from being forced to accept depreciated paper by the state, while at the same time *their* out-of-state creditors insisted on hard money. In the meanwhile, the mass of tobacco piled up in state warehouses, and the states found it impossible to sell it anywhere near the price that it had paid. Eventually the state had to take a 50 percent loss on the tobacco. By the end of the decade, North Carolina was forced to begin calling in and destroying its paper money.

Georgia had a similar experience; the legislature issued £30,000 in 1786 to pay Revolutionary veterans, and the bills were made legal tender for all payments: the issue was made at the behest of the rapidly expanding settlers in the backcountry. The money began to depreciate immediately, and Savannah citizens wisely and increasingly refused to take it despite the law. In only a year, the Georgia paper had fallen to a discount of four to one, and it ceased to be legal tender in 1790.

The New Jersey issue was essentially a land bank, pushed through by the Assembly over the opposition of the Council. The legislature finally passed an emission of £100,000 in legal tender bills in May 1786, all to be loaned on the security of real estate. Local vigilante associations terrorized merchants and traders into accepting the paper at par, but they could not terrorize New York and Philadelphia merchants, and the paper issue quickly began to depreciate by 15 percent. By 1789 the money was too valueless to pass in circulation.

The New York paper issue again belies the "radical-farmer-debtor," "conservative-merchant-creditor" dichotomy. £200,000 were issued in 1786, of which three-fourths was to be loaned on real estate or specie security, and one-fourth to pay interest to public security-holders. Staughton Lynd points out that New York City's leading conservative newspaper, the *New York Daily Advertiser*, approved the paper issue, as did the highly conservative Bank of New York. The conservatives were content that the paper was not declared legal tender for new debts, only for old ones. It should be noted that the New York radical leaders were opposed to legal tender, and most were opposed to the paper money.[17] The paper generally passed at a discount of up to 12 percent.

---

[17]Professor Lynd concludes:

Seven states issued paper money during the Confederation period, and of these Rhode Island was undoubtedly the most enthusiastic. A state in which there had previously been a rash of armed resistance to tax collection, Rhode Island issued £100,000 in 1786, a sizable amount considering its small population. The money was all to be loaned on land—the bill having been put through by the rural farmers over the determined opposition of the Providence merchant community. Rhode Island not only offered a very low interest rate on its loans; it provided a particularly severe set of legal tender laws and punishments. Indeed, a person accused of the heinous crime of refusing to accept the new bills at par was to be tried in a special court, without benefit of jury trial or even of the right of appeal. This brutal attack on the creditors and on merchants impelled mass resistance by the merchants and traders. Many merchants, despite the law, refused to accept the notes, and even closed their stores in protest. Farmers, in turn, pledged to boycott the sale of their produce to Providence. Customers rioted and tried to force tradesmen to accept the notes at par, and many traders and creditors were forced to flee the state. Finally, determined judicial resistance against the coercive acts led, after a furious struggle, to the repeal of these notorious laws in December 1786. The notes depreciated rapidly after that, down to 10 percent of face value by the end of 1788, and the legal tender clause was at last repealed in 1789.

Rhode Island was far more successful in her treatment of public creditors. The creditors were forced by law to accept redemption of their credit in the rapidly depreciating paper. In that way Rhode Island was able to rid her citizens of virtually the entire burden of state debt by 1790, and the debts were repaid at minimum sacrifice to the people of Rhode Island.

Because of its prominence in the politics of the late nineteenth century, the paper money question has often been considered the central issue dividing radicals from conservatives in the Critical Period. It was nothing of the kind. ... The allegedly extremist victory was, in fact, a mild inflationary measure rapidly acquiesced in by all groups in the community, just as in other cities. ... What all creditors feared in paper money was not inflation as such. ... [but] that it might be made a legal tender.

Staughton Lynd, "The Revolution and the Common Man: Farm Tenants and Artisans in New York Politics, 1777–1788" (Unpublished Ph.D. dissertation, Columbia University, 1962), pp. 212–13.

Of the six states that did not issue paper money during the 1780s, Connecticut managed to escape its distress by the far sounder method of emergency tax reductions and tax abatements. Delaware was in the trading and financial area of Pennsylvania, and hence Pennsylvania's bank and state paper circulated there. Virginia's opinion was staunchly hard money, this sentiment being shared by its liberals as well as conservatives, so there was little struggle there.

A strong drive for paper money arose in Maryland in 1786, and the Inflationist Party called for £350,000 of paper notes, of which £200,000 was to be lent to land owners. The Maryland Senate blocked the bill that was passed by the House in late 1786. Like Connecticut, Maryland, after outbreaks of armed attacks on her tax collectors, was partly able to stave off a drive for paper money by abating tax collections and suspending the forced sale of property of delinquent taxpayers. In New Hampshire too, the grievous burden of taxes led to the march of a large armed mob upon the capital in September 1786. The mob besieged the legislature and urged the issue of paper money; but a counter gang of citizens and militia drove off the rebels, and the voters of the towns firmly rejected a paper-money scheme referred to them by the legislature. Conservative Massachusetts, the hardest pressed of all, refused to issue paper or to grant any relief in taxes or in executions for tax delinquency.[18]

---

[18][Editor's footnote] Jensen, *The New Nation*, pp. 313–26; Nettels, *The Emergence of a National Economy*, pp. 81–88.

6

The Burdens
of Federal Public Debt

Part of the drive for state paper money came from the public creditors as well as the states; for the federal creditors were anxious to get paid
by *some* organ of government, and after the collapse of Robert Morris'
nationalist program they began to agitate for the states to assume their
share of the federal debt. Hence, the nationalists came to see that public
creditors could prove to be a troublesome two-edged sword. This process was accelerated by Congress' difficulties in raising its requisitions
and its inability to drive through any impost, which meant it was unable
to pay interest on the federal debt. Pennsylvania began the process of
state assumption during the war, and when Congress defaulted on payment of interest on its loan certificates in 1782, Pennsylvania assumed
payment of the interest to its citizens. Pennsylvania, New Hampshire,
and New Jersey quickly issued paper monies to pay the public creditors
who, while preferring specie, also preferred state paper to nothing at
all or to highly depreciated "indents"—paper certificates of interest—
which Congress had begun to issue after 1784, and which exchanged on
the market for one-fourth to one-eighth of their face value.

In 1787, short of specie and lagging in requisitions, Congress finally
allowed the states to service interest on the federal public debt in whatever type of money they chose. The paper-issuing states, furthermore,

began, one by one, to assume the federal securities held by their citizens. Pennsylvania's paper money issue enabled her to assume over $5 million of federal debt, exchanging it for new state securities, Maryland assumed several hundred-thousand dollars' worth during the 1780s, and New York, in its paper-money bill of 1786, undertook to assume all federal securities in exchange for state notes. New York thereby assumed over $2.3 million of federal securities. By the end of 1786, indeed, the New York, Pennsylvania, and Maryland state governments had assumed nearly $9 million of federal securities—one-third of the total principal of the public debt. New England and the South, with few federal securities extant in their states, accumulated little further federal securities, but it was still true that the states were acquiring more and more federal debt and that this "portended an end to major Congressional receipts and disbursements; the servicing of the debt bypassed Congress, and state revenues were committed to local purposes."[19] The nationalist program, based on centralized public debt, was increasingly in danger by the late 1780s. Congress, pressed for revenue, was forced to default on payments of its debt to France and Spain.

By the end of 1786, then, the nationalist program was in full rout. Congress had failed to aggrandize itself into the dominant power: it could not achieve a federal navigation act or more importantly a federal impost for its own source of tax revenue. Its requisitions were failing and its eagerly assumed public debt was rapidly being whittled away by the states, and it could not even meet any of the payments on its $10 million of foreign debt. Lacking independent federal revenue, the natural course would have been the disintegration of federal credit and power, and a full resumption of the decentralized policies that had been the initial consequence and the long-range promise of the American Revolution. Soon, as a congressional committee recommended in August 1786, Congress would have had to accept defeat and distribute all of the public debt among the states and let them pay or get rid of the debt as they wished. As Professor Ferguson concludes:

> The idea was supremely practical; it accorded with the nature of the Union and the predilections of the states. But it signified the complete abandonment of any effort to strengthen

---

[19]Ferguson, *The Power of the Purse*, p. 234.

Congress under the Articles of Confederation. Most of the states would probably have retired the bulk of the debt by cheap methods. Congress would have been left with depleted functions and little reason to claim enlarged powers. Creditors would have attached themselves to the states, and no ingredients would have remained to attract the propertied classes to the central government.[20]

In the days before corporations (except for the few banks), public debts provided one of the few markets for security speculation. Of the federal debt, loan certificates, amounting to about $11 million, had originally paid interest and were the "blue chips" of the federal security market. After 1782, the federal government defaulted on interest payments, and consequently the market price of loan certificates fell to about 20 to 25 percent of the nominal price. More speculative were the final settlement certificates paid to civilians and largely to soldiers at the end of the war; they sold during the 1780s at 10 to 15 percent in those states which paid interest on public securities merely in "indents," which were paper certificates of interest to be redeemed in the future. In those states that decided to support the securities more firmly, notably Pennsylvania, which backed them with taxes and assumed them on its own, the securities exchanged at 30 to 40 percent.

Whereas the more highly prized loan office certificates often remained in the hands of the original owners, the army final settlement certificates were quickly sold by the receiving soldiers and officers and found their way into the holdings of speculators, often very large ones. By 1787, those securities not redeemed by the states were almost all in the hands of secondary rather than the original owners. New York City became the center of this new public security trade and also the clearing house for investment of foreign capital. Foreign investment began to accelerate with the establishment in Europe of Daniel Parker from Watertown, Massachusetts, an associate of Robert Morris; as well as Gouverneur Morris; William Constable; Andrew Craigie; and William Duer. Parker also interested a group of Dutch bankers in American public securities.

---

[20]Ibid., p. 241.

As federal securities moved from original owners to brokers and speculators, the concentration of holdings sharply increased. In Massachusetts, original holdings of federal securities generally amounted to less than $500 for any one person; but by 1790, the top 7 percent of all subscribers owned 62 percent of the federal debt, while the lowest 42 percent of holders owned less than 3 percent of the debt. Sixty-one percent of the securities were owned by citizens of Boston. Similarly in Pennsylvania, 3 percent of the holders owned 40 percent of the securities and 9 percent of the holders held 61 percent of the debt. Again, the great bulk of public securities had been transferred by the late 1780s to a relatively few large speculators. In Maryland, the sixteen biggest speculators, or 5 percent of the total, held over 50 percent of the federal debt. Again, Rhode Island's 2.2 percent of leading debt owners held nearly 40 percent of the total debt.

Overall, taking Massachusetts, Maryland, Pennsylvania, and Treasury registers for interstate holders, the 280 largest holders owned nearly $8 million of federal securities, or two-thirds of the ones recorded in these sources. In contrast, holders of less than $500 of securities owned only 2 percent of the total. Fewer than 3,300 individuals held the roughly $12 million in securities recorded in the Treasury and in the above states.[21]

---

[21][Editor's footnote] Ibid., pp. 220–86.

PART II

The Western Lands
and Foreign Policy

7

The Old Northwest

With the cession of the claims of Virginia and other states to the lands of the Old Northwest, and the passage of its Ordinance of 1784 (applying to *all* western lands), Congress had nationalized the public domain and pledged itself to allow full self-government to any settlers of new territory whenever the territory should amass a population of 20,000 or more. New states were to be carved out of these territories when their population *equaled* that of the free citizens of the smallest of the existing states.[1]

On May 20, 1785, Congress adopted the Ordinance of 1785, which elaborated a detailed policy for Congress on surveys and sales of the western lands. The Ordinance provided for congressional surveyors to map out the land before sale, and for the land to be divided into New England-style "townships" and parceled out into rigid rectangular surveys of six square miles in the New England fashion. This contrasted to the natural boundary method of surveying used in the South. The rigid rectangular method compelled the purchases of sub-marginal land within an otherwise good "rectangle." Townships would be divided into minimum units of 640 acre sections, and these sections could be sold at public auction with a minimum imposed price of $1.00 per acre payable in specie or the equivalent in public securities. This minimum land price was high and discouraged settlement as frontier lands in the

---

[1][Editor's footnote] For more on the western lands, see Rothbard, *Conceived in Liberty*, vol. 4, pp. 1483–86, 1527–29; pp. 369–72, 413–15.

states were selling on much more favorable terms. Furthermore, each township would be forced to pay $36 to Congress for its (unasked for) surveying. This provision reflected the desire of Congress to milk revenue from the purchasers of western land, a desire that came higher than any attention to the rights or the needs of the settlers themselves. This imposed great hardship on the settlers, and insured that wealthy speculators would buy most of the land tracts. Indeed, large speculative land companies were influential in inducing Congress to set the high minimum price and the minimum acreage for land sales. Four sections of land in each township were to be reserved to Congress, to be distributed as it saw fit, and one section was forced to be set aside for public schools. One-third of the gold, silver, or copper to be found on the western lands was also to be reserved to the sovereign Congress—a policy all too reminiscent of royal reservations in colonial days—but this assertion of power was never applied and became a dead letter. The liberals in Congress, led by David Howell of Rhode Island and Melancton Smith of New York, narrowly managed to expunge a section that would have compelled the establishment of the religion of the majority of the local inhabitants.

The relatively liberal Ordinance of 1785, as well as the superior Ordinance of 1784, was a reflection of Virginia's previous triumph over the powerful companies of land speculators that had dominated the politics of Maryland, New Jersey, and other Middle Atlantic states, but this triumph proved to be short-lived, for there soon followed an orgy of congressional privileges to land speculators. Hardly had Congress begun the laborious process of surveying (which it had insisted on monopolizing) when it controverted its previously moderate liberal policy of land distribution and fell prey to the wiles of new groups of land speculators.

A group of New England ex-army officers of the Revolutionary War, headed by Generals Rufus Putnam and Samuel Holden Parsons, had long intrigued to grab large tracts of western lands. Finally, in 1786, Putnam and Parsons organized a statewide convention in Boston of Massachusetts veterans to form a joint-stock company called the Ohio Company of Associates (no connection with the pre-revolutionary Ohio Company formed by Virginia speculators). The new Ohio Company asked for the huge grant of one million acres. When Parsons' request made little headway, the company sent one of its organizers to lobby Congress, the Reverend Manasseh Cutler of Ipswich Village, Massachusetts, former lawyer and army chaplain. Cutler's wily lobbying made a deep imprint upon Congress, whose president was the highly receptive General Arthur St. Clair, an old-time Pennsylvania speculator in western lands and one of the leaders of the diehard conservative Republican Party in Pennsylvania. Cutler cemented his success by linking his fortunes to the New York reactionary William Duer, an old business associate of Robert Morris and the powerful secretary of the Board of the Treasury established by Congress. The influential Duer, who would handle the financial arrangements of the mammoth land sale, was eager to acquire a million or more acres of Ohio land east of the Scioto River and west of the Ohio Company tract. Linking forces, Cutler and Duer—over the impassioned objections of New York's radical Congressman Abraham Yates—pushed through Congress in the autumn of 1787 a gigantic deal for land monopoly. Cutler and the Ohio Associates were sold a huge tract of 1.5 million acres in Ohio, partially payable in land bounty certificates owed to the Continental Army, certificates that were selling for ten cents on the dollar on the open market. As a result of this and other special deductions, the Ohio Company was allowed to pay for their huge tract of land eight to ten cents an acre, in contrast to the one dollar required of ordinary purchasers of smaller sections at public auction. Thus were the at least moderately liberal provisions of the Ordinance of 1785 swept away on behalf of these influential land monopolists. Even more monopolistic was the similar privilege granted to Duer's "Scito Project," which bought nearly 3.5 million acres along the Ohio River of land originally arranged for Cutler. Much of the initial payment by Cutler, which launched the contract, was secretly advanced to him by Duer.

In order to cement these speculative projects, something had to be done to fasten the rule of the land companies over the western settlers. As a result, Cutler was instrumental in changing America's entire land policy by replacing the Ordinance of 1784 with the Ordinance of 1787. Thomas Jefferson's highly liberal Ordinance of 1784, allowing full self-government to settlers as soon as a territory reached a population of 20,000, greatly inconvenienced the land companies, for it meant that Congress and its favored land speculators might lose control of the West to the actual settlers. Indeed, settlers were increasingly squatting and developing western land in complete disregard of Congress or the land companies, thus challenging the authority of both august institutions. As early as 1785 Congress prohibited all settlement north of the Ohio River and soon sent troops to the frontier to burn the cabins of the squatters. But the settlers stubbornly returned to their lands when the troops departed. One settler put the case for all of them with great cogency:

> All mankind ... have an undoubted right to pass into every vacant country, and to form their constitution, and that ... Congress is not empowered to forbid them, neither is Congress empowered from that Confederation [of the U.S.] to make any sale of the uninhabited lands to pay the public debts, which is to be by a tax levied and lifted by the authority of the legislature of each state.[2]

The Northwest Ordinance, satisfying the aims of the land companies, was adopted on July 13, 1787, to apply only to the territory north of the Ohio River. While the system of land sales was continued along the lines of 1785, settler self-government was replaced by territorial government in the hands of Congress. Specifically, Congress would appoint a governor, a secretary, and three judges to govern and apply any laws they chose from the thirteen states. The settlers would be allowed to elect an assembly, but the appointed governor had an absolute veto on all legislation. The governor could choose a council from men nominated by the assembly. Furthermore, the governor (and Congress) were to have full control over the militia and the appointment of militia officers. The entire plan was almost a parody of royal colonial government. After the population reached 60,000 it might vote a constitution and establish a state government. Land-company domination of the new government for the Northwest Territory was revealed in the first congressional appointments: General Arthur St. Clair as governor and General Samuel Holden Parsons as one of the judges.

One of the most important provisions of the Northwest Ordinance was the prohibition of slavery (and servitude) in the Northwest Territory. The clause was passed without southern opposition, apparently because the South had little hope of slavery being established north of the Ohio; furthermore, the clause was offset by the agreement that fugitive slaves in the West from other states might be apprehended and

---

[2]Jensen, *The New Nation*, p. 357.

returned. A crucial difference, moreover, from Jefferson's original plan of 1784, was that slavery was outlawed only in the Northwest rather than in the entire western public domain.

Other large land grants in the Ohio region rapidly followed. In 1788 John Cleves Symmes, a wealthy and influential politician from New Jersey, was sold 330,000 acres of Ohio land on the Miami River, west of the other grants and on the same bargain terms. Also, Connecticut, in return for surrendering its claims to western lands, was granted in 1786 a tract of 3.5 million acres bordering on the bottom of Lake Erie. The bulk of this area, known as Connecticut's Western Reserve, was in turn sold to the Connecticut Company in the mid-1790s.

Despite the huge subsidies, the schemes of the Ohio and Scioto Companies quickly collapsed. The Ohio Company did little more than found Marietta, at the mouth of the Muskingum River; while the fly-by-night Scioto Company collapsed, succeeding only in the fiasco of swindling French settlers in founding the village of Gallipolis. The land was actually owned by the Ohio Company, so when the settlers arrived, they found their deeds to the land worthless. Symmes' venture also fared none too well, although he succeeded in founding the town of Cincinnati. By 1790, there were several thousand American inhabitants of the Northwest Territory distributed between Cincinnati, Marietta, and Gallipolis. Governor St. Clair's exercise of autocratic power soon led him into trouble with the American settlers and the Indians, who were understandably bitter at the invasion of lands that they claimed they never ceded to the white man.

The Indians, indeed, had cause for complaint. Congress earlier had arrogantly pronounced the western Indians subjects of the United States who had forfeited their rights by their hostility to the American cause during the Revolution. In particular, all Indian titles to their lands were declared void, and Indians were peremptorily ordered to move west of the Miami and Maumee Rivers—in short, to evacuate all their towns and hunting grounds in the Ohio country. To prevent American exercise of sovereignty over them, the Indians of the Northwest met at a general conference at Sandusky and at Niagara in the fall of 1783 and the summer of 1784, to plan confederation against American aggression.

An even greater obstacle to effectuating an American takeover of the Northwest was the British insistence on retaining the key Northwest forts of Oswego, Niagara, Detroit, and Michilimackinac.[3] The British army, remaining there to protect the British fur trade from American and settler invasion, encouraged the Indians in joint resistance against the menacing prospect of an American invasion. To the anguished American outcry that the British occupation was in direct violation of the peace treaty, the British could promptly reply with a *tu quoque*: for after all, the Americans were completely violating the treaty clause pledging no legal obstacles to a collection of prewar debts owed to British subjects, and they were also making no effort to comply with the treaty's restoration of confiscated Loyalist property. Despite its affirmation, Congress could not force the states to collect prewar British debts; indeed, attempts in various cities caused riots and threats of assassination against the would-be debt collectors. The Americans, in their turn, used as *their* excuse for violating the treaty a previous British violation: evacuating British troops had taken with them several thousand black slaves, some of whom were allowed their freedom, while others were sold again into slavery in the West Indies.[4]

The Continental Army had disbanded with the advent of peace, and the states would not stand for such a gross assumption of central power as a peacetime standing army. But Congress evaded this clear policy by creating a temporary western force, made up of militia from several states interested in grabbing the Northwest. This small contingent under the command of General Josiah Harmar of Pennsylvania was, however, scarcely in a position to attack the British and Indian forces in the Northwest. Indeed, their only action was to burn private settlements which had dared to venture north of the Ohio River in defiance of congressional will. During the remainder of the 1780s congressional policy toward the Indians could best be described as two-faced. Thus, the Northwest Ordinance piously pledged that "the utmost good faith shall always be observed toward the Indians; their lands and property shall never be taken from them without their consent ..." Yet, Governor Arthur St. Clair was at the same instructed by Congress not to

---

[3]British troops also remained in the northern New York forts of Oswegatchie, Pointe-aur-Fer, and Dutchman's Point.

[4][Editor's footnote] Southerners also argued that the debts were incurred during an unjust mercantilist regime. See Rothbard, *Conceived in Liberty*, vol. 3, pp. 1071–72; pp. 307–08.

"neglect any opportunity … of extinguishing the Indian rights to the westward as far as the River Mississippi."[5]

Before St. Clair's appointment, a bizarre movement developed for a new state of Illinois, stimulated by Congress' Ordinance of 1784. The war-created Illinois County of Virginia had collapsed late in the conflict. After the war, however, the adventurer John Dodge, former Indian agent for Virginia in Illinois, seized the military command of the village of Kaskaskia and proceeded without authorization of any kind to govern and terrorize its French citizenry. Dodge and Dorsey Pentecost, former head of the Virginia militia in the west, cooked up a petition for a new state of Illinois, but the petition had few supporters and the movement got nowhere.

Meanwhile, directly to the east of the Northwest Territory, the state of Pennsylvania was succeeding in expanding its territory at the expense of other states and the nascent new-state movements. In accordance with a bi-state agreement of 1779, the long-disputed Pennsylvania-Virginia boundary was finally settled in 1785, with Pennsylvania acquiring Pittsburgh and environs. Further east, a congressional court in 1782 arbitrarily awarded Pennsylvania jurisdiction over the Connecticut settlers of the Wyoming Valley, but on condition that the land titles of the settlers be upheld. Pennsylvania ignored this proviso and promptly sent militia to drive out the settlers, spurred on by the speculative land claims of leading Pennsylvania legislators. Connecticut's Susquehanna Company, organizers of the settlement, defended its colonists, and civil war raged, the settler resistance being led by frontiersmen John Franklin, under the Company promise of land grants. Ethan Allen and his Green Mountain Boys went down to aid the Wyoming settlers. Franklin proposed the formation of a new state of Westmoreland, to include the Susquehanna Valley of New York as well as Wyoming Valley in Pennsylvania. Oliver Wolcott of Connecticut drafted a constitution for Westmoreland, but the state of Connecticut completely betrayed its colonists and left them to the mercies of Pennsylvania, in return for the retention of the Ohio Western Reserve in 1786. Pennsylvania's jurisdiction was firmly resisted by the embattled settlers until Pennsylvania finally agreed to confirm the land titles of the pre-1782 settlers. John

---

[5]William T. Hagan, *American Indians* (Chicago: University of Chicago Press, 1961), p. 42.

Franklin, however, was seized and tried by the Pennsylvania authorities.[6]

---

[6][Editor's footnote] Jensen, *The New Nation*, pp. 169–70, 276–81, 327–39, 350–59; Burnett, *The Continental Congress*, pp. 682–88; Nettels, *The Emergence of a National Economy*, pp. 142–55; Thomas Perkins Abernethy, *Western Lands and the American Revolution* (New York: Russell and Russell, 1959), pp. 309–10; A.M. Sakolski, *The Great American Land Bubble* (New York: Harper & Brothers Publishers, 1932), pp. 99–123.

8

The Old Southwest

In the Southwest the Americans faced an at least equally difficult situation. At the end of the war, about 10,000 American settlers lived in these southwestern enclaves: central Kentucky, what is now northeastern Tennessee on the Holston River, and on the Cumberland River in north-central Tennessee. To the south, Spain claimed all the land south and west of the Tennessee River, covering western Tennessee and what is now Mississippi and Alabama. The Spanish claim, by conquest and occupation, was in fact far more tenable than that of America, which had sent no settlers into the deep Southwest. *Its* only claim was based on the peace treaty in which Great Britain had transferred lands no longer in its effective possession. Spain, too, tried to use the Indians of the Southwest as a buffer against American expansion.

Despite these hazards, the coming of peace saw the beginning of a flood of migration westward into the settlements of Kentucky and western Tennessee, doubling their population in one year. Many of the new settlers came armed with land-company grants, veterans' land rights and other such special privileges granted by Virginia and North Carolina, and were even able to oust many of the original settlers from the land. Dissatisfaction was particularly rife in western North Carolina, where the conservative-dominated legislature in 1783 threw open the western country to an orgy of speculative land grants. After doing so, North Carolina cunningly ceded its western lands to the Confederation Congress on condition that all of its speculative land grants be validated. But now the Holston River settlers, taking advantage of the cession and of the recently passed Ordinance of 1784, elected a convention which met in late August to form their own government and looked forward to becoming a new western state. The guiding spirit of the new-state movement was Colonel Arthur Campbell, of Washington County in southwestern Virginia, who urged the formation of a new state of Franklin to consist of what is now eastern Tennessee, chunks of southeastern Kentucky, southwestern Virginia, western North Carolina, northwest Georgia, and northeastern Alabama. However, the Holston convention of December 1784 was more modest and confined itself to Holston territory that North Carolina had already ceded; in accordance with the Ordinance of 1784 the convention declared a new state of Franklin, elected John Sevier governor, and asked Congress for admission as a new state. Campbell, however, persisted in leading a movement in Washington County to secede from Virginia and join the new state of Franklin. Campbell persuaded the county not to send any delegates to the Virginia House and he organized meetings condemning the oppression of Virginia's tax and militia laws. Throughout 1785 Campbell waged a successful struggle with Governor Patrick Henry, an opponent of secession, over retention of his and his followers' county offices.

In November 1785 a decisive confrontation occurred in the Franklin convention. On one side were the conservative forces, led by Governor Sevier, who had opposed the Franklin movement at the beginning and who wanted to remain a quasi-adjunct of North Carolina, limiting Franklin territory to North Carolina cessions and retaining a North Carolina type of constitution. In particular, Sevier wished to keep a North Carolina land law and a judicial system to foster land speculation, for Sevier himself was a leading land speculator. Thus, Sevier managed to reintroduce into the Holston settlement the hated land laws and land grants of North Carolina. In opposition, Arthur Campbell, the Reverend William Graham, and the Reverend Samuel Houston, led a struggle for a greater Franklin to include southwestern Virginia, and to form a new frame of government free from North Carolina's influence and based on highly liberal and radical principles. Campbell's proposed constitution would have instituted a one-house legislature, universal manhood suffrage, voting by secret ballot, and a referendum of *all* bills to the people before they could become law. In short, the legislature would propose, and the people would dispose of, all legislation; the people, in effect, would have been a second house of the legislature. But Sevier's victory at the convention meant that the claims of North Carolina land speculators remained essentially intact, and Campbell understandably lost interest in his own Franklin movement.

Meanwhile, North Carolina, reacting in horror to the new state of Franklin, repealed the cession of its western lands to the United States in the autumn of 1784. Sevier could not risk his popularity by acceding to North Carolina sovereignty, but he was, as we have seen, successful in keeping Franklin in the North Carolina orbit. The state remained precariously independent, however, and virtual civil war within Franklin erupted in 1787 as North Carolina tried to reestablish jurisdictions. In every Holston county there was now dual power, each with a set of Franklin and a set of North Carolina officials. Generally, the northern Holston counties were willing to return to North Carolina, while the southern counties, encroaching on Cherokee territory, were more fiercely committed to independence for fear that North Carolina would not defend their right to exist.

Another western land scheme, the Muscle Shoals project, was a land company attempt to grab and settle land at the bend of the Tennessee River south of the North Carolina line and hence under Georgia's asserted jurisdiction. Two of the main rulers of North Carolina, Congressmen William Blount and Governor Richard Caswell, both conservatives and inveterate land speculators, organized a land company with other leading western figures, including John Sevier. Also included were a set of influential Georgia politicians who obtained an agreement from Georgia in early 1784 to establish there a county of Tennessee. Georgia appointed a board of commissioners to report on the lands and function as Justices of the Peace for the county; three of the seven commissioners were members of Blount's Muscle Shoals Company. Sevier, one of the commissioners, was made colonel commandant of the county. The difficulties of the state of Franklin, however, as well as the growing disenchantment of Georgia officialdom, blocked the advance of the Muscle Shoals scheme during 1784. When Georgia proved reluctant to get involved with the Indians in the area, Blount and the other promoters turned to South Carolina, another state with claims in the region. Influenced by General Wade Hampton, one of the organizers of Blount's company, South Carolina made large grants of land in the "Bend of Tennessee" area during 1786. Georgia was also persuaded, after a struggle, to grant large tracts of land to the commissioners of the new "Tennessee County."

With the advent of peace, the citizens of the Kentucky region had begun a drive for independence from Virginia and for statehood. Particularly grievous to the Kentucky land speculators was Virginia's recent tax of five shillings per hundred acres on all large Kentucky land grants. This action turned the leading Virginians living in Kentucky, most of whom were land speculators in Virginia grants, in favor of a statehood which they had previously opposed. This, plus other tax burdens, the lack of independence of the Kentucky militia, and poor judicial service from the state of Virginia, ignited the postwar Kentucky statehood movement. Proceeding very cautiously, the voters of Kentucky, in three separate elections and three conventions at Danville during 1784–85, deliberated until finally unanimously demanding Virginia's recognition as a "free, sovereign, and independent republic." The goal was a separate state and then admission to the U.S. Virginia, in gentle resignation, resolved in June 1786 to accept Kentucky as a separate state if requested by another convention, the acceptance to take effect when Kentucky would in turn be accepted by Congress. One vital clause was Virginia's insistence that Kentucky retain the validity of all land claims previously established under Virginia law—a clause that dampened some of the ardor of the Kentucky settlers for independence. Indeed, the Kentucky statehood movement had been captured by the Virginia land speculators from the original liberal settler-oriented advocates led by Arthur Campbell. Kentucky's seemingly imminent statehood, furthermore, was challenged during 1786 by its preoccupation with combating Indian forays.[7]

---

[7][Editor's footnote] Jensen, *The New Nation*, pp. 327–37; Abernethy, *Western Lands and the American Revolution*, pp. 288–324.

9

The Jay-Gardoqui Treaty and the Mississippi River

The settlers who poured into the Southwest after the war some-how expected that they would be able to trade down the Mississippi River. The Mississippi, rather than the east-west trade across the almost impassable Appalachian Mountains, was the natural trading route for the western inhabitants. Yet, it should have been evident to them that Spain, in unchallenged possession of both sides of the lower Mississippi (even the aggressive United States did not dispute Spain's possession of West Florida below the 31st parallel), had no particular reason to open the Mississippi to American trade. Hostile to the new republic and understandably fearful of its potential expansion westward and southward, Spain was in no mood to relax prevailing mercantilist poli-cies for the benefit of the United States. The Americans, to be sure, argued that Britain had granted the U.S. free navigation of the Missis-sippi in the peace treaty, but here American arguments were even more absurd than in their claims to the Southwest above the 31st parallel. Since Britain had granted West Florida to Spain, Britain had no power whatever to grant any aspect of the Mississippi, and hence the free navigation clause in law or in reason was meaningless. Yet, the western migrants who should have realized the situation reacted in anger and shock when they discovered that Spain proposed to keep the Missis-sippi closed to their trade.[8]

---

[8][Editor's footnote] For more on the Mississippi question in the Treaty of Paris, see Rothbard, *Conceived in Liberty*, vol. 4, pp. 1470–79; pp. 356–65.

With the advent of peace, Spain closed the lower Mississippi River to American trade in early 1784, raising a storm of shock and bitter protests and even rumbled threats of war by some Americans. Alarmed at this frenzied reaction, Spain sent Don Diego de Gardoqui as a special envoy to New York City, where Congress was now sitting, to negotiate a treaty. The idea was to regularize all outstanding questions: territorial, political, and commercial, between the two nations, and to do this before the population explosion in the West built up enormous pressure against Spanish territory. Spain was prepared to yield a substantial amount. In particular, they were prepared to grant to the U.S. the right to trade in Spain and Spanish colonial ports, a trade that America had enjoyed during the war and had supplied hard cash for American exports. The port of Havana was particularly important in the trade with the Spanish colonies. On boundary questions, Spain was also prepared to be extremely generous, and for the sake of American quiescence was willing to abandon its well-founded claim to all the land south and west of the Tennessee River, and to be content with the Yazoo River parallel at the northern boundary of West Florida. This would have yielded all the land north of the mouth of the Yazoo, including what is now western Tennessee, most of Mississippi and Alabama, and northwestern Georgia. In return, Spain sought a mutual guarantee of boundaries, which would have meant a permanent alliance in the Western Hemisphere. On the Mississippi River question, however, Spain was adamant, and Gardoqui was not permitted to yield on it.

Gardoqui arrived at New York in July 1785 and launched continuing negotiations with John Jay, Congress' Secretary for Foreign Affairs. Jay was sympathetic to these just and highly favorable terms, but was hamstrung by congressional orders to conclude nothing without congressional approval, nor to yield an inch of insistence upon the "right" of free American navigation of the Mississippi or on the American claim to push Spain's West Florida boundary down to the 31st parallel. The latter claim was advanced on the absurd ground that Britain had so defined West Florida in the peace treaty—at a time when West Florida, whose boundary had always been at the Yazoo, was in Spanish possession.

Jay and Gardoqui came to agree, along Spanish-proposed lines, on a projected treaty of commerce and alliance for thirty years. The alliance provided a mutual guarantee of boundaries in the Western

Hemisphere. In the commercial clauses of the treaty, Spain granted American merchants commercial reciprocity between the U.S., Spain, the Canary Islands and such ports as Havana. The merchants of either nation were to be given the treatment accorded to each country's own citizens. The merchants were to be free to introduce all manufactures and products of either country, except tobacco, with tariffs to be worked out on a principle of reciprocity. As a special bonus, Spain agreed to help the United States oust Britain from her military forts in the Northwest Territory and to guarantee the purchase in specie of a certain amount of American hardwood every year.

Jay and Gardoqui were thus in close agreement on the terms of the proposed treaty. There remained, however, the big stumbling block of the congressional mandate for free navigation of the Mississippi. As a result, Jay decided to propose to Congress that it agree to forbear using the Mississippi for the duration of any agreed-upon treaty. In this way, Congress would not even be ceding the principle of navigation in approving the proposed treaty.

No more reasonable proposal could have been put to Congress, which received the plan at the end of May 1786. Short of making war upon Spain, which almost no one was willing to undertake, Americans would not be trading down the Mississippi in any case. Such an American claim, moreover, was unheard of in international law or polity. For the mere forbearance of exercising this "right," America was being offered the privilege of a highly favorable trade with Spain. Yet the proposal generated a fierce controversy and split Congress into two sectional camps.

To the northern delegates there was no problem; the Jay proposal was intelligent and judicious, and it provided a welcome and important trade for America.[9] Furthermore, there was a healthy distrust of

---

[9]Historians have tended to slight the advantages and manifest justice of the Jay-Gardoqui treaty. Thus, Samuel Flagg Bemis, after conclusively demonstrating the absurdity of the western claim of a "right" to navigate the Mississippi, suddenly turns upon Jay in a burst of patriotic fervor and vainglory. Samuel Flagg Bemis, *Pinckney's Treaty: America's Advantage from Europe's Distress* (New Haven, CT: Yale University Press, 1960), p. 88. On the other hand, properly appreciative of the Jay-Gardoqui treaty is Forrest McDonald, *E Pluribus Unum* (Boston: Houghton Mifflin, [1979] 1965), pp. 144–46.

the West and a realization that accelerating migration there was generating a potentially aggressive and even separatist people, sharply cut off as they were from commerce from the East by the Appalachian Mountains. The fact that land speculators in the East opposed migration in order to keep new settlers there and thus appreciate the value of their lands, does not negate the cogency of the northern position. The southern states, however, trapped in a precarious hold on the southwestern settlers, were heavily immersed in speculation in western lands, including several members of Congress. The South was largely politically and economically committed to support the western hysteria about a Jay sellout of their frenetic claims. James Madison, Patrick Henry, and Thomas Jefferson were among the Virginians in opposition. Some southerners, in contrast, were able to rise above these political and personal considerations: George Washington generally favored the treaty, as did Richard Henry Lee and his nephew Henry Lee, a member of Congress. Henry Lee's arguments for the great advantages of a "free liberal system of trade with Spain" were really not belied by his acceptance of a bribe from Gardoqui, who was ever ready to ply sympathetic Americans with his favors.

There was another important reason for the sharp North-South sectional split on the western issue. For already slavery, rapidly disappearing in the northern states, was becoming a sectional issue. To all Americans the *West* meant the *Southwest*, for the area north of the Ohio was not only unsettled, it was largely under the control of the British military outposts. It was the Southwest that was receiving a heavy influx of new settlers. Therefore the rapid admission of new western states would magnify the political strength of the southern slave states and diminish the strength of the free North. Here was another favor propelling both southern enthusiasm, and northern hostility, toward western expansion.

Finally, after a furious struggle, Congress at the end of 1786 passed a motion by the Massachusetts delegation to abandon its insistence on Mississippi navigation and on the 31st parallel in its instructions to John Jay. The vote was seven to five, strictly sectional, with every state north of Maryland voting for repeal, and every state from Maryland southward voting opposed (Delaware was not in attendance). But the vote was a pyrrhic victory; any treaty would need the vote of nine states for approval and the southern states gave notice that they would do battle to the end. Blocked by implacable southern hostility, further negotiations had become useless, and Gardoqui broke them off in the spring of 1787. Gardoqui, moreover, had now realized that the western hysteria was now escalating into profound disillusionment with a United States that could have passed such a treaty. As a result, many in the West were beginning to toy with the idea of seceding from the United States altogether, and in some way linking up with Spain to secure free navigation of the Mississippi. In truth, the secession movement and the proposed linkage with Spain was a highly sensible western turn toward their natural southern route of trade and communication.

The idea of western secession and subsequent linkage with Spain was first broached to the fascinated Gardoqui at the end of August 1786 by Dr. James White, a congressman from North Carolina. White, a highly educated speculator in Cumberland land, was a friend and business associate of William Blount and Governor Richard Caswell, two of the dominant men in North Carolina. Shortly after his bold proposal, White was chosen for the important post of Superintendent of Indian Affairs for the Southern Department. The Spanish Foreign Minister, delighted by White's suggestion, instructed Gardoqui that westerners could be sure of the free use of the Mississippi should they secede and then ask Spain for protection.

Meanwhile, Kentucky politics were undergoing an upheaval. In the fall of 1786 Kentucky's military and political leader, George Rogers Clark, had raided, confiscated, and destroyed the property of several Spanish merchants in the Vincennes area of the Illinois territory. Moreover, Clark encouraged rumors that he was planning an attack on the Spanish Southwest territory to drive the Spanish out of the Mississippi. The fabulous young adventurer and intriguer General James Wilkinson, who had only come to Kentucky a few years earlier, was able to use this incident as the lever for Clark's political downfall. Wilkinson, now the political leader of Kentucky, also conceived of the idea of western secession as well as a tie-in with Spain.

In the summer of 1787 the daring Wilkinson, determined to be the "George Washington of the West," went along to New Orleans and there presented his scheme to the eager Spanish officials. In the interest of secession and linkage with Spain, Wilkinson advised Spain to stand firm on the Mississippi question, while at the same time he now urged friends in Congress to accept the Jay-Gardoqui Treaty, thus providing a double impetus for western revolt. Taking a secret oath of allegiance to Spain, Wilkinson persuaded the Spaniards to grant him the lucrative personal right to trade with New Orleans so as to build up a Spanish connection with the West.

In Kentucky, political power was in the hands of Wilkinson's group who was involved in the secession scheme. Members included Harry Innes, Benjamin Sebastian, and George Muter. In addition, the Wilkinsonian John Brown was elected Kentucky delegate to the Confederation Congress. Virginia Governor Edmund Randolph, a business associate of Wilkinson's and a heavy speculator in Kentucky lands, seemed undisturbed by hints of plans for western independence.

During 1788 the various western threads began to tie together: James Robertson, undisputed head of the Cumberland settlement, declared his willingness to join the Kentucky plans, and James White, traveling far for the cause, inducted John Sevier of the State of Franklin into the secession plan. This was not difficult, since Sevier was about to be arrested for treason to North Carolina for his Franklin activities. Sevier wrote Gardoqui of his support and asked for loans and military aid from Spain. Robertson, too, wrote to the Spanish governor of Louisiana, Esteban Miró, and proudly informed Miró that they had just succeeded in getting North Carolina to organize the Cumberland territory into the "District of Mero" named in the governor's honor. Sevier also tried to induce the Spanish to approve the Muscle Shoals project and grant it an outlet to the Gulf of Mexico.

When Congress postponed the question of Kentucky's admission into the Union because of the current changeover to the Constitution of the United States in mid-1788, Wilkinson saw that the hour of decision had arrived. Now in July 1788, a Kentucky convention was in session to frame a constitution for the new western state. Wilkinson, Brown and their colleagues tried hard at this convention, and at another convention in November, to push through the formation of Kentucky as an independent state and therefore a state free of the Union. But the true motives of the planners had now become public, aided by the apostasy of George Muter, and Kentucky decided to ask Congress humbly for admission to the Union. The leaders of Kentucky, lacking Wilkinson's bold imagination and insight into western problems, had dealt a grave blow to the idea of western secession.

At the end of the year Virginia passed another act confirming the secession of Kentucky, but this time its terms of the bequest were harsher. Virginia veterans were to be allowed unlimited time to lay their claims to bounty lands in Kentucky; furthermore, Kentucky was to be required to pay her part of Virginia's public debt. These harsh terms encouraged renewed attention to the proposal by Wilkinson, thus keeping alive the idea of secession on behalf of Spain. Kentucky refused to accept the conditions, and Virginia then agreed to rescind them in another act of separation at the end of 1789. The rest was routine: a convention completed the formation of the state of Kentucky in mid-1790 and Congress agreed to admit the new state to the Union in February 1791, and it officially became a state in June 1792.

The rebellious lands of the Tennessee area were similarly quieted by a worried North Carolina, which agreed in early 1790 to cede its western lands to the United States. In 1790 Congress promptly created and organized the Southwest Territory consisting of North Carolina's seceded western lands and a narrow strip southward that had been seceded to the U.S. by South Carolina in 1787. This step effectively ended the Southwest movement for secession from the U.S. The leaders of the secession intrigue were shrewdly coopted into the United States system: John Sevier, for example, was pardoned for this "treason" by North Carolina and given a handsome appointment as Brigadier General by that state; James Robertson was also made a Brigadier General. Andrew Jackson, a young North Carolina lawyer who recently moved to the Cumberland and became an ardent secessionist, was made Attorney General of the Mero District. Finally, none other than William Blount, the dominant political force in North Carolina and extensive speculator of the southwestern lands, was appointed governor of the Southwest Territory as well as Superintendent of Indian Affairs for the region.

While western intrigues with Spain were progressing, Britain, ensconced in the Northwest, was by no means quiescent. Britain's idea was to promote a different type of secession of the West—a secession that would link up with Britain and proceed to open up the Mississippi River by driving the Spanish out of the area. During 1788, Lord Dorchester, Governor General of Canada, dispatched the veteran Tory Dr. John Connolly to sound out western leaders in Pittsburgh and Kentucky on this scheme. James Wilkinson expressed interest, and evidently kept the idea in reserve in case the Spanish project should fail. Several Pennsylvanian and western leaders were favorable to the scheme and a Committee of Correspondence was created in Kentucky to promote the plan.

In response to the rising pressures for western separation, the northern states became frightened at these rumblings and decided to reverse the decision of 1786 and reaffirm a hard line on Mississippi navigation. In September 1788, the North Carolina delegation urged stridently and preposterously that Congress resolve that the United States "have a clear, absolute and unalienable claim to the free navigation of the River Mississippi," which was supported not only by treaties but also purportedly "by the great law of nature." John Jay apparently felt it necessary to make public confession of his sins and he told Congress that "*circumstances and discontents*" had changed his views on the question of Mississippi navigation. Congress then resolved "that the free navigation of the River Mississippi is a clear and essential right of the United States," and Gardoqui, seeing that further negotiations would be useless, promptly sailed for home in October 1789.[10]

---

[10][Editor's footnote] Bemis, *Pinckney's Treaty*, pp. 1–148; Abernethy, *Western Lands and the American Revolution*, pp. 317–53.

10

The Diplomacy of the Confederation

Not all the diplomacy of the postwar period was such a failure as the negotiations with Spain and Great Britain. As soon as the peace treaty was signed, America, freed from the fetters of British mercantilism and eager to trade with all nations, instructed the peace commissioners (John Jay, John Adams, and Benjamin Franklin) to negotiate commercial treaties with all willing countries. While peace negotiations were still underway, Franklin had already signed a treaty with Sweden in April 1783. The treaty was based on the libertarian American "Plan of 1776" for freedom of trade and the safeguarding of neutrals' rights: in particular, restricting contraband that could be seized by belligerent partners, the freedom of neutral shipping between belligerent ports, and the principle that free ships make free goods. The Swedish treaty made the further liberal addition of agreeing to convoy each other's neutral ships in time of war.[11]

In 1784 Congress established another treaty commission, with Thomas Jefferson replacing John Jay. Their new instructions—in the "Plan of 1784"—added advanced libertarian features to the old Plan: e.g., providing immunity to civilians and unfortified towns during war, prohibiting privateering between the treaty parties in case of war between them, and restricting the scope of blockades. But the most creative innovation in the Plan for protecting neutrals' rights was a

---

[11][Editor's footnote] The Plan of 1776 refers to the agreement made with France to recognize American independence and promote free trade. Rothbard, *Conceived in Liberty*, vol. 4, pp. 1346–53; pp. 232–39.

new rule on contraband. Previously, warring nations could confiscate contraband articles even on neutral ships; now contraband was to be purchased, rather than seized by force (John Adams, indeed, wished to abolish the contraband category altogether and thus preserve neutral rights totally).

The first treaty concluded under the new instructions was signed with Prussia in 1785. This admirably advanced treaty not only provided for neutral convoys, but also for purchase of contraband and abolition of all privateering between the two countries, even if they were at war. These provisions were, in the words of Franklin, "for the interest of humanity in general, that the occasions of war, and the inducements to it, should be diminished." The ultimate goal of these endeavors, according to Jefferson, was to be "the total emancipation of commerce and the bringing together of all nations for a free intercommunication of happiness."

In colonial days British payment of tribute had protected American shipping from depredations by pirates from the Barbary States of North Africa. The good offices of Spain, however, enabled Adams and Jefferson to conclude a favorable treaty in 1787 with the Sultan of Morocco. Exacting only nominal tribute, the Sultan agreed on friendly peaceful commercial relations and on treating captives of any mutual wars of the future as prisoners of war, rather than slaves, as had been the custom. However, the rulers of the other Barbary States—Algiers, Tripoli, Tunis—continued to prey on American ships and enslave their sailors or hold them for ransom. For a peace treaty they demanded from the United States a large tribute. The aggressive Jefferson preferred war to tribute and tried to organize a joint European war against the Barbary pirates, but Congress would not support this bellicosity. Thus, John Adams trenchantly pointed out that the demanded tribute would be far cheaper than any American war against Barbary, but John Jay, the Secretary for Foreign Affairs, preferred to do nothing about Barbary in order to win American public opinion for his nationalist schemes: the lure being the use of national force to the benefit of American shipping in the Mediterranean. This Mediterranean trade particularly included exports of fish, wheat, and flour. In fact, Jay could breezily write upon hearing of Algiers declaring war against American shipping: "This war does not strike me as a great evil. The more we are ill-treated abroad, the more we shall unite and consolidate at home. Besides, as it may become a nursery for seamen, and lay the foundation for a respectable navy, it may eventually prove more beneficial than otherwise." In short, welcome pillaging of American ships so as to seduce the public into looking for a strong national government for protection.

As for Great Britain, it not only refused to leave the Northwest forts, but also to sign any commercial treaties with the United States. Here, Prime Minister William Pitt the Younger yielded to the pressure of British shipowners and American Tories in Canada who wanted a monopoly of the British West Indies export trade. Indeed, although John Adams was sent as Minister to Great Britain, Britain refused to send even a diplomatic representative to the new nation. Instead, Britain intrigued not only with Indians and westerners, but also with the independent state of Vermont. Still kept out of the Union, Vermont was at least willing to listen to the idea of Union with Canada, since its natural trade route was the St. Lawrence River. The British as late as 1789 talked with Ethan and Ira Allen about a commercial treaty and possible reunion with Britain. Vermont, however, decided against this course and would eventually be admitted as the first new state of the Union in early 1791.[12]

---

[12][Editor's footnote] Nettels, *The Emergence of a National Economy*, pp. 5–6, 67; Jensen, *The New Nation*, pp. 161–68, 211–13; Dumas Malone, *Jefferson and the Rights of Man* (Boston: Little, Brown and Co., 1951), pp. 22–33; Chilton Williamson, *Vermont in Quandary, 1763–1825* (Montpelier: Vermont Historical Society, 1949), pp. 156–61, 294.

PART III

The Nationalists Triumph:
The Constitutional Convention

11

Shays' Rebellion

Massachusetts suffered particularly from the economic aftermath of the Revolutionary War as its fisheries trade was cut off and its exports to the West Indies were sharply curtailed. Furthermore, the grandiose postwar funding of the wartime Massachusetts debt, which ballooned from £100,000 to £1.5 million after the war, placed a particularly heavy tax burden on its citizenry. While Congress was reevaluating its currency at a depreciation of forty to one, and other states were depreciating at higher rates, Massachusetts stubbornly and absurdly insisted on redeeming its notes at their full value when they were issued. Interest, furthermore, was paid in specie. In addition, reliance on poll and special excise taxes placed an enormously heavy burden on the poorer farmers of western Massachusetts. The courts of the western counties not only exacted high fees, but were also the hated instrument of the enforcement of the tax burden, which included imprisonment of public and private debtors as well as the selling of many debtors into servitude to pay off the debt; some were imprisoned for owing only six shillings! All the debtors' property except clothing was subject to court seizure. We have already noted the swarm of petitions and the more insurrectionary anti-tax, anti-court movement in the west before the end of the war, headed by the Reverend Samuel Ely and propelled by these distressed circumstances.

The nationwide depression that struck in 1784 hit the already depressed Massachusetts particularly hard. In 1784 alone there were over 2,000 suits for recovery of taxes and other debts in Worchester

County alone, and over ninety insolvent debtors were sent to jail in Worchester in the following year. Hampshire County saw its common pleas courts crowded with over 800 debt cases in 1785 alone. Lands in the western counties dropped precipitously in value, and numerous distressed citizens of Massachusetts packed up and emigrated westward.

Yet western Massachusetts did not erupt immediately as might have been expected. The reason was probably that the Massachusetts General Court cut taxes in the towns enormously during 1784 and 1785, assessing only 140 towns in the prior year and none at all in the latter. The taxes were replaced by a stamp tax, which fell on the press, and transfer of documents had to be modified quickly. Furthermore, the plight of debtors was slightly eased in 1784 by increasing the maximum amount of debt suits which could be handled by local justices of the peace, who charged far lower fees than did the courts of common pleas. However, the backcountry attorneys who earned far more from the more expensive common pleas litigation insisted still on taking these small debt cases there, much to the anger of the western farmers and debtors. Many of these attorneys, furthermore, were government officials interconnected with the county judges, an interconnection that angered the citizens of the country even more.

Finally, in early 1786, the masses of western Massachusetts began to erupt once again. From their state government they demanded a lowering of taxes, especially poll taxes, which now accounted for an enormous 40 percent of the state's revenue, a lowering of judicial fees and increased simplification and greater efficiency in the judicial system, and the lowering of government salaries and expenses. The protestors also opposed the acceleration of Massachusetts' assumption of public debt, the payment of 6 percent interest in specie annually, and the redemption of the notes at their full face value. In short, they objected to excessive burdens on the taxpayer for the benefit of the cliques of public creditors, mainly eastern merchant-speculators who had purchased the debt at a great discount. Western Massachusetts soberly asked for redemption of the securities at their market value and not their face value.

Overall, the basic program of the people of western Massachusetts was eminently libertarian. They also asked for emission of state paper money and a law that would exempt personal property of debtors from executions. Yet, in the spring of 1786, the General Court brusquely dismissed the western pleas and piled insult upon injury by raising taxes on polls and estates. Indeed, to make up for the tax moratorium in 1785, the General Court in the following year raised the assessed tax burden on the towns to over £300,000—the highest in a five-year period. Of this amount, nearly £130,000 was for payment to public creditors on their securities, going mainly into the hands of speculators. This tax burden was even greater in real terms since prices and property values had declined in the depression, thus making given nominal taxes a heavier burden in real purchasing power and in relation to the incomes of the people. To this oppression was added an expanded work of legal fees for lawyers, judges, and court clerks—fees for less efficient judicial service in the courts.

Apparently it took a lawyer to know a lawyer, for one of the leaders of the western anti-attorney campaign was the lawyer Thomas Gold, a relative of the highly conservative congressional delegate from the West, Theodore Sedgwick. Gold denounced the "Oppression, Extortion & Malpractices of the Attorneys" and introduced a bill abolishing the common pleas court in favor of justices of the peace, as well as opening up the legal profession to freedom of entry for every man. The bill was killed in the Massachusetts Senate.

Thus, none of the westerners' grievances were met by the General Court in the spring of 1786; instead their demands of protest were brusquely dismissed. And not only in the West: no sooner did the legislature disperse on July 8 when the eight towns of Bristol County in southeastern Massachusetts met and called for a new constitutional convention for Massachusetts. The Bristol towns demanded the suspension of suits for debt and tax collection for nine months and an emission of paper money largely to pay the public debt. As an ultimate demand the Bristol towns asked for abolition of the Massachusetts Senate as an economical move, and significantly urged—as in the case of the battle against the Crown—that government officials be made dependent on the *annual* vote of their salaries by the House. In short, these liberals acted against the postwar buildup throughout Massachusetts of a state bureaucracy bent on continuing their permanent salary.

Further conventions were soon held in Worchester, Berkshire, Hampshire, and Middlesex counties. The Hampshire convention began with an advanced meeting of a few towns at Pelham, which then circulated to the entire county. The convention met in Hatfield on

August 22 and represented no less than fifty towns, the largest convention yet held in Hampshire County. The delegates were elected and paid by the towns and included some of the most prominent citizens of the county: e.g., the great family scion William Pynchon of Springfield, John Hastings of Hatfield, and the merchant Benjamin Ely of West Springfield. The Hatfield convention drew up a comprehensive list of twenty-five grievances that summed up the libertarian program of the Massachusetts radicals. Grievances included the exactions of state government; the stamp tax on newspapers; excessive poll, post and other taxations; high judicial and lawyers' practice fees; and "the existence of" the common pleas (civil) and general session (criminal) courts. Hampshire also followed Bristol in calling for a constitutional convention and urged reapportionment, abolition of the Senate, and making appointed government officials subject to annual vote of their salaries. The Senate was not only criticized as expensive, it had also blocked freedom of entry to the legal profession as well as instituted the tax on polls and estates. Furthermore, its membership was legally confined to the highly propertied class, and the senators were also elected by large districts, and not individual towns, which made them remote from the people.

Not all from the West favored the Hatfield resolution. Hatfield itself objected to the paper-money clause. More serious were the defections of the towns of Springfield and Northampton. The conventions of Berkshire, Worchester, and Middlesex counties were also rather milder than that of Hampshire. All the county conventions, however, caused a wave of hysteria by Massachusetts conservatives who ranted about treason and even sinister British influences. The towns of Cambridge and Medford, annually rejecting an invitation to take part in the Middlesex convention, opined that annual elections of House representatives were enough of a means of exerting the public will and gaining redress of grievances. The radicals rebutted by pointing to the obstructive Senate. The city of Boston, conveniently forgetting its own "illegal" and revolutionary past, saw only subversion and British machinations in the protest movement. And the chief justice of the Massachusetts Supreme Court declared that all conventions, especially Hampshire's presumption of criticizing the Massachusetts constitution, were to be illegal and dangerous.

The Hampshire convention, along with all the others, had carefully insisted that all protests be peaceful, but the protesting masses realized that only by direct action—only by taking responsibility for their own lives and fortunes—could any substantial gains be made. A few days after the Hatfield convention, an armed mob of about 1,500 assembled in Northampton and seized the county courthouse to block any sessions of the courts. The insurgents appointed a committee to "request" adjournment of the courts, to which the judges hastened to reply. The idea was to close the courts until redress of the people's grievances were achieved; the rebels surely compared the "great scarcity of cash" among the people to the handsome salaries of the appointed government officials. The leader of the successful Northampton mob was Captain Luke Day of West Springfield, a landowner who raised his own insurgents and drilled them. Assisting Day in the court seizure were Captain Joseph Hinds of Greenwich and Lieutenant Joel Billings of Amherst.

The Northampton uprising set the spark for armed mobs in the other protesting counties, and courts were forcibly closed in the counties of Worcester, Middlesex, and Bristol. When Governor James Bowdoin called out the Worcester County militia against the rebels, the militia, in a classical revolutionary mood, refused to turn their guns against their friends and neighbors. A mob of rebels were thus able to close the Worcester courthouse. When the town of Concord went against the tide to vote condemnation of the Hampshire and Worcester uprisings, Job Shattuck marched into Concord with one hundred supporters and picked up another one hundred within the town. Ignoring the numerous pleas of the Middlesex convention, Shattuck and his mob seized the courthouse at Concord and closed the court of common pleas. In Bristol County the rebels were also able to overrule the militia and force the closing of the courts.

On September 13 the courts of Berkshire County, scheduled to sit at Great Barrington, were seized by an armed mob of 800 men coming from twenty-three towns in the county. When the militia was called to march against the rebels, the bulk of it actually deserted to the enemy. After the judges prudently decided to close the courts, the mob forced the common pleas judges to sign a declaration that they would not open the courts until the Massachusetts constitution had been revised. The triumphant mob released all the debtors from the Great Barrington jail. One observer marveled that "not one act of private outrage was committed during the whole transaction. ... Does history exhibit such another transaction as this, yet every citizen secure in his person and property?" The observer noted that the Hampshire and Worcester court closings had been similarly scrupulous and orderly.

Deeply involved in the Berkshire rebellion was the formerly conservative William Whiting, a prominent physician and chief justice of the Berkshire court of common pleas. Whiting had collaborated in the insurgents' plans and had published his support for the rebellion and his condemnation of the legislature for conspiring against the liberties of the people. Whiting particularly attacked the speculators benefiting from the state's redemption of any notes at face, rather than market, value.

The Berkshire closing stirred Governor Bowdoin the next day to call an emergency session of the Massachusetts General Court for September 27. But on the twenty-sixth, the Supreme Court was scheduled to sit in Springfield in Hampshire County, and there was grave danger that the grand jury might indict the Northampton rebels. To prevent any coerced closing of the courts, General William Shepard of the county militia occupied the courthouse himself with 800 men, 200 of whom consisted of "the most respectable and opulent gentlemen" of Hampshire County. The general also illegally helped his men to arms from the federal arsenal in Springfield.[1]

Against this formidable force marched approximately 1,100 rebels who sent a committee headed by a young former debtor from Pelham, Captain Daniel Shays, to make their demands of the Supreme Court: to dismiss the militia, to hear no suit for debt until grievances were redressed, and to take no action on grand jury indictments. The court refused the demands but found it could not round up enough people for a grand jury. Meanwhile, as the opposing forces watched each other warily, the rebels put a sprig of hemlock in their hats, while the government forces countered with slips of white paper. Finally, the court agreed to close, and General Shepard surrendered the courthouse; the rebels had won a significant victory.

---

[1]Taylor, *Western Massachusetts in the Revolution,* p. 146. [Editor's remarks] Ibid., pp. 125–46; Jensen, *The New Nation*, pp. 307–11.

The Massachusetts Supreme Court was also scheduled to hold a session in Great Barrington, Berkshire County, in mid-October, but again a mob of several hundred angry men gathered to block it, and the conservative leader Theodore Sedgwick only saved himself by fleeing to Stockbridge. The Supreme Court canceled its session; the courts in five Massachusetts counties had now been forcibly closed by the armed people.

One striking feature of the Shaysite rebellion was the defection of the leaders of the old Constitutionalist movement: a defection of older militants that has been a common feature of all radical revolutionary movements in history. The Reverend Thomas Allen and Berkshire sheriff Caleb Hyde, old Constitutionalist leaders, were violently opposed to the Shaysites—a movement that formed the logical continuation of the Constitutionalists, albeit more daring and revolutionary.

While many were harassed debtors, the rebels, or "Regulators" as they called themselves, were by no means rabble. In addition to Chief Justice Whiting, two Berkshire justices of the peace and a Bristol justice of the peace openly supported the rebellion, as did many gentry and professional people. Many leading property owners headed the insurrection, attacking especially the idea of redeeming the public debt at face value and in specie. Leading supporters of the rebellion were former House members from Berkshire, Benjamin Ely of West Springfield and Leicester Grosvenor of Windsor. Particularly strong in the rebellion were former soldiers and officers of the Revolutionary Army—men who were understandably bitter at seeing the army notes which they had sold to eastern speculators at depreciated rates now being redeemed at full face value in interest and principal by the eastern-dominated state government. Redemption, furthermore, was paid in specie and secured by high taxation.

The conservatives demagogically raised the nationalist hue and cry that the insurrection was secretly a British plot to subvert the government, but there is no evidence of British incitement, and the insurgents angrily denied the charge. Indeed, many of the western Massachusetts Tories were opposed to the rebellion.

The Massachusetts General Court met on September 27, 1786, to confront the crisis. The reactionary Governor Bowdoin naturally advocated the use of force, and the conservative-run Massachusetts Senate urged the coercion and the suspension of the basic individual right of *habeas corpus*. However, the less conservative Massachusetts House decided first to hear the numerous grievances of the rebels. But angered by a letter of defiance from the insurgents, the House agreed to suspend *habeas corpus*; moreover, the General Court passed repressive anti-riot acts and gave the governor and council the right to imprison without bail anyone they chose to hold inimical to the safety of the state. Furthermore, the Supreme Court was given the power to try the supposedly dangerous folk in any county it wished, rather than before a jury of their peers in their home districts.

To balance this repression, the General Court decided to make a few halting concessions to the protestors. Specifically, it permitted the payment of taxes in commodities as well as specie, permitted for eight months the payment of debts in appraised real estate instead of specie, exempted clothing and needed instruments from execution, and made all suits for debt (except real estate) arguable before justices of the peace. Furthermore, the legislature sweetened the pill of repression further by granting an indemnity to all rebels who had ceased their activity and taken an oath of allegiance before January 1, 1787, and it prudently postponed the reopening of the Hampshire and Berkshire courts.

By November 18 the General Court adjourned, confident that its blend of big stick and small, but widely trumpeted, carrot would quell the insurrection. And it is true that a disorganized Hampshire convention, held untimely in November during the legislative session, secured little support. The General Court, however, had not postponed the reopening of the courts in the counties of Bristol, Middlesex, and Worcester. On November 21 the armed rebel forces of Shays, Day, and Thomas Grover, 200 strong, seized possession of the Worcester courthouse and forced the judges to withdraw. Job Shattuck and Oliver Parker of the gentry of Groton organized a concerted county-wide attack on the Middlesex courthouse. But the Worcester rebels failed to arrive, and the Bristol movement reneged at the last moment and surrendered to the allegedly good deals of the General Court. Betrayed, the Shattuck forces fought bitterly but were finally defeated, and Shattuck, Parker and several other revolutionary leaders from Groton and Shirley were imprisoned under the new repressive legislation. From that point on the insurrectionary movement was confined to the western counties of Worchester, Hampshire, and Berkshire. The Worcester courts were again closed on December 5 as the rebels marched against the courthouse.

There had never been an overall organization to the Regulator rebellion, but now in December the insurgents began to organize more formally on military lines. The Hampshire insurgents formed a "Committee of Seventeen" as captains and six organized county regiments. Chairman of the committee was John Powers of Shutesbury. It is clear that the name Shays' Rebellion is a misnomer because Shays was never any more than one of the leading military captains of the insurrection. In fact, there is evidence that Shays was one of the most reluctant of the rebel leadership. At the end of December, 300 organized rebels headed by Shays, Day, and Grover marched into Springfield and easily forced the closing of the new session of the Hampshire court.

Thus, by the end of 1786, it was clear to the conservative rulers of Massachusetts that the Regulator rebellion in the West could not be crushed by the county militias. Actually, they could have simply allowed the western courts to remain closed, as had held true during and after the Revolutionary War. But the forces of conservatism could not leave the people of the interior alone, and instead they felt the rebellion to be a threat to their mystical sovereign power. Hence, Massachusetts prepared to escalate the violence and proposed to raise an army against its own citizens, and it appealed to Congress for aid.

Congress was indeed worried at this libertarian upsurge, for those oppressed by taxes and imprisonment to pay for the public debt began to be inspired by the Massachusetts example. As early as July 1786, conventions were held in New Hampshire to protest taxes needed to pay the public debt. In September, a mob demanding paper-money relief for debt suits and court fees laid siege to the New Hampshire legislature at Exeter and threatened the lives of the recalcitrant legislators. The New Hampshire rebels, too, were wildly attacked as levelers of property and condemned as opponents of "law and government." And former rebels from Massachusetts were soon causing trouble in Litchfield County, Connecticut. In the South, too, radical uprisings were erupting. As early as 1785 South Carolina insurgents were stirred by heavy taxes to pay public debts at face value and had closed many courts in the state; in Maryland, mobs closed many courts and rioted during 1786 and 1787.

The new revolution was clearly spreading. Congress was also worried about the federal arsenal, an enclave of federal power in Springfield. The arch-reactionary Secretary of War, General Henry Knox, had investigated the scene in the autumn of 1786 and now warned hysterically of the danger of social revolution, while Congressman Henry Lee of Virginia ranted of the "dreadful work" that was leading inexorably to "anarchy."

Congress unanimously decided on October 20, 1786, to raise a special body of continental troops to crush Shays' Rebellion and called upon New England to raise the men. However, it secretly and fraudulently concealed its purposes by pretending that the troops were for crushing the Northwest Indians. Congress, however, kept from its eagerly sought taxing power, had to raise the money for the troops by borrowing and requisition, and neither source could raise the funds in time. Knox managed to send troops to Springfield by February 1787, but by that time the insurrection was nearly over.

The Massachusetts General Court had even less money to organize a state army of counterrevolution; but a hundred odd "public spirited" wealthy men contributed over £5,000 to finance the huge 4,400 man army formed out of the militia of five counties. The new army was put under the command of General Benjamin Lincoln. Triumphant *within* their home territory, the rebels could not be expected to vanquish such a formidable force gathered from outside counties. Marching westward, Lincoln's army permitted the Worcester courts to open on January 23, and the insurgents retreated westward to Palmer in Hampshire County. The desperate rebels seized supplies from conservative opponents, burned their buildings, and looked longingly at the federal arsenal in Springfield, manned by 1,100 militia under General Shepard. Moving on Springfield were Luke Day in West Springfield with 400 men, Eli Parsons of Adams with 400 Berkshire Regulators, stationed to the north at Chicopee, and Daniel Shays with 1,200 men east of Springfield at Wilbraham. Meanwhile, under the pressure of Lincoln's advancing army, the insurgents had radically scaled down their demands to complete indemnity, the release of Shattuck and the other Middlesex prisoners, and a provision of the settlement of grievances at the next legislative session.

Shays now organized a joint Shays-Day attack on Springfield and moved himself to the attack on January 25. However, Day could not join Shays until the twenty-sixth, and the government forces intercepted Day's message to Shays to that effect. As Shays besieged the fort, one volley into the ranks unaccountably scattered the rebels, who retreated to Ludlow without firing a single shot. This ignominious defeat caused dozens to desert the rebel ranks.

Marching northward, Shays joined Parsons and retreated further to South Hadley, while Day's forces were dispersed by the combined governmental forces of Lincoln and Shepard. Confronting each other at Hadley, Shays and a committee of rebel officers headed by Francis Stone asked the General Court for a general pardon as the terms for laying down their arms—a petition backed by ten Massachusetts towns. Thwarted by the legislature, Shays retreated northeastward to Petersham. In a forced march at night through a snowstorm, General Lincoln reached Petersham, and the rebels surrendered *en masse*. The main leaders, however, did not surrender and fled to surrounding states.

In the meanwhile the Berkshire rebels became restive, resisted attempted arrest, and tried to open a second front against Lincoln. However, the county militia under General Patterson defeated the Berkshire rebels in a series of skirmishes, and Lincoln's arrival in Pittsfield on February 10 spurred a rash of surrenders under Lincoln's terms of pardoning all arrested men who would take an oath of allegiance. The determined hardcore of Berkshire, however, escaped westward to New York from where they were led by Captain Perez Hamlin to conduct guerrilla raids against Massachusetts.

By the end of February 1787, the Massachusetts Regulator rebellion had been crushed; Massachusetts asked the neighboring states to cooperate in stamping out the remaining guerrilla forces. Only Connecticut responded readily, while in independent Vermont the people welcomed the fleeing rebels with Shays himself at their head. In fact, Vermont itself had its own Regulator rebellion at the same time as in Massachusetts, and was directed similarly against the courts. On October 31, 1786, thirty armed Regulators of eastside Vermont led by Robert Morrison, a blacksmith, and Benjamin Stebbins, a farmer, had marched to Windsor to close the courts. The stern line of the sheriff and state's attorney, however, was able to disperse the rioters, and Morrison and others were arrested; after this the sheriff fell upon a group of rebel followers who were planning to rescue their colleagues and arrested them as well. Still, the remaining band of eastside Regulators were considering another rescue attempt but were dissuaded by a force of 600 militia assembling at Windsor. The westside Regulator rebellion in Vermont was more short-lived; a mob attempt to break up the Rutland County court led by Assemblyman Jonathan Fassett was foiled by the militia. The militia surrounded the rebels, who quickly surrendered. Fassett was fined and unanimously expelled permanently from his seat in the Vermont Assembly.

Hence, when Shays' Rebellion reached its climax in January 1787, the Vermont rebellion had already fizzled out and could not be revived. The people of Vermont, however, were still sympathetic, and Governor Thomas Chittenden delayed moving against the Shaysites. Soon, however, Chittenden did move. First, he warned the Vermonters not to aid the Massachusetts rebels, and then he proceeded to raise troops to round them up.

The Massachusetts General Court, meeting after the crisis in mid-February 1787, quickly proceeded to a nakedly vindictive attack on the former rebels with the Disqualifying Act; no amnesties were allowed to any former rebel that was an important officer, to citizens of other states, to any former member of the legislature, to anyone ever a delegate to any state or county convention, or to anyone holding a civil or military office. Even the supposedly "amnestied" rank and file of the Regulators were forbidden to vote, hold office, serve on a jury, teach school, operate an inn, or sell liquor for three full years. This bitterly harsh reprisal defeated its own purpose because even conservatives and moderates, such as George Washington and General Lincoln, attacked the punishment as overly severe. Lincoln declared in a cold and calculated analysis that to deprive the rebels of their full rights would rejuvenate the movement. Full amnesty, on the other hand, would "be the only way ... to make them good members of society and to reconcile them to that government under which we wish them to live."[2] A commission of three, including General Lincoln, extended pardons to nearly 800 Shaysite sympathizers. But fourteen of them, of whom

---

[2]Taylor, *Western Massachusetts in the Revolution*, p. 164. [Editor's remarks] Ibid., pp. 146–64; Main, *The Antifederalists*, pp. 21–28, 61–67; Frederic F. Van de Water, *The Reluctant Republic: Vermont, 1724–1791* (Cornwall, NY: Cornwall Press, 1941), pp. 330–33; Williamson, *Vermont in Quandary*, pp. 168–71.

five were from Hampshire and six from Berkshire, were indicted for "treason" to Massachusetts, convicted, and sentenced to death by the Supreme Court. Many others were fined and imprisoned.

By the late 1780s, the old Massachusetts Left had become so conservatized that Sam Adams' reaction to the rebels was as bigoted and uncomprehending as any conservative's. Like the city of Boston, Adams simply painted the Regulators as disorderly guerrillas and attacked them as greedy men and subversive British agents. In fact, it was precisely the ex-radical Adams who, as an appointee of the vigilant Governor Bowdoin on the Massachusetts Council, pushed through the Senate the suspension of *habeas corpus* and led in urging the maximum force against the Regulator movement. It was also Adams who led the fight for a maximum policy of revenge and the execution of the Shaysite leaders.

At this point, however, buoyed by his great popularity and the harsh repression of the Shaysites, the moderate John Hancock swept back into the governor's seat and crushed Bowdoin in the 1787 elections. Hancock also brought with him a liberal General Court. The turnover was enormous: nearly three-fourths of the House representatives were new, as well as over half of the Senate. The new legislature promptly repealed the harsh Disqualifying Act, and Governor Hancock pardoned with full amnesty for anyone who would take an oath of allegiance to the state. Only nine leaders were exempted from the amnesty, but soon all of them under the death penalty were pardoned by Hancock. Day was captured by New Hampshire in January 1788 and was pardoned. The following month, Shays and Parsons recanted their evils, promised good behavior, and soon received pardons, with the provision that neither could ever hold civil or military office in Massachusetts.

The newly liberal legislature passed reforms to address some of the grievances of the interior: the tender law was extended, clothing and various goods were exempted from execution, the imprisonment for debt was virtually abolished for debtors who could not pay for their room and board, and poll and state taxes were dramatically lowered. Moreover, court fees were sharply reduced, and Hancock voluntarily lowered his salary by nearly one-third. However, the General Court refused to issue future paper money, scale down the debt, refine the appropriation of excise revenues, or crack down on the practices of the legal profession. Nevertheless, in the final result, after peaceful protest had failed, the Regulator rebels, by taking to arms and engaging in illegal acts, were able to push through substantial liberal reforms. Thus, direct armed insurgency came to provide the necessary impetus to enact liberal parliamentary reforms.[3]

The reform policies and their drastic lowering of direct taxes weakened the grandiose Massachusetts debt-funding program. As a result, the public creditors in Massachusetts came to support a strong central government with taxing power to assume their claims as they were now doubtful of Massachusetts ever being able to pay its debts. The propertied men of Massachusetts shifted *en masse* into the nationalist camp, and Shays' Rebellion conservatized many of the state's leaders who now felt that the state government and the Confederation were too weak to prevent such tax uprisings from occurring.

Shays' Rebellion served as a spur to nationalist sentiment in other states by providing fuel for demagogic attacks about dangers of weak government under the Confederation. General Knox lost no opportunity in whipping up a scare campaign about the rebellion and damning the system of "vile state governments" as "sources of pollution" and were therefore directly responsible. George Washington was apparently frightened enough by the Shays episode to return to politics to push the nationalist cause; the young Connecticut-born lecturer and textbook writer Noah Webster denounced the rebellious state, urged national government, and even called for a "limited monarchy" to block the "ignorance and passions of the multitude." Above all, perhaps, Alexander Hamilton raised the charge of anti-Shayism hysteria. Brusquely dismissing the real and intense grievances of the people of western Massachusetts, Hamilton thought that the intention of the rebels was to abolish all debts, abrogate contracts, and generally to establish some vague kind of subversive and egalitarian government. Only a strong national government, opined Hamilton, could save America from the army of future and greater Shayses and their "spirit of licentiousness." And, in a sense, the liberal reformist Regulators who followed after the

---

[3]On Shays' Rebellion, in addition to Taylor, *Western Massachusetts*, see Richard B. Morris, "Insurrection in Massachusetts," in Daniel Aaron, ed., *America in Crisis* (New York: Knopf, 1952), pp. 21–49. [Editor's remarks] John C. Miller, *Sam Adams: Pioneer in Propaganda* (Stanford, CA: Stanford University Press, 1936), pp. 373–76.

rebellion were, to Hamilton, as dangerous and subversive as the insurrection itself. George Washington and James Madison also dismissed Shaysite grievances and wanted to confiscate the arms of the rebels. Both Madison and Washington believed the rebellion was designed to abolish all debts and redistribute property.

Outside the ardent nationalist camp, opposition to the Shaysites was far more sober and subdued. Benjamin Franklin refused to get excited about the rebellion. More interesting was the reaction of Thomas Jefferson, minister to France. Until now a political moderate, Jefferson was still opposed to any modification of the debt process or to popular acts against the courts. But, it was remarkable that while all the other major leaders of America were being pushed rightward by the Shaysite turmoil, Thomas Jefferson, in contrast, moved sharply leftward. Jefferson began to realize that repression was far worse than rebellion and that in the non-governmental body of the people was to be found far more wisdom and justice than in the government. Rebellion is a voluntary education, he began to conclude, and he also reflected on the whole of government: "were it left to me to decide whether we should have a government without newspapers or newspapers without a government, I should not hesitate a moment to prefer the latter."

Here was a decidedly anarchistic statement, and this sentiment was refined by a critically important letter that he wrote at the time to his old friend James Madison, who was worried about the Shaysite troubles in Massachusetts. There were three types of societies, wrote Jefferson: "1. Without government, as among our Indians. 2. Under governments wherein the will of every one has a just influence, as is the case in England to a slight degree, and in our states, in a great one. 3. Under governments of force: as is the case in all other monarchies and in most of the other republics." Jefferson went on to declare that the first anarchistic form was probably the best, "but I believe it to be inconsistent with any degree of population." Next best was democracy, under which "the mass of mankind ... enjoys a precious degree of liberty & happiness." True, democracy may be turbulent, as presumably in the Shay episode, "But weigh this against the oppression of monarchy, and it becomes nothing. ... [and] even this evil is productive of good. It prevents the degeneracy of government and nourishes a general attention to the public affairs. ... It is a medicine necessary for the sound health of government."[4]

[4]Thomas Jefferson to James Madison, January 30, 1787, in Malone, *Jefferson and the Rights of Man,* pp. 156–60. [Editor's remarks] Ibid., pp. 160–66; Jensen, *The New Nation,* pp. 107–08, 249–50, 365; John C. Miller, *Alexander Hamilton and the Growth of the New Nation* (New York: Harper & Row, 1959), pp. 142–45.

12

The Annapolis Convention

By 1787, the nationalist forces were in a far stronger position than during the Revolutionary War to make their dreams of central power come true. Now, in addition to the reactionary ideologues and financial oligarchs, public creditors, and disgruntled ex-army officers, other groups, some recruited by the depression of the mid-1780s, were ready to be mobilized into an ultra-conservative constituency. Inefficient urban artisans who wanted a central protective tariff to secure a nation-wide market from more efficient British competition; merchants who wanted central navigation acts and other subsidies; western land speculators who wanted to prevent settlers from following the natural course of secession and collaboration with Spain; southern land speculators and settlers who wanted to drive Spain out of control of the Mississippi River; northwestern land speculators, fur traders, and expansionists who wanted an aggressive foreign policy to force the British out of their northwestern forts; southern slave owners who wanted to expand the realm and political rights of the slave states; commercial farmers who wanted an aggressive foreign policy to force open the European and West Indies ports and wage war against the Barbary coast nations; public debt-owners frightened by the legislation whipped up over Shays' Rebellion; all these forces coalesced behind a radically nationalist program that urged the creation of a new government to rival or parallel the political structures exactly before the Revolutionary War. They wanted a strong central power that would control an aggressive national army and navy, wield a national taxing power to decimate the rights of the states and individuals, and federally assume public debts and army pensions.

Basically, urban merchants and artisans, as well as many slaveholding planters, united in support of a strong nation-state that would use the power of coercion to grant them privileges and subsidies. The subsidies would come at the expense of the average subsistence yeoman farmer who might be expected to oppose such a new nationalism.[5] But against them, to support a new constitution, were the *commercial* farmers aided by the southern plantation-farmers who also wanted power and regulation for their own benefit. Given the urban support, the split among the farmer, and the support from wealthy educated elites, it is not surprising that the nationalist forces were able to execute their truly amazing political *coup d'état* which *illegally* liquidated the Articles of Confederation and replaced it with the Constitution. In short, they were able to destroy the original individualist and decentralized program of the American Revolution. Superior leadership and personality were critical factors in their victory. One of the important reasons was that the nationalist leaders of the different states were wealthier and better educated, generally knew each other, and could even communicate quickly. On the other hand, the "Anti-federalists" were scattered, poorer, and tended to be less educated and from more remote locations.[6] And finally, in state after state, the Left no longer had effective

---

[5]In 1785 Nathan Dane of Massachusetts noted that resistance to stronger government came from "the yeomanry or the body of the people." Similarly, in 1786 the French Minister to the United States, Louis Otto, observed that the common people recognized that a stronger government meant "a regular collection of taxes, a strict administration of justice, extraordinary duties on imports, rigorous executions against debtors—in short, a marked preponderance of rich men and of large proprietors." Main, *The Antifederalists*, p. 112.

[6]As historians have pointed out, "Antifederalist" is a misnomer, deliberately placed on the opposition by the victorious nationalists, who cunningly appropriated to themselves the benign term "Federalist." In reality, those who wanted to adhere to the Confederation were the true "Federalists"; the nationalists who wanted a counterrevolutionary move toward the old colonial system of central and executive power were the real opponents of federalism. But the terms are too deeply grounded in American history to uproot at this juncture. But let it suffice to record the injustice experienced by the Antifederalists and the unscrupulous treaty of terms that was being put over on the American public. As one New York

or brilliant leadership, the natural leaders of the Antifederalists were either confused or had gone over to the nationalist camp on the Right.

The nationalists had tried legal and constitutional means to attain their ends, but each had failed on the ironclad requirement of the Articles of Confederation that amendments must be approved by every state. In 1786 the final nationalist attempt to grant Congress the power to levy an impost was blocked by New York. Now, in 1786, the conservatives made a final attempt to affect a legal review of the fundamental constitutional government of the United States. At the beginning of the summer, Congress appointed a committee that, on August 7, proposed some fundamental amendments to the Confederation. The amendments, drawn up largely by Charles Pinckney of South Carolina, granted Congress the exclusive power of regulating foreign and domestic commerce and levying duties on imports and exports, empowered Congress to enforce its regulations upon the states, gave Congress the exclusive power of making treaties, and established and empowered a federal court, which could take appeals from state courts. These amendments Pinckney proposed were, however, shot down by Congress. There was scarcely any likelihood of the unanimous approval by the states, and, in any case, a more likely route was coming to view. This new route promised a devious and hidden channel toward an illegal and thoroughly revolutionary *coup d'état* that would entirely eradicate the Confederation and replace it with a new centralized Constitution.

It all started innocently and innocuously enough; indeed, it started precisely as a way that the states could handle interstate problems themselves without turning to a central arbiter and regulator. Virginia and Maryland, whose natural boundary was the Potomac River, were anxious to open it up for navigation; the anxiety was especially propelled by the western land speculators in both states who wanted to provide an alternative route for western trade so that the Spanish Mississippi might not exert a fatal block on western settlement. But first Maryland and Virginia had to agree on use of the river. Consequently, in March 1785 commissioners from the two states met at Alexandria to consider

---

writer, "Countryman," correctly observed in December 1787, after the Constitution was ratified, this "was the way some great men had to deceive the common people, and prevent their knowing what they were about." Ibid., p. xxv.

navigation on the Potomac and also on their other joint boundary, the Chesapeake Bay. The commissioners adjourned to Mt. Vernon where, at the end of March, they quickly came to a fruitful agreement: all the joint waters were to be a free and common highway with citizens of each state free to use each other's harbors. Tonnage duties exacted from ships entering both Maryland and Virginia would be equally divided between the states. All costs of public expenditures for navigation on the Potomac would be shared equally, while Virginia would pay five-eighths of the just expenses of navigation on the Chesapeake Bay. The commissioners also agreed to recommend uniform commercial regulation and imposts, a uniform currency, a joint Chesapeake navy, and an annual commercial conference between the two states.

The commissioners were understandably pleased with their success. Indeed, around this time an assembly of wealthy citizens of both states organized two companies, both of which were partially owned by George Washington, to exploit navigation on the Potomac. Pennsylvania, which had concluded a navigation agreement of its own on the Delaware River with New Jersey two years before, was as interested as the Maryland and Virginia land speculators in extending a route from the Potomac to the Ohio River. Hence, the commissioners decided to invite Pennsylvania to join Virginia and Maryland in a pact for common collaboration on the Ohio. The commissioners, who were heavily nationalist, had no definite nationalist aim in mind; quite the contrary, the agreements were compacts between the states themselves.[7] Neither did Maryland have such a design in mind when it ratified the Mt. Vernon agreement in November 1785, a month after Virginia had done so, and enthusiastically proposed another conference that would include Delaware as well and handle all the remaining contractual commercial problems in the Chesapeake-Potomac area.

It was at this point that devious and sinister machinations began to enter the scene. For in the Virginia legislature the ultra-nationalist leader James Madison, who had pushed for the Alexandria treaty, saw the opportunity to transform the proposed meeting into a way to

---

[7]For a corrective to the usual accounts that make the steps from Alexandria to the Constitution seem natural, see McDonald, *E Pluribus Unum,* pp. 235ff. [Editor's remarks] Burnett, *The Continental Congress,* pp. 663–65; Jensen, *The New Nation,* pp. 418–21.

strengthen the power of Congress. On January 21, 1786, at the very end of the session of the Virginia legislature, Madison pushed through a proposal for a convention of commissioners from *all* states to provide for uniform commercial regulations and for "the requisite augmentation of the power of Congress over trade." As one of the selected Virginia commissioners, Madison called such a convention for Annapolis on September 11. In his words, the location was chosen "to avoid the neighborhood of Congress, and the large commercial towns, in order to disarm the adversaries to the object, of insinuations of influence from either of these quarters." Madison was so cautious about the meeting that he only told his close personal friends that its true objectives were not for commercial arrangements but instead the beginning of political reform.

Only nine states, however, decided to send delegates to the Annapolis Convention, and one of the recalcitrant was Maryland, presumably disgruntled at this complete perversion of the original aim of the conference it had proposed. Without Maryland there, the original members of the Chesapeake-Potomac agreement could not at all be persuaded. Furthermore, only five of the states—New York, New Jersey, Pennsylvania, Delaware, and Virginia—bothered to send delegates in time to even attend the convention. Moreover, of the twelve delegates sent by the five states, only did three states (New Jersey, Delaware, and Virginia) send the required number of delegates to Annapolis. Delegates for Massachusetts and Rhode Island were on their way, but the convention adjourned before they could arrive. It was clear that the Annapolis Convention could be only a total failure.

But the nationalist leadership possessed the capacity of turning a seemingly utter defeat into another step on the way toward victory. With the veteran reactionary John Dickinson, representing Delaware in the chair, the outstanding nationalist theorist Alexander Hamilton was able to draft a report for a committee of five leading delegates: Chair Egbert Benson, conservative lawyer for Dutchess County, New York, and a leading attorney for the New York oligarchy; Tench Coxe, a brilliant young Philadelphian merchant and advisor to Hamilton on ultra-nationalist economics; Abraham Clark of New Jersey, one of *the* originators of the idea of calling a constitutional convention; George Read of Delaware, an ultra-conservative economically affiliated with the Robert Morris interests and who had initially opposed American independence; and Virginia Governor Edmund Randolph, a leading southern planter who exerted a moderating influence on the resolutions of the committee (although James Madison was not on the committee, he played a critically important role in the entire proceedings). The committee's report was unanimously approved by the full convention on September 14 and sent to Congress as well as the several states. It called for another all-state convention, this time to propose a comprehensive revision of the Articles so as "to render the Constitution of the Federal Government adequate to the exigencies of the Union." But Hamilton mendaciously hastened to assure everyone that this would be a legal revision—in short, a revision that would have to be approved first by Congress and then by every state in order to go into effect. His resolution affirmed that a revision to be recommended by the general convention would be reported "to the United States in Congress assembled, as when agreed to by them, and afterwards confirmed by the Legislatures of every State." The new convention of commissioners from each state was called for the following May in Philadelphia.[8]

---

[8][Editor's footnote] Burnett, *The Continental Congress*, pp. 665–68; Miller, *Alexander Hamilton and the Growth of the New Nation*, pp. 136–41.

13

The Delegates of the Convention
and America's Great Men

From the very beginning of the great emerging struggle over the Constitution the Antifederalist forces suffered from a grave and debilitating problem of leadership. The problem was that the liberal leadership was so conservatized that most of them agreed that centralizing revisions of the Articles were necessary—as can be seen from the impost and congressional regulation of commerce debates during the 1780s. By agreeing in principle with the nationalists' call for central power, but only opposing the change going too far, the Antifederalist leadership threw away its main weapon and found itself ready to be antagonized by the forces of the counterrevolution. The nationalist leaders, in contrast to their wavering opponents, knew exactly what it wanted and strove to obtain the most possible. The initiative was always in the hands of the Federalist Right, while the Antifederalist Left, weakened in principle, could only offer a series of defensive protests to the reactionary drive. The battles were consequently fought on the terms set by the aggressive nationalist forces. Thus, such distinguished liberal leaders as Timothy Bloodworth of North Carolina; James Warren and Elbridge Gerry of Massachusetts; George Mason, Patrick Henry, and Richard Henry Lee of Virginia; George Bryan of Pennsylvania; and Governor George Clinton of New York; had all at one time or another conceded the necessity of strengthening the central power, particularly in imposts and regulation of commerce. A real libertarian Left existed only in such thoroughly disaffected areas as Shaysite western Massachusetts, western Rhode Island, and inland areas of upstate New York. As a result of his ambivalence, Governor Clinton had allowed Hamilton his head in selecting delegates for the Annapolis Convention. And the most that the liberals did was, like Patrick Henry and Richard Henry Lee in Virginia, to live aloof and refuse to attend the Constitutional Convention. Only a few writers and pamphleteers, largely in New England, raised the torch of all-out opposition from the very beginning.[9]

In October 1786 Virginia was the first state legislature that approved the call for a convention for constitutional revision, and it did so overwhelmingly. In a tactical masterstroke James Madison and Alexander Hamilton persuaded the enormously prestigious George Washington to agree to place himself at the head of Virginia's delegation, and he later became presiding officer of the Constitutional Convention. As the front man, he put his unquestioned reputation at the service of the nationalist designs. No more apt evaluation of Washington's character and role at the convention has been written than this delightfully caustic appraisal:

> Washington, at fifty-four (or at any other age), could have added little to the intellectual average of any convention, and his knowledge of what to do in one barely extended beyond rules of order. But that was all he needed to know, for any assembly he attended was likely to elect him presiding officer. He had two attributes that, even without his unparalleled prestige, prompted men to choose him The Leader; and it mattered not that one of the attributes was trivial and the other he carried to the point of triviality, nor did it matter that for the last third of his life he was largely (and self-consciously) playing a role. The first attribute was that he looked like a leader. In an age in which most Americans stood about five feet five and measured nearly three-fourths that around the waist, Washington stood six feet and had broad, powerful shoulders and slim hips; and he had learned the trick, when men said something beyond his ken, of looking at them in a way that made them feel irreverent or even stupid. The other attribute was personal integrity. At times, Washington's integrity was bewildering, for his artlessness and his susceptibility to flattery led him to endorse actions that less scrupulous but more cagey men might shun; and at times it could be overbearing, stifling. But it was unimpeachable, and everyone knew it, and that, above all, made Washington useful.

---

[9]Main, *The Antifederalists*, pp. 113–16.

Others would do the brain work and the dirty work; Washington needed only to be there, but if there was to be a national government he absolutely had to be there, to lend his name to the doings.[10]

Polar opposite to Washington in characteristics stood the theoretician James Madison, who was equally important to the nationalist cause. In McDonald's words:

> Madison, at thirty-seven (or at any other age), was Washington's opposite. Few men looked less like a leader: scrawny and pale, a bookworm and a hypochondriac, he owned a physical presence as uncommanding as one was likely to meet. But his knowledge of what to do in a convention was vast, and his talents for doing it matched his knowledge. ... at base he was a brittle, doctrinaire theorist. But these very attributes were useful (practical, free-wheeling politicians can always use a good theoretician, much as practical, freewheeling businessmen can use a good lawyer); and together with persistence, shrewdness, and devotion to the nation, they made him a priceless member of the nationalist group in the convention.[11]

Out of its seven-man delegation, other prominent Virginia notables included conservative Governor Edmund Randolph, who later moderated at the end of the convention, and the liberal-moderate George Mason.

It was, of course, critical for right-wing design that Alexander Hamilton be selected as a delegate to the convention for New York. But, with Governor Clinton largely in conflict with the New York legislature, the going would not be easy. The liberal-oriented Clinton was greatly disturbed at the odd turn that the Annapolis Convention had taken and now strongly affirmed that no such major centralizing revision of the Confederation was necessary. In fact, the Assembly, which again turned down the congressional impost plan in its 1786 session, waited until early 1787 to report disapproval of the proceedings at Annapolis. But coincidentally, a change of events proved that luck was

---

[10]McDonald, *E Pluribus Unum*, pp. 262–63.
[11]Ibid., pp. 263–64.

with the nationalists: news came of Shays' Rebellion striking upstate New York, of the British maintaining their prohibition on American trade with the British West Indies, and of new depredations of Barbary pirates. Under the pressure of their circumstances the Clintonians reluctantly joined the nationalists in mid-February and agreed to send delegates to Philadelphia and recommend the act to Congress. However, doughty old Abraham Yates, lawyer, pamphleteer, and former shoemaker from Albany and Clinton's man in the state Senate, now led the last-ditch radical effort to New York's participation. Yates warned of the dangers of an "aristocracy, king, despot, unlimited power, sword and purse," but the moderate-right coalition managed to override his opposing resolution to block any changes to the Articles which weakened the New York Constitution. Yates' resolution was defeated in the Senate by the thinnest of margins: one tie-breaking vote made by its president, Pierre Van Cortlandt. Therefore, on February 20, New York instructed its delegates in Congress to recommend participating in the Philadelphia Convention.

The struggle over naming the delegates occurred in early March. The Antifederalists preferred to elect by joint ballot of both houses of the legislature because this would have insured an all-liberal delegation dominated by the more moderate Clinton-controlled Assembly. But the more conservative Senate, led by the oligarch Peter Schuyler, insisted on separate voting. The result was a deal by which, for its three delegates, New York chose the Federalist Alexander Hamilton and two staunch Antifederalists from Albany: Robert Yates, a distinguished justice on the New York Supreme Court, and John Lansing, a wealthy lawyer appointed mayor of Albany. Since Yates and Lansing were Clintonian officeholders and had voted against the congressional impost, an Antifederalist majority of the delegation was assured. While Yates and Hamilton were chosen virtually unanimously, the Senate hotly argued to accept the result of a deal between Lansing for the liberals and James Duane of the conservative New York City oligarchy. Characteristic of the sectional splits in New York, Lansing won in the Assembly by 26-23, Lansing carrying the will of the upstate counties (except for Albany) and the swing Long Island counties, while Duane carried accordingly the city vote: New York City and Albany, as well as Richmond County. Hamilton, furthermore, was repeatedly defeated in attempts to add Chancellor Livingston, Egbert Benson, Duane, and especially John Jay, to the New York delegation in order to increase the Federalist voice.

Pennsylvania hastened to send delegates to the convention with more dispatch than New York. Most fortunately for the nationalists, the conservatives had won a significant victory in the fall elections of 1786 that weakened the radical majority in the legislature. The election, furthermore, truly revealed a sharp sectional divide within Pennsylvania, with the conservatives in control of the southeast around Philadelphia and the radicals generally dominant elsewhere. The conservatives moved swiftly and ruthlessly to impose their program. Thus, in March 1787 the legislature voted to re-charter the Bank of North America, though its charter was limited to fourteen years, its capital reduced to two million, and its loans in goods and real estate restricted. The conservatives also moved quickly to choose conservative delegates to Congress. For its eight delegates, Pennsylvania ruthlessly chose an all-nationalist delegation with the single exception of the aging opportunist Benjamin Franklin. Apart from Franklin, the oligarchy, headed by Robert Morris, scintillated in Pennsylvania's delegation: Robert Morris, Gouverneur Morris (now residing in Philadelphia), James Wilson, Thomas Fitzsimons, George Clymer, and Thomas Mifflin. Only Jared Ingersoll was a member of the radical Pennsylvania Constitutionalist Party and was the son-in-law of the wealthy Philadelphia speculator and financier, the moderate Constitutionalist Charles Pettit. Unsurprisingly, every single one of the Pennsylvanian delegates came from Philadelphia.

While the states began to send delegates to the forthcoming convention, it was by no means certain that the Congress would put its imprimatur on the meeting. Rufus King, a young congressman from Massachusetts, expressed an intelligent puzzlement: if the convention is to stay within the framework of legality and Congress is to ratify the result, then what is the point of not having Congress itself do the revising? King and his colleague Nathan Dane advised Massachusetts not to send men to the convention, and Massachusetts was strongly opposed to agreement. In mid-October of 1786, Congress referred the proposal to a grand committee that showed no sign of doing anything about it. But Shays' Rebellion was now frightening respectable Massachusetts opinion into a far more nationalist mood, and Rufus King, reflecting this change, began a steady shift into the nationalist camp. As a result, on February 20, 1787, the grand committee ratified approval of the new convention by a mere majority of one vote. King and Dane, however, insisted that the convention be expressly and unambiguously limited to legal review of the Articles. The Congress, therefore, adopted on February 21, over the opposition by the rest of New England, the Massachusetts Resolution endorsing the convention, but only "for the purpose of revising the Articles of Confederation … and reporting to the United States in Congress assembled and to the States respectively such alterations and amendments." No contract could be more explicit. Massachusetts' approval followed the next day, and thus by the opening of the Constitutional Convention.

By May 14, the opening date for the convention, all but two states had chosen delegates. One, New Hampshire, finally chose a delegation in June, which arrived in Philadelphia at the end of July, after the important part of the convention had been concluded. Rhode Island, however, a state that had learned its radicalism the hard way for stopping taxes and public debts, stood steadfast as the lone holdout, refusing to have anything to do with the convention. However, General James Varnum, the Rhode Island nationalist, went to Philadelphia as a lobbyist and unofficial representative of the Rhode Island conservatives. Even with twelve states' support, only Virginia's and Pennsylvania's eager delegates had made the trek to Philadelphia by the official opening date of May 14. It was only on May 25 that a quorum of seven states had appeared, and the Philadelphia Convention was finally ready to begin.[12]

The gathering at Philadelphia was a distinguished one as each state tended to select its leaders for this clearly important event: this in itself lent a strong conservative bias to the proceedings, for the distinguished men were generally wealthy and educated. In the case of the delegates, almost all were merchants, large landowners, or lawyers tied in with these interests, and many were relatively young men. Apart from such specific common aims as the coerced payment of the public debt and

---

[12] [Editor's footnote] E. Wilder Spaulding, *New York in the Critical Period, 1783–1789* (New York: Columbia University Press, 1932), pp. 184–88; Brunhouse, *The Counter-Revolution in Pennsylvania*, pp. 191–202; Burnett, *The Continental Congress*, pp. 669–79; McDonald, *E Pluribus Unum*, pp. 259–70; Forrest McDonald, *We the People: The Economic Origins of the Constitution* (Chicago: University of Chicago Press, 1958), pp. 21–25.

the opening of foreign ports to American commerce, such men were the power elite of their states, and a power elite naturally wants to expand its power and, therefore, its scope to a broad national scale. The "Great Man" is likely to be a man where his fortune or power has been aided, in one way or another, by the State; and, on the other side of the coin, he is an influential man who stands in a likely path to reach out and use the levers of State power for his own advantage. Hence, *ceteris paribus*, the more distinguished any given gathering, the more statist and reactionary it will likely be. The classic injunction of Lord Acton applies to the history of the Constitution:

> I cannot accept your canon that we are to judge Pope and King unlike other men, with a favourable presumption that they did no wrong. If there is any presumption it is the other way against holders of power, increasing as the power increases. ... Power tends to corrupt and absolute power corrupts absolutely. Great men are almost always bad men, even when they exercise influence and not authority: still more when you superadd the tendency or the certainty of corruption by authority. There is no worse heresy than that the office sanctifies the holder of it.[13]

Furthermore, while it was true that nationalism was newly dominant among the urban artisans, it was also true that the proportion of nationalists was greater among the rich and the eminent than among the poor and the nameless, so that again any distinguished gathering of the two was bound to be united on behalf of the conservative cause.

It must be noted that among this gathering of America's Great Men there were conspicuous absences. These were men who were more often than not deeply skeptical or at least ambivalent about the prospects of a convention. Two of the most distinguished, John Adams of Massachusetts and Thomas Jefferson of Virginia, were away as ambassadors to England and France, respectively. Ultra-nationalist John Jay of New York was deliberately not chosen by the largely Antifederalist legislature. Richard Henry Lee and Patrick Henry of Virginia, on the other hand, were chosen as delegates but declined to attend—undoubtedly from deep suspicion; the doughty Patrick Henry declared that he "smelt

---

[13]Lord Acton to Mandall Creighton, April 5, 1887, in J.E.E. Dalberg-Acton, *Essays on Freedom and Power* (Boston: Beacon Press, 1948), p. 364.

a rat." Henry Laurens, eminent merchant and planter of South Carolina, was too sick to attend. Thomas Paine of Pennsylvania was out of politics in Europe trying to raise financing for a bridge project he had organized. Sam Adams, too, was highly skeptical and was influential in getting the Massachusetts Resolution to restrict the scope of the convention and remain with the Confederation. Governor John Hancock of Massachusetts did not have himself selected as a delegate, probably for similar reasons. The old Adams-Lee Left, in short, was marked and almost forgotten by its absences—not only for the convention, but as a cohesive force in American political life as well. Maryland's top oligarchs, such as Samuel Chase and Charles Carroll of Carrollton, also held aloof, and that state sent its second-rank leadership to the convention. And in North Carolina, Willie Jones, the wealthy planter who led the liberal wing of the state, was chosen as a delegate but declined to attend, for Jones would have had to serve with the entire leadership of the highly conservative oligarchical nationalist men of the state led by William Blount.[14]

Overall, seventy-four delegates from twelve states were selected by state legislatures for the Philadelphia Convention, of which nineteen refused, for one or another reason, to attend. Only a handful of attending delegates could be considered leading liberals, all of whom were moderates like George Mason of Virginia or Elbridge Gerry of Massachusetts, who were sympathetic to the convention as a device for strengthening the Articles. It was only as the true dimensions of the nationalist design began to unfold that these moderates started to grow wary and eventually go into opposition. Nationalist strength tended to come not only from the wealthy and eminent *per se*, but also from the urban commercial interests, merchants, and artisans, the majority of

---

[14]As we have seen, Blount and much of his clique were leading speculators in western lands. They were also, seemingly paradoxically, at the same time nationalist and intriguing with Spain for secession of the West from the Union. The paradox is resolved in the fact that *either* a strong national government in control of and pushing the interests of the western lands, or a Spanish secession, would greatly raise the value of the western lands. On Blount and his group, see Main, *The Antifederalists*, pp. 33–38, and Abernethy, *Western Lands and the American Revolution*. [Editor's remarks] McDonald, *E Pluribus Unum*, p. 60; McDonald, *We the People*, pp. 30–34.

commercial farmers, and leading urban-exporters. In short, nationalist strength came from men who supported centralizing tariffs and navigation laws, raising the value of their public securities, and an aggressive foreign policy, all at the expense of the taxpaying inland farmer.[15] And surprisingly, in seven of the twelve states, no representation whatever at the convention was allowed to the inland farmers, which was a clear and enormous weighting of the convention in favor of the nationalist forces. Typical was Massachusetts; of the four delegates who attended, three were from the commercial seaboard, and one was a conservative follower of Theodore Sedgwick from the commercial Connecticut valley town of Northampton. None of the numerous small inland towns were represented, to say nothing of the Shaysites from the West. The two New Hampshire delegates came from the main commercial seaboard town of Portsmouth and Exeter—again no representation from the oft-disgruntled northwestern interior. None of the three Connecticut delegates represented the inland subsistence farmer of the North, and all came from commercial towns east of the Connecticut Valley. In Pennsylvania, as we have seen, the situation was particularly blatant as every one of the eight delegates were from Philadelphia (seven from the city proper, and one from the surrounding countryside).

In the South, representation was similarly weighted in favor of men of the most conservative means, the large-planter dominated coastal

---

[15] It certainly seems reasonable to suppose that the public creditors, especially the federal creditors, favored a strong central government to assume and fund their debt as they had been at the end of the Revolutionary War. While this is certainly true, the famous controversy over the Charles Beard Thesis of public creditors providing the big impetus for nationalism at the Constitutional Convention is weakened when one notes that (a) many of the leading Antifederalists held large amounts of public securities; (b) as Professor Dorfman has pointed out, some securities were being held to short-sell, and therefore the holders assumed their prices would decline. But the crucial consideration is that Beard and his followers have had to rely solely on security ownership data for the year 1790. Buying securities *after* the Constitution was submitted in 1787 or later ratified was only good sense, and therefore holdings in 1790 say nothing about the utterly different situation in 1787, the relevant time for influencing the creation of the Constitution. Ferguson, *The Power of the Purse*, pp. 337–41; Joseph Dorfman, "Review of Ferguson, *The Power of the Purse*," *The William and Mary Quarterly* (April 1961): 275–77.

plains. In South Carolina, the four delegates were all large lowland planters residing in Charlestown—not one representative of the small-farm backcountry. The five North Carolina delegates all came from the commercial large-planter dominated northeastern section of the state. In Virginia's complex politico-economic geography, there were seven or eight major sections, of which two, the lower river valleys and especially the old feudal North Neck oligarchy of the Potomac, were the conservative, large-planter ones. Of the seven-man Virginia delegation, two men came from the North Neck and four from the lower river valleys; only James Madison, from Orange County, did not fit this picture, and he came from an area not too far from the upper Rappahannock.[16]

What of the other five states? Democratic Georgia, it is true, sent two delegates from the East and two from the West, but as will be seen below, it was overwhelmingly Federalist at this picture. For its part, Maryland was always accessible to the sea and was ultimately all eastern planter-run Tidewater. Delaware distributed its five delegates between New Castle County and the two southern agricultural counties, but the whole of the small state was largely a tributary of Philadelphia and the Delaware River, and consequently Delaware, too, was overwhelmingly nationalist. New Jersey had no east-west division in the commercial agricultural as did most of the other states. Instead, it had two areas, one (East Jersey) awarded to New York City, the other (West Jersey) awarded to Philadelphia, both nationalist cities. It is no surprise then that the state was overwhelmingly nationalist throughout the 1780s. Only in New York, therefore, was there a sectional-political struggle in which the interior was firmly represented and, therefore, the Antifederalists predominated (and even here the Antifederalists came from the commercial Hudson Valley town of Albany).

---

[16] Jackson Turner Main, "Sectional Politics in Virginia, 1781–1787," *The William and Mary Quarterly* (January 1955): 96–112, and Main, *The Antifederalists*, pp. 28–33. [Editor's remarks] Ibid., 114–18; McDonald, *We the People*, pp. 21–37.

PART IV

The Nationalists Triumph: The Constitution

14

Elections in the Bicameral Congress

The nationalists who went into the convention agreed on certain broad objectives, crucial for a new government, all designed to remodel the United States into a country with the British political structure. They had the ultimate advantage of any group that knows what it wants in advance of a convention. First, there must be an overriding sovereign government with independent power to tax, regulate, and coerce states and individuals. Second, an independent and oligarchical executive administration and upper legislative house must be created and elevated to weaken the democratic and representative lower legislative house. There would, however, be vigorous discussion on the nature of representation in the bicameral Congress—would it be proportional to population or based on equality of voting, and would slaves be included? It was on these issues that voting would be bitterly debated among the nationalists, between large and small states and North and South.

When the Constitutional Convention opened on May 25, 1787, its first act was a foregone conclusion: unanimous selection of George Washington as its presiding officer; it was all too symbolic that Robert Morris was the man to make the nomination. Next came the adoption of voting rules for the convention. The Pennsylvanians had the presumption to urge voting by population, but Virginia, fearing hostility from the small states, vetoed the move, and voting was established as in the Congress: one vote per state and voting by majority of states, a simple majority resolving all issues. Another rule made all votes taken to be permanent, subject to reopening later in the convention. Particularly important was the decision, now and afterward, to hold the entire convention in strictest secrecy in order to make sure that the public would not know what was going on until the convention presented its conclusions as a *fait accompli*. Here was a perfect setting for the pursuance of the nationalist design. This secrecy rule, proposed by Pierce Butler of South Carolina, was to be demonized by Thomas Jefferson as "abominable."

The Virginia delegation arrived early and hammered out a common program. On May 29, Virginia opened proceedings with Governor Edmund Randolph presenting its revolutionary resolutions to the convention, which were written largely by James Madison. Randolph, who had been quickly influenced by Madison on the deficiencies of the Articles, made clear that the Virginia Plan was directed "against" democracy. Randolph conceded, wrote Robert Yates of New York in alarm, that the proposal was "not intended for a federal government—he meant a strong *consolidated* union, in which the idea of states should be nearly annihilated." Specifically, the Virginians recommended:

1. Voting in the national legislature to be proportionate to tax revenue or population, rather than by equality of states.

2. Two branches of the national legislature, the lower house to be selected by the people of each state, not by the state legislatures.

3. Election of the smaller upper house for long terms by the lower house out of persons nominated by the state legislatures.

4. Congress to be empowered "to legislate in all cases to which the separate States are incompetent," the ramifications to be presumably decided by Congress, and Congress to have veto power over all state laws which it considered to be inimical to the Confederation, and to force the states to obey. Thus the rule of the state legislatures were to be enormously

reduced to being a pool for nominations for the national upper house.

5. Establishment of a national executive to be chosen by the Congress, its salary to be fixed and chosen by Congress, and the executive to be limited to a single term.

6. A national judiciary of supreme and inferior courts, and with supreme jurisdiction for interstate cases.

7. The creation of a Council of Revision composed of the executive and some of the national judiciary to examine every act of the legislature and to exert a veto power over it, which could be overridden.

8. Finally, this government would be submitted by the old Congress, not to state legislatures as under the Articles, but to special state conventions chosen by the people for this purpose.

In the course of clarification of their resolutions, it quickly became clear that the Virginians had wanted not a "merely federal" union, but a "*national* government ... consisting of a *supreme* judicial, legislative, and executive.*" In short, the Virginians meant political revolution rather than reform of the Articles of Confederation. Gouverneur Morris further clarified the nationalist view: the old federal government was "a mere compact resting on the good faith of the parties" while the new national government was to have "a compleat and *compulsive* operation." It was these revelations that made Charles Cotesworth Pinckney of South Carolina and Elbridge Gerry of Massachusetts grow restive. This was illegal, revolutionary, and violated the express instructions of Congress and some states to confine themselves to revising the Articles. Pinckney expatiated that the convention should really be at an end, while Gerry called on the delegates to create a "federal" rather than "national" legislature, executive, and judiciary. But the convention ignored the protests and fatefully resolved that "a national government ought to be established consisting of a supreme legislative, judiciary, and executive." This critical resolution, moved by Pierce Butler of South Carolina, passed by 6-1-1 (Yes: Massachusetts, Pennsylvania, Delaware, Virginia, North Carolina, and South Carolina; No: Connecticut; Divided: New York

147

between Hamilton for and Yates against).[1] The Virginia Plan then went into the Committee of the Whole and the convention spent the next two weeks debating it. This was in itself a benefit for the nationalists because they were able to get from the beginning the frame of reference for the convention's debates.

One crucial debate concerned Virginia's demand over proportional representation in Congress (either by population or by contributions of revenue) and the issue of election of congressmen by popular vote. Here had been one of the critical debates in writing the Articles of Confederation a decade before. There were, in fact, two main reasons for the nationalist emphasis on these issues. One was the desire of the populous states to dominate the new government by ensuring that there would be no equality of states' voting. In particular Virginia, Pennsylvania, and Massachusetts were anxious to get this dominance as they were the largest states, with nearly half of the American population between them. James Madison of Virginia and James Wilson and Gouverneur Morris of Pennsylvania led the drive for proportional representation. In contrast, the small states, even the most nationalist of them, were bitter from the start; George Read, a conservative from Delaware, even threatened to lead Delaware out of the convention if the large states insisted on this plan since the state had instructed their delegates not to change "the rule of suffrage." Under the Delaware threat, the convention agreed to postpone the explosive question of proportional representation in Congress.

But there was another, subtler reason for this nationalist clause— a reason which has again been foreshadowed in the original debates over the Articles. This was the demagogic, supposedly democratic, opportunism by the anti-democrats to use popular election of the large house to destroy the power of the state legislatures, which were severely hated by the nationalists as being overly democratic and inimical to a powerful central government. Thus, democracy could be thwarted

---

[1][Editor's footnote] Rothbard presents votes on several resolutions in the form of Yes-No-Divided. Recall that Rhode Island declined to attend the convention and New Hampshire arrived late. Delegates from several states periodically left (including at one point the entire New York delegation, which was continually split between Hamilton versus Yates and Lansing), and this explains why the total number of states in the vote counts was not always uniform.

with this seemingly democratic solution. This clause of popular election of the lower house of Congress was opposed from two directions: by those critical of national government, and by anti-democrats, often the same people who didn't understand the intricacies and subtleties of the nationalist machinations. Thus, on the one hand, Roger Sherman of Connecticut demanded continued election of the lower house by the state legislatures. Otherwise, state governments would be critically weakened by the national government. On the other hand, Sherman, the South Carolinians, and Elbridge Gerry, frankly frightened by the Shaysite Rebellion, warned of the evils of popular election in Congress.

The idea of direct popular election of Congress was defended by George Mason, a liberal who didn't grasp the nationalist designs. Answering Gerry and Sherman, Mason simply defended such an elected lower house as the "grand depository of the democratic principle of the Govt." James Madison, who *did* understand what was going on, shrewdly provided lip-service to the necessity of popular election of *one* legislative branch as "essential to every plan of free Government." But then he revealed the purpose of the plan by assuming that popular elections would be refined "by successive filtrations" and that such filtrations of the Senate (the upper house), the judiciary, and the executive would effectively place the all-powerful national government beyond popular control. The even franker James Wilson laid bare the Machiavellian design of the nationalists: popular election of the House would free the national government from state control and thus raise "the federal pyramid to a considerable altitude" by giving it "as broad a basis as possible." Thus, national power could really be removed from more popular control while at the same time, popular election would mislead the people into placing their necessary confidence in the government. For "no government could long subsist without the confidence of the people. In a republican Government this confidence was peculiarly essential."

Wilson added that a large-scale government would naturally give this confidence because of the vainglory of the masses: "The people he supposed would be rather more attached to the national Govt. than to the State Govts. as being more important in itself, and more flattering to their pride." Furthermore, any danger from excessive democracy could be met by making the elective districts *large* and therefore remote from control by the people themselves. One amusing incident occurred when George Read, exasperated at John Dickinson of Delaware's wish to allow some room for the states in the American system, revealed his eagerness to see the total abolition of the states: "We must look beyond their continuance. A national Govt. must soon of necessity swallow all of them up. They will soon be reduced to the mere office of electing the national Senate." Read attributed any reluctance to "interested men" in state governments. James Wilson, alarmed at Read's imprudent frankness, hastened to assure everyone that the states would not be abandoned; in fact, they might well remain provided they were "restrained to certain local purposes." With Read refusing to take the hint and repeating his pronouncements, it is doubtful that Wilson's attempt to soothe proved much comfort for the few liberals present. Finally, after lengthy debate, the convention voted, on June 6, to elect the lower house of Congress by the people rather than by the state legislatures. The vote was 8-3; the three objecting were Connecticut, New Jersey, and South Carolina.

In the course of the debate on this question, Madison returned to the scene with a general defense of the concept of strong central government. In what is surely one of the most specious and overrated arguments for wide-ranging government ever provided (and foreshadowing his argument in *The Federalist No. 10*), Madison insisted that one of the main purposes of government was to defend the rights of various types of minorities. To do so, the bigger and farther-reaching government the better, for then it would be difficult for any *one* majority to form out of the great multiplicity of minority interests. As Madison put it:

> Where a majority are united by a common sentiment and have an opportunity, the rights of the minor party become insecure. In a Republican Govt. the Majority if united have always an opportunity. The only remedy is to enlarge the sphere, & thereby divide the community into so great a number of interests & parties, that in the 1st. place a majority will not be likely at the same moment to have a common interest ... and in the 2d. place ... they may not be apt to unite in pursuit of it.

It should be evident that, first, coalitions to form a majority are not very difficult and, second, the centralizing of power into one large juggernaut provides far more of an opportunity—and more of an incentive—for trampling the rights of minorities. The stakes are larger and

150

restraints weaker, not greater, because power is concentrated and consolidated. On the contrary, it is the fragmentation of power into many small local units that is likely to make oppression of minorities more difficult. Furthermore, minorities tend to have more control in smaller political units since they are more likely to have effective representation in them. In other words, the smaller the political unit, the harder it is for any one minority to coerce another, and the greater control each minority has.

In fact, Madison's real argument here was worded in deceptive language. What Madison and his fellow nationalists were really anxious to secure were the rights of minorities against the majority, or more specifically, oligarchical rule by a specialized minority at the *expense* of the majority. What central government power made easier was just such minority rule, for central government was both stronger and more remote from the knowledge, vigilance, and control of the people. The larger the scope and strength of government, indeed, the more difficult it is for a knowledgeable majority to form and unite to rise up *against* its remote oligarchical and bureaucratic rule.

The unrealism of Madison's theory can be seen from the only true examples which were given of supposed majorities trampling over the minority that made strong central government necessary: "Debtors have defrauded their creditors. The landed interest has borne hard on the mercantile interest." But the reality of the 1780s was that the landed farmers were being oppressed by the public debt and tax structure imposed by merchant-public creditors, and that such attempts as Shays' Rebellion to break off their yoke were one of the important factors in pushing the nationalists to form the Constitutional Convention. In short, strong centrist government was partly devised to reimpose the minority mercantilist yoke upon the majority, which was being thwarted in some of the states.[2]

The next critical debate was over the upper house (the Senate), which Virginia had proposed to have elected by the lower house of Congress, thus assuring large state nationalist domination of the Senate as well as

---

[2]Many historians have represented the struggle as being over paper money and *private* debts, but as has been seen, almost all groups favored paper money inflation of one form or another. The main conflict of private debtors was the highly justifiable one of imprisonment for nonpayment of debts.

the House. Here the resistance was too great, and only Massachusetts and South Carolina backed the Virginia Plan. James Wilson insisted on crushing the states completely by also electing the Senate according to popular vote, while George Read was by far the most reactionary in advocating the executive appointment of senators from members of state legislatures. John Dickinson protested that he opposed any "attempt to abolish the States" altogether. The result, on June 7, was unanimous agreement to have senators selected by the separate state legislatures.

Thus, by early June, the convention had decided on election of the lower house of Congress by the people of various states, and election of the senators by the state legislatures. But one critical point about the representation had yet to be settled: *how many* representatives would be granted to each state? This struggle had been postponed when the Delaware delegates threatened to walk out should representation be proportionate, as in the Virginia Plan, to population in the apportionment of both houses of Congress.[3]

---

[3] [Editor's footnote] Max Farrand, *The Records of the Federal Convention of 1787*, vol. 1 (New Haven, CT: Yale University Press, 1911), pp. 30–37, 48–50, 135–37. Farrand's records are based largely off of James Madison's own personal notes.

15

The Nature of National Power

At the end of May, the convention approved with little debate the severely national power granted to Congress, including the absolute power to act when it deemed the states to be "incompetent" and to veto all state laws it held to violate the constitution or any national treaties (a device added by Benjamin Franklin). Charles Pinckney, John Rutledge, and Pierce Butler of South Carolina expressed worry over the sweeping nature of congressional power; Randolph rather ingeniously denied any intention to destroy state power, while Madison held that broad national consolidation would override any contrary wishes for a limited enumeration of power. For his part, James Wilson asserted brusquely "that it would be impossible to enumerate the powers which the federal Legislature ought to have"; its power must, in short, be boundless. Finally, the convention granted Congress the absolute power to act whenever states were not competent by a vote of 9-0-1; only Connecticut failed to agree due to the actions of Roger Sherman. Madison did opportunistically prefer an amendment of the clause authorizing force against the states because force, Madison correctly observed, "would look more like a declaration of war, than an infliction of punishment."

Extended discussion did arise, however, over the nature of executive power. What specific form should it take? Should it, for example, be single or *plural?* Predictably, the ultra-nationalists, led by James Wilson, Charles Pinckney, and John Rutledge, urged a single executive (which would concentrate the most power and be closest to an American monarchy). Roger Sherman urgently insisted, in opposition, that the executive was only an instrument for carrying out the will of the legislature and, therefore, the members of the executive should be left to the discretion of Congress. Edmund Randolph passionately warned that a single executive would be "a foetus of monarchy." He suggested instead a plural three-way executive. Randolph insisted that he would be opposed to a single executive as long as he lived. The "permanent temper of the people," Randolph warned, "was adverse to the very semblance of Monarchy." To this, Wilson and the other ultra-nationalists hastened to assure the convention that there was no resemblance whatever to the British monarchy.

Wilson's use of dramatic rhetoric toward the necessity of concentrated power was advanced even further by South Carolina's Pierce Butler, who declared that a single executive would in some way "be responsible to the whole, and would be impartial to its interests." Butler was particularly concerned to have a single "impartial" executive for conducting military actions. For his part, James Wilson seems to have deplored the use of the alleged devotion of the Founding Fathers at Philadelphia to "checks and balances" in government; instead, a plural executive was rejected by him because it allowed for more disagreement, which would have prevented the effective and unchecked actions of the national government. On June 4 the convention fatefully acceded to Wilson's desire for a single executive. The vote was 7-3, New York, Maryland, and Delaware objecting. Virginia's delegation was split 4-3 in favor of Wilson's scheme over its own; George Mason, Edmund Randolph and John Blair were overruled by nationalists James Madison, George Wythe, and James McClurg, joined by a rare George Washington tie-breaking vote.

James Wilson, on June 1 and 2, continued to promote his emphatically ingenious scheme for the reality of tyranny unopposed in a plebiscitary-democratic form. Wilson, in short, called for replacing the Virginia Plan's selection of the executive by Congress. Instead, the executive would be chosen directly by the people, voting in state districts to choose electors, who in turn would select the executive. Thus, in the name of popular election, the executive would be removed from its natural dependence in the body making the laws (the legislature) and exist independently and remotely in its own power base, ostensibly subordinate to the broad public, but in reality removed from effective public control. The insulation from public control was further ensured by the device of the Electoral College, which placed the executive far removed from popular choice. Wilson also repeated his argument for a popular election of the lower house, since only with this would the people truly be inclined to place their confidence in their national rulers.

Roger Sherman, as in so many other issues, cogently opposed the ultra-nationalist schemes. Sherman "was for the appointment by the Legislature and for making him absolutely dependent on that body, as it was the will of that which was to be executed. An independence of the Executive on the supreme Legislative, was in his opinion the very essence of tyranny if there was any such thing." Finally, Wilson's proposal was beaten down by 8-2, with only Maryland and Pennsylvania in favor. The convention promptly agreed that Congress would elect the single executive for a term of seven years; again the vote was 8-2, with Pennsylvania and Maryland voting no. The lengthy seven-year term, however, was a victory for the nationalists. It was proposed by Charles Pinckney and attacked by Gunning Bedford of Delaware, who called for a three-year term. The seven-year clause was passed by the close vote of 5-4-1 (Yes: New York, New Jersey, Pennsylvania, Delaware, Virginia; No: North Carolina, South Carolina, Georgia, Connecticut; Divided: Massachusetts). The nationalists won another handful by overwhelmingly crushing an intelligent proposal by John Dickinson, a veteran conservative worried by excessively nationalist trends, that the executive be removable by Congress with a majority of the state legislatures.

On June 4 the question of the preferred veto power for a Council of Revision ran into the sensible theory that judges should not be part of a vetoing council because they were also the arbiter of the constitutionality of laws. There was also a remarkable clause pushed by the ultra-nationalists James Wilson and Alexander Hamilton to give the executive an *absolute* veto power over Congress, a vast power that they somehow contended would not be "too much exercised." Its very existence would "preserve harmony and prevent mischief," i.e., it would ensure the subservience of Congress to the supreme will of the executive. Even so strong a nationalist as Pierce Butler balked at this, warning of another Oliver Cromwell, and James Madison felt that the people were not yet ready "to give such a prerogative."

To meet this new threat by the ultras, George Mason rose to the height of his eloquence and thundered that the executive would be a

155

monarchy even *more* dangerous than the British because it was elected. Mason "hoped that nothing like a monarchy would ever be attempted in this Country. A hatred to its oppressions had carried the people through the late Revolution." The Wilson-Hamilton proposal for absolute veto was defeated unanimously by the states. The single executive, however, was given veto power that could only be overridden by two-thirds of each house of Congress, and the veto was vested in him alone and not in a Council of Revision. The requirements for overriding the veto were so stringent that an elective monarchy in the United States may be said to have been imposed in any case.

Who would appoint the judiciary? The Virginia Plan's appointment of the Supreme Court by Congress was fought by Wilson, who urged that the executive, "a single, responsible person," be given the power to appoint the entire judiciary; again, all power would be concentrated in the president. But this time John Rutledge balked at the specter of monarchy, and Sherman and Pinckney urged the original Virginia Plan. James Madison, however, proposed and carried a compromise for selection of the Supreme Court by the Senate.

A particularly severe struggle occurred over the role of the inferior courts. The moderates, led by Rutledge and Sherman, wanted *no* inferior courts whatever, all original cases could be heard in the state courts, and the federal Supreme Court would then be limited to an appellate role, which would be sufficient to ensure national uniformity. Any structure of federal inferior courts would pose a severe threat to state power and raise the potential for a national dictator. Madison, for several reasons, led the nationalist fight for a body of inferior courts with full jurisdiction in many cases, thus would the federal judiciary be "commensurate to the legislative authority."

Rutledge's proposal to eliminate the clause establishing federal inferior courts passed, on June 5, by a narrow vote of 5-4-2 (Yes: Connecticut, New Jersey, North Carolina, South Carolina, Georgia; No: Pennsylvania, Delaware, Maryland, Virginia; Divided: Massachusetts, New York). But just when it seemed that the Right had suffered a significant loss, the nationalists bounced back to capture once more, as in the case of the executive veto power, the essence of their goals at the expense of a slight loss of the form. Wilson and Madison ensured that Congress "be empowered" (though not compelled) to establish inferior courts and won by a vote of 8-2-1, Connecticut and South Carolina being opposed and New York divided. Again the nationalists won the essence of their demands.

At this early date in the convention, the nationalists began to hint of their essentially revolutionary design to not submit the new Constitution as a legal amendment to the Articles. Roger Sherman objected to the Virginia Plan idea of submitting their decisions to state conventions with the consent of Congress; why not ratify them in the state legislatures? Madison fell back on the Wilsonian pseudo-democratic rhetoric, while Rufus King let slip the real reason for the sudden accession of democratic form by the nationalists: "A Convention being a single house, the adoption may more easily be carried thro' it, than thro' the Legislatures where there are several branches. The Legislatures also being to lose power, will be most likely to raise objections." In other words, there was no chance of ratification in the state legislatures, and the electors chosen by state conventions could be more easily "persuaded." After the convention was softened up with this skirting with illegality, James Wilson offered a truly subversive direction: why allow the bulk of the states to be blocked by the "inconsiderate or selfish opposition of a few [States]"? Why not just choose ratification after only a certain number of states—Pinckney helpfully supporting nine? The issue was postponed by the possibly stunned assemblage, with no comment made on this blunt proposal to scrap the unanimity proposal of the existing Confederation.

Thus, by June 7, the nationalists, though forced to make a few concessions, had so far carried the substance of their program: the creation of a supreme national government and a Congress empowered to act whenever it thought the states were incompetent to veto any state laws it felt threatened the Constitution or national treaties, though it was not empowered to coerce the states; an independent and powerful single executive chosen by Congress for seven years with a nearly absolute veto power over Congress; a national supreme judiciary appointed by the Senate and a system of inferior courts established by Congress and appointed by the president, the judges all to be appointed for life terms; a bicameral Congress, with the lower house elected by the people; and the Constitution would be submitted to state conventions rather than legislatures, and potentially secured through a union of nine states rather than by unanimous ratification. The election of senators in the upper house by state legislatures was the only substantial setback so far for the nationalist cause.

On June 8 the exultant nationalists moved to further augment the central power even more; Congress had already been given the absolute power of vetoing state laws deemed to be unconstitutional or in violation of national treaties. Now the emboldened nationalists moved to crush the states altogether, as Charles Pinckney proposed that Congress have the absolute power to veto all state laws whatsoever. James Madison seconded with an impassioned plea for such total power as "absolutely necessary to a perfect system"; in fact, the absolute veto was the least that could be done. James Wilson's frenzy was, predictably, even greater, as he thundered that "We are now one nation of brethren. We must bury all local interests & distinctions."

The opposition to all this fire-eating was weak; once again, the liberals and moderates were stymied by their agreement with the fundamental tendency and direction of the nationalists, though not with the length to which the ultra-nationalists pushed the logic of their views. Only Gunning Bedford delivered an opposition of any force or spirit. Bedford spoke up for the several states in danger of being crushed by the advancing juggernaut of Pennsylvania and Virginia, who "wished to provide a system in which they would have an enormous & monstrous influence." Yet the Pinckney proposal for a universal congressional veto over the states was defeated by the tremendous margin of 7-3-1. Voting for the nationalist dream, indeed, were precisely the three big states: Massachusetts, Pennsylvania, and Virginia. Virginia's delegation was again split, Mason and Randolph objecting, while McClurg and Blair followed Madison's lead. Delaware was the divided state, and the conservatives Read and Dickinson were blocked by Bedford and Richard Bassett.[4]

---

[4]Ibid., pp. 54–68, 88, 98–102, 119–23, 164–67.

16

The Debate Over
Representation in Congress

The stage was now set for one of the great titanic struggles of the Philadelphia Convention: the postponed question of the nature of representation in Congress, and specifically on the Virginia Plan of proportional representation. William Paterson and David Brearley of New Jersey took the occasion to launch a full-scale counterattack on the large-state nationalist junto. Brearley opened by pointing to the convenient solution of the question that had already been hammered out in the formation of the Articles: equal voting by each state. Only in that way could the smaller states avoid being surrounded by Massachusetts, Pennsylvania, and Virginia. Paterson was even more pointed, sternly reminding the convention that the express object was to amend the Confederation, and that

> the articles of confederation were therefore the proper basis of all the proceedings of the Convention. We ought to keep within its limits, or we should be charged by our constituents with usurpation. ... the people of America [are] sharpsighted and not to be deceived. ... The idea of a national Govt. as contradistinguished from a federal one, never entered into the mind of any. ... We have no power to go beyond the federal scheme, and if we had the people are not ripe for any other.

Paterson also threatened that Wilson's hint at a new national confederation of states would not include the small state of New Jersey, which would never accept the proportional representation plan of American nationalism.

159

If representation was to be proportional, then some specific plan would have to be selected. On June 11, Roger Sherman proposed a significant compromise: that the House be chosen in proportion to the respective number of free persons, while the Senate consist of one vote per state. In this way, the lower house would be chosen on a national basis, elected by the people to their number, while the Senate would be chosen equally by the state legislatures.

Immediately, the issue arose of the *kind* of proportional representation in the lower house. John Rutledge and Pierce Butler urged representation proportional to the revenues supplied by each state; as Butler put it with unmatched candor: "money was power; and that the States ought to have weight in the Govt.—in proportion to their wealth." By a vote of 7-3-1, the convention then affirmed *some* principle of representation for the lower house as opposed to equality of states; New York, New Jersey, and Delaware voted no, while Maryland was divided.

It was at this point that a fateful issue was injected into the proceedings: slavery. For if the proportion was to be according to population, the South wanted slaves included in the population figures. Wilson and Pinckney proposed that the proportion of each state in the lower house include every free person, including bond servants, plus three-fifths of all "other persons," except Indians. Wilson's excuse was that Congress had already recommended, and eleven states had approved, that revenue quotas under the Articles would be so apportioned—a specious argument, since levying taxes and granting representation are scarcely the same thing. In addition, "as Luther Martin told the Maryland legislature, taxing slaves discouraged slavery, while giving them political representation encouraged it."[5] At this juncture there was very little debate, and only Elbridge Gerry cogently pointed out that if the slaves were property, there is no more reason to represent them then the "cattle & horses of the North." In the vote, the three-fifths clause was approved by no less than nine states to two, only New Jersey and Delaware, the champions of the small states, voting against.

The next order of business was the Senate. Roger Sherman, seconded by Oliver Ellsworth of Connecticut, made a very strong plea

---

[5]Staughton Lynd, "The Abolitionist Critique of the United States Constitution," in Martin Duberman, ed., *The Antislavery Vanguard* (Princeton, NJ: Princeton University Press, 1965), p. 217.

for each state to have one vote in the Senate. Implicitly adding Connecticut's withdrawal threat to Delaware and New Jersey's, Sherman warned that "Every thing he said depended on this. The smaller States would never agree to the plan on any other principle than an equality of suffrage in this branch." It has been remarked that it was with this touchy issue of representation in Congress that tempers began to flare and withdrawals threatened. Yet, despite Sherman's stringent plea, the vote for equal state voting in the Senate was rejected and a Wilson-Hamilton motion for the same method of apportionment as in the lower house was approved by the same closest of margins, 6-5. The votes were: for equal voting by states: Connecticut, New York, New Jersey, Delaware, Maryland; for proportional voting as in the House: Massachusetts, Pennsylvania, Virginia, North Carolina, South Carolina, Georgia. In short, the small states and New York for equal voting; the large northern states plus the slaveholding South for the large-state nationalist plan of proportional representation.

We may now pause to consider the question: why did such smaller states as North Carolina, South Carolina, and the really small state of Georgia (and often joined by Maryland) take the large-state view, and also their victory? A Georgia or a South Carolina might be a nationalist for many reasons, but why generally a large-state nationalist? The answer is that these southern states, in which slavery played an integral role in the economy and society, expected the slave states to multiply in population and soon outweigh the North. Already the slave states were almost on a population parity with the predominantly free states. And the lands approximately ready for settlement were the Southwest, where Kentucky and Tennessee were already expanding rapidly, while the unsettled North was commanded by British army forts. Evidence of great expectations abounds; thus, James Madison wrote to Thomas Jefferson during the spring of 1787 that representation by population would be adopted because it would be "recommended to the Eastern States by the actual superiority of their populousness, and to the Southern by their expected superiority." Both South and North agreed on the essentials of the question: later in the convention, George Mason would look forward to the day "as soon as the Southern & Western population should predominate, which must happen in a few years," and Gouverneur Morris would concede the necessity of accepting the "vicious principle of equality" in the Senate "in order to provide some defence for the N. states" against a preponderance of southern and western power.[6]

After the crucial vote on representation in the Senate, the convention proceeded, by similar close majorities, to vote for referral of the new Constitution to conventions in the various states. Terms of appointment were decided for Congress, and in both cases the longest of the terms considered were chosen: three years for the lower house, and seven for the Senate. Madison led the fight from the nationalists for long terms, while Gerry argued for annual house elections to provide a popular check on their representatives.

The Committee of the Whole had now made up its decision on the Virginia Plan, and the nationalist triumph was seemingly complete. The committee made its report to the convention on June 13. The Virginia Plan had been essentially adopted whole. A supreme national government, the Congress of which could veto all state laws it considered unconstitutional and in violation of national treaties; a powerful single executive, chosen for a long term of seven years by Congress, with a nearly absolute veto power over Congress; a Supreme Court appointed by the Senate and a system of inferior federal courts authorized, which would be appointed by the president; a bicameral Congress, the lower house elected by the people on the basis of population including three-fifths of slaves, and an upper house selected by state legislatures on the same basis; the Constitution to be submitted to state conventions after approval by Congress; all this symbolized a total smashing large-state nationalist victory. The voting, especially in the close small- versus large-state conflict, had been made possible by the absence of two small states from the convention: Rhode Island, which refused to attend, and New Hampshire, whose delegates had not yet arrived.

But the small-state nationalist bloc, albeit joined with the liberals, had only begun to fight. To block the acceptance of the Virginia Plan Report on June 15, William Paterson outlined the contrasting New Jersey Plan. This last-ditch measure was successful in blocking ready acceptance of the Virginia Plan Report of the thirteenth, and both plans were now referred back to the Committee of the Whole.

---

[6]Ibid., pp. 230–32.

The New Jersey Plan had been drawn up by a bloc of members of full delegations from New Jersey and Delaware, who were small state nationalists, and Connecticut and New York, who were liberals and moderates. The Plan's main difference from Virginia's was that, while it gave greatly increased power to the federal government, it at least tried to maintain the semblance of a confederation, and it gave the smaller states a voice in that confederation. Instead of the Virginia Plan's bicameral legislature, the New Jersey Plan stuck with the current confederation's unicameral legislature, and each state had only one vote. The federal government also had no veto power over state legislation. There was a federal judiciary and a plural federal executive, and while the latter had no command of the army, it had the power to "call forth" the confederation and "enforce and compel an obedience" to congressional laws and treaties.

It was at this point that Alexander Hamilton decided to get into the act. Outnumbered on his own delegation, Hamilton was, rather surprisingly, not playing a leading role in a convention he had been instrumental in promulgating; and besides, from his extensive position on the ultra-right he was getting restive at the meager concessions to liberals that he saw being made. Hence, with more than one constitutional plan now being offered, on June 18 Hamilton presented his own. Reviewing briefly the history of federal unions (Greece, Germany, Switzerland), Hamilton quickly concluded that federalism was hopelessly weak and ineffective, and that therefore "we must establish a general and national government, completely sovereign, and annihilate the state distinctions and state operations." Deploring even republicanism in itself, Hamilton pointed uncritically to the British monarchical government as the model for American framers to follow. Attacking the masses of the people as "turbulent and changing" and filled with fervor, Hamilton called upon the convention to give to the few who "are the rich and the well born" a permanent share in national power. In a bizarre *non-sequitur*, Hamilton maintained that making the rich and well-born into a national ruling class would most assuredly give them a vested interest in the system, and "they therefore will ever maintain good government." Only such a permanent ruling class could "check the imprudence of democracy." Indeed, no democratically elected executive, even as conservative a one as under the Virginia Plan, can be of any value; only the British-style executive will at all suffice. The

163

nationalistic Virginia Plan in general did not go far enough in increasing the power of the government, for it was "but *pork still, with a little change of the sauce*" [italics in original]. Pushing for what was in effect an elective, powerful monarchy, Hamilton called for a national executive elected *for life*, and one, moreover "who dares execute his powers"; the executive to be elected remotely from the public by electors chosen in the various states. Hamilton also urged a Senate elected for life, also independently by electors.

In Hamilton's dream state, there were to be no restrictions whatsoever on the absolute power of the central government. The Congress was to have "the unlimited power of passing *all laws* without exception" [italics in original], and the executive to have absolute veto power. Also, an executive office in each state would be appointed by the president with absolute power to veto all state laws, and all militia officers were to be appointed by the national government. In addition to a Supreme Court, Congress was to appoint inferior courts in every state "so as to make the state governments unnecessary." Alexander Hamilton had conclusively described the matter for his dream state— his ideal polity—and no clearer blueprint could have been devised for absolute despotism.

Significantly enough, one of the reasons given by Hamilton in the alleged necessity of replacing the Confederation with a strong national government was the weaknesses of the war power. Under the Confederation, the military was weak "and it is evident they [the Confederation] can raise no troops nor equip vessels before war is actually declared." It has often been insisted that one of the major impulses behind the nationalist drive was a desire to replace the foreign policy of the United States under the strictly limited government of the Confederation with an aggressive foreign policy along the model of all Great Powers.

The Hamilton speech struck the members of the convention with the force of a thunderclap. To the liberals and moderates, this was the corporeal embodiment of their fears of the nationalist designs. To his fellow counterrevolutionaries, Hamilton's candor was a terrible indiscretion, a mighty embarrassment, the imprudent revelation of all their fantasies they knew could not be achieved. As Professor Miller writes: "With good reason, therefore, Madison exclaimed that Hamilton was up to his old trick of letting the cat out of the bag; and this time the cat was a particularly ugly specimen that seemed quite capable of breaking up the Convention."[7] Madison and Wilson rushed to denounce Hamilton's plan, both of them hyperactively assuring everyone that they were deeply devoted to preserving the rights and powers of the states, these absolutely necessary institutions. Hamilton himself added that he did not exactly want to abolish the states *altogether*, only to make them mere administrative subdivisions of the national government—hardly an explanation calculated to soothe the feelings of the moderates. Only the highly conservative George Read, of all the delegates, subscribed with enthusiasm to Hamilton's idea; indeed, he went even a step further to urge the obliteration of even the states as administrative subdivisions, and then representation by eventually new administrative districts. The nationalist disapproval, however, killed the Hamilton Plan completely.

The convention's Committee of the Whole turned to consider the New Jersey Plan. James Madison delivered the large state nationalist attack, e.g., a newly revised Articles would not prevent the states from violating national treaties, would not ensure good state laws, and did not supply sufficient force to suppress state insurrections such as Shays' Rebellion. After Madison's speech, on June 19 the convention voted 7-3-1 to reject the New Jersey Plan in favor of the agreed Virginia Plan. Voting to scrap the New Jersey Plan for the Virginia Plan: Massachusetts, Connecticut, Pennsylvania, Virginia, North Carolina, South Carolina, Georgia; voting against scrapping: New York, New Jersey, Delaware; Maryland was divided. The Virginia Plan was now before the full convention as the basis for further work. Each clause of the Plan would now again be taken up in turn.

On the initial first clause of the Virginia Plan: to establish a "supreme national government," Wilson, Hamilton, and King argued in favor, Wilson being careful to absolve himself from Hamilton's design. Luther Martin of Maryland cogently set forth the state-sovereignty position:

> the separation from G. B. placed the 13 States in a state of nature towards each other; that they would have remained in that state till this time, but for the confederation; that they entered into the confederation on the footing of equality; that they met now to amend it on the same footing, and that he

---

[7] Miller, *Alexander Hamilton and the Growth of the New Nation*, p. 172.

could never accede to a plan that would introduce an inequality and lay 10 states at the mercy of Va. Massts. and Penna.

To this argument, Wilson and Hamilton replied with another one of their ingenious fancies: that somehow the Declaration of Independence meant that the states became independent first as united and not as separate entities. As a semantic concession to the moderates, proposed by Oliver Ellsworth, the word "national" was replaced throughout by "the United States." But the *supremacy* of the central government—the real point of this clause—remained.

The next point was a bicameral Congress, and here the liberal-moderate bloc counterattacked strongly, a remarkable development, since at the end of May this clause had passed almost unanimously in the Committee of the Whole. On behalf of the Confederation, John Lansing of New York moved that Congress shall consist of a single body. George Mason of Virginia delivered a speech against, but Lansing was supported by Roger Sherman and Luther Martin. The vote on June 20 was surprisingly close, and Lansing's motion for a unicameral Congress was defeated by only 4-6-1 (Yes: Connecticut, New York, New Jersey, Delaware; No: Massachusetts, Pennsylvania, Virginia, North Carolina, South Carolina, Georgia; Divided: Maryland). The bicameral clause was adopted the next day by 7-3-1 (Connecticut switching its vote from the day before).

Next came the question whether the lower house of Congress would be elected by the people. Charles Cotesworth Pinckney of South Carolina led the attempt to throw out this clause and revert to the election by the state legislatures. Hamilton led the defense of this key part in the nationalist program. But only Connecticut, New Jersey, and Delaware joined South Carolina in supporting election of the lower house by the state legislatures. And only New Jersey (with Maryland divided) held out to the last against popular election of the lower house. The convention did agree, however, to lower the congressional term from three to two years.

The next clause of the Virginia Plan was the selection of the Senate by the state legislatures—one of the few concessions that the nationalists had been forced to make in the Committee of the Whole. Until now the division of the states had not precisely been small versus large; it had rather been the South *plus* the two large states of the

North (Massachusetts and Pennsylvania) against the smaller states of the North. Now, on June 25, came the first purely sectional split of the convention. A motion to postpone consideration of the Senate until the three-fifths clause of representation in the House was settled mobilized the five slave states (the South from Maryland to Georgia) in favor of postponement, and the six northern states opposed. The nationalists, led by James Wilson, launched an assault to reverse their concession and elect the Senate by electors chosen by people in the several states. The convention, however, voted overwhelmingly to keep the concession of election by state legislatures; only the ultra-nationalist delegation from Pennsylvania and Virginia voted no.

The term of senators was then taken up; the moderates arguing for a shorter term than seven years to provide a popular check on the senators, and the reactionaries arguing for longer terms for the opposite reason. In a sense, the debate turned not so much on whether the proposed term should be lengthened from seven years to nine, or down to six or four, as to where the major threat to liberty laid. Madison, leading the nine-year proponents, trumpeted again on his formulaic theories and warned of the evils of majority rule, specifically the suffrage of the mass of the poor. In short, Madison and his nationalist cohort saw the main danger to liberty in the people and wished to build up an even stronger oligarchical rule in central government to exert power against the menace of the people. In this aim, Madison was backed by Wilson and Read, while Hamilton and Gouverneur Morris argued life terms for the senators. On the other hand, the liberals located the major threat to liberty precisely in the oligarchical threat the nationalists were happy to fasten over the people; the way to guard against the danger of government was to weaken the oligarchy and bureaucracy and multiply popular checks upon the rulers. Here, indeed, was the basic political issue between Left and Right in the United States. Thus, Roger Sherman, in the course of this debate, eloquently declared: "Govt. is instituted for those who live under it. It ought therefore to be so constituted as not to be dangerous to their liberties. The more permanency it has the worse if it be a bad Govt. Frequent elections are necessary to preserve the good behavior of the rulers."

James Wilson, in his speech for lengthening the Senate terms, raised an interesting point, for it showed the importance that the nationalists gave to foreign affairs and to an aggressive foreign policy designed to aid merchants in pursuing their trade. Wilson asserted that since the Senate will have the power to make wars and treaties, "it ought therefore to be made respectable in the eyes of foreign nations. The true reason why G. Britain has not yet listened to a commercial treaty with us has been, because she had no confidence in the stability or efficacy of our Government. 9 years with a rotation, will provide these desirable qualities."

After hearing the importance of the various arguments, the actual voting was another climactic event: the convention voted *not* to extend Senate terms to nine years *and* to cut the term to six. Only Pennsylvania and Virginia, joined by Delaware, voted to extend; to cut to six years, many nationalists decided to vote for, while four states (New York, New Jersey, South Carolina, Georgia), held out for a still shorter term. The decision for six years scarcely differed from the reported Virginia Plan.[8]

It was on June 27 that the convention reached the most fateful point of all, on which acrimony had spread and walkouts had been threatened: the apportionment of voting in the two branches of Congress. Luther Martin led a lengthy assault on proportional representation in the lower house. The separate states were still sovereign, said Martin, and had not abdicated; furthermore "an equal vote in each State was essential to the federal idea." Acrimony over the debate mounted so alarmingly that Benjamin Franklin, at one point, frantically called for a turn to religion and prayer to seek a solution. At one point in the debate, on June 29, Dr. William Samuel Johnson of Connecticut resurrected a compromise made earlier by his Connecticut colleague Roger Sherman: that the upper house of Congress have equal representation by each state while the lower house be elected by proportional representation. But Madison, Hamilton, Gerry, and the nationalists would have none of this. Madison declared frankly that "the states ought to be placed under the control of the general government—at least as much so as they formerly were under the king and British parliament."

---

[8][Editor's footnote] For more on Rothbard's views regarding short terms and compulsory rotation, see Murray Rothbard, "Bureaucracy and the Civil Service in the United States," *Journal of Libertarian Studies* (Summer 1995): 16–28; Rothbard, *Conceived in Liberty*, vol. 4, pp. 1239–43; pp. 125–29.

Finally, in one of the fateful votes of the convention, the body voted on June 29 to establish suffrage in the lower house by some proportionate ratio and not by the equality of the Articles of Confederation. The vote was very close: 6-4-1 (Yes: Massachusetts, Pennsylvania, Virginia, North Carolina, South Carolina, Georgia; No: Connecticut, New York, New Jersey, Delaware; Divided: Maryland). Once again the lineup was Massachusetts, Pennsylvania and the South against the rest.

The convention now came to an issue even more crucial than the previous one: the pattern of representation in the Senate. Until this point, the Virginia Plan as represented by the Committee of the Whole had been scarcely changed in any respect; but now the frantic liberals, moderates, and small state nationalists opened a desperate assault on the plan's selection of senators also by proportional representation. Oliver Ellsworth of Connecticut made a strong plea for equality of voting as basic in the Connecticut Compromise scheme, and he trenchantly warned that no state north of Pennsylvania but Massachusetts would accept proportional representation in both branches of Congress. But the large-state nationalists were brutally adamant. James Wilson took the tactic that this separation of the states might *just* as well be *made.* Sneering at the states and their very existence, Wilson refused to accede to such a supposedly pernicious system of representation where a minority could rule the majority. Wilson, however, did use the effective argument that governments were made for men, not for "imaginary beings called States." While joining Wilson in worrying about the rights of the national majority being destroyed by a minority, Madison added a shrewd, if overdrawn, point: the real struggle was not so much small state versus large but "by other circumstances ... principally from [the effects of] their having or not having slaves. ... the great division of interests in the U. States. ... did not lie between the large & small States: It lay between the Northern and Southern ..."

For his part, Rufus King of Massachusetts threatened a breakup of the convention and declared his absolute refusal to come under a government founded in a "vicious principle of representation" (i.e., equality of voting by states). Jonathan Dayton of New Jersey promptly attacked King's argument, and Luther Martin of Maryland insisted that he could never accept federation on an unjust principle (inequality of voting).

The small state leader Gunning Bedford of Delaware then asserted "that there was no middle way between a perfect consolidation and a mere confederacy of the States." Bedford also insisted that the large-states bloc *include* those states that would soon become large: Georgia, South Carolina, and North Carolina. The large states, Bedford pointed out, were trying to oppress the small, and their power will be abused. Bedford trenchantly declared "*I do not, gentlemen, trust you*. If you possess the power, the abuse of it could not be checked; and what then would prevent you from exercising it to our destruction?" [italics in original] Bedford concluded with a counter-threat of his own. Should the large states separate from the small, then "the small ones will find some foreign ally of more honor and good faith, who will take them by the hand and do them justice." Never had the convention been closer to permanent split and dissolution, which now seemed imminent. At this point, Alexander Hamilton, discouraged, his plan dismissed and his vote continually overruled in his own delegation, left for home.

On July 2 Ellsworth moved that each state be allowed one vote in the Senate. On this crucial vote, the convention split evenly, 5-5-1. Voting yes: Connecticut, New York, New Jersey, Delaware, Maryland; No: Massachusetts, Pennsylvania, Virginia, North Carolina, South Carolina; Georgia was the surprise, it divided between Abraham Baldwin "aye" and William Houston "nay." In a very real sense, it was this young western-Georgia lawyer Baldwin who saved the Constitutional Convention and the new Constitution, for without his switch vote, the equality of the states would have lost, the small states would have walked out, and the Constitution would not have been formed or, if formed, never ratified.

At this point it should have been clear that the alternative was either something like the Connecticut Compromise or dissolution. Yet the supposedly level-headed practical framers and moderates of the convention: Madison, Wilson, Washington, and Hamilton, were bitterly opposed to any such compromise as destructive of their basic nationalist design. General Charles Cotesworth Pinckney of South Carolina moved to create a committee from each state to propose a compromise. Not only did the nationalists lose in their opposition to Pinckney's proposal; but the composition of the committee spelled an anti-large-state nationalist triumph. Of the members, only Elbridge Gerry of Massachusetts was a moderate large-state nationalist, while the committee included such staunch small-state leaders as William Paterson, Gunning Bedford, and Oliver Ellsworth; liberals such as Luther Martin and Robert Yates; and such compromisers as Abraham Baldwin of Georgia, William Davie of North Carolina, John Rutledge, George Mason, and Benjamin Franklin. No such major ultra-nationalist leaders such as Madison and Wilson were included on this committee.

The committee had been handed the problem of representation in both the Senate and House, and on July 5 it delivered its report. The committee recommended equal voting by states in the Senate and proportional voting by population in the House, and one congressman for every 40,000 people, including three-fifths of the number of slaves, with a minimum of one representative for each state. Here indeed was a threat to the large-state nationalist bloc, for their cherished principle of proportional representation in both houses was abandoned. In the height of this blow, the committee's concession of allowing the House to originate all money bills and leaving the Senate unable to amend them was scarcely any consolation to their designs.

To this compromise, the large-state nationalists were adamantly opposed, and Madison launched the attack with a bitter rejection of "departing from justice" by granting equality in the upper house. Madison made clear that he would rather split the Union and form a separate nation with the large states and simply let the small ones exist as best they could. In this, Madison displayed not the broad flexible nature of the compromiser that has often been attributed to him, but rather the rule-or-ruin tactician of the hardline ultra-nationalist who settled for nothing less than total victory and was willing to see the Union dissolve rather than give up his program.

Gouverneur Morris of Pennsylvania was even blunter. Grandiosely designating himself as a "Representative of the whole human race," Morris urged the large states to go ahead heedless of the public opinion, which "could not be known" anyways, and the smaller states would have to go along, whether by persuasion or by force. For "this Country must be united. If persuasion does not unite it, the sword will." Returning to the attack in a second speech, Morris thundered that the compromise failed "to protect the aggregate interest of the whole." In particular, contended Morris, "he had seen no [provision] for supporting the dignity and splendor of the American Empire." For the states, Morris would just as soon see "all the Charters & Constitutions of the States … thrown into the fire, and all their demagogues into the ocean." James Wilson joined his fellow nationalists in demanding their version of "justice and right," while Gerry and Sherman argued meekly for compromise, and small-state nationalist William Paterson was more impressive in opposing the large-state nationalists.

In the midst of the debate, the convention entered a complex and equally significant and bitter struggle over the lower house of Congress. If it was argued that representation there would be proportional, the next logical question was: proportional to what? Gouverneur Morris now moved to push the convention into an even more reactionary stance than what had been reflected in the Virginia Plan: to make representation proportional not only to the number of people, but also to *wealth*. Morris conjoined wealth and power and maintained that life and liberty were not nearly as important as property. Life and liberty, he speciously declared, were better defended in the "savage State"; the purpose of society and government was only to secure property. Therefore property had to be represented in government. Morris also brusquely declared that the Atlantic states should be secured in a fixed domination over the national government over new and future western states. Morris was supported in this call for dominance by wealth and seacoast by King, Gerry, and the South Carolina coastal planter delegation.

This question was referred to a committee of five, headed by Morris, which reported on July 9 for apportionment by wealth *and* number. The committee proposed an initial House based vaguely on such an ambition, and warned that the Virginia Plan's apportionment of one representation for every 40,000 would make Congress too large and would soon give dominance to the western states. The committee recommended that western representation be doled out "in safe proportions." To replace these vague injunctions, a new committee under Rufus King was appointed, which recommended an apportionment based on the three-fifths slave clause, and even more than three-fifths for slaves. The slavery issue was by now in the thick of the debate over representation in the lower house, and here North and South squabbled bitterly. King declared that "he was fully convinced that the question concerning a difference of interests did not lie where it had hitherto been discussed, between the great & small States; but between the Southern & Eastern." Therefore, he had been ready to make concessions in the proposed national apportionment to the South, concessions which some in the South, such as Charles Cotesworth Pinckney, did not think sufficient. The northern surrender to the slave states was at the heart of the new American Constitution, and the concession on House apportionment was one of the crucial elements in that surrender. King, at the heart of this concession, was later to declare that the three-fifths clause "was, at the time, believed to be a great one, and has proved to have been the greatest which was made to secure the adoption of the Constitution." In a speech at the convention, King shined great light on the reason for this meek submission to a system which everyone in the North abhorred. The reason was economic interest: "If the [Northern states] expect those preferential distinctions in Commerce & other advantages which they will derive from the connection they must not expect to receive them without allowing some advantages in return."

At the same time William Paterson attacked the very idea of slave representation: slaves are only property of the masters, they have no free choice or personal liberty, and consequently are not represented in the southern state legislatures: so why then in the Congress? Furthermore, this would constitute an encouragement to the slave trade. In a reply, Madison cynically suggested his own pro-large-state, pro-slave-state "compromise": that the House represent all free people in proportion to their number, and that the Senate represent the nation in proportion to everyone, free and slave.

The King Committee suggestion was agreed to on July 10, by 9-2, only South Carolina and Georgia holding out for even more concessions to slavery, while the other southern states were already content with the apportionment concession. But now the future, as well as the initial allocation of votes in the lower house, had to be decided. Accordingly, Edmund Randolph of Virginia and Hugh Williamson of North Carolina suggested the next logical step: that federal censuses be taken periodically on the population of the various states, and that apportionment in the House be periodically updated to account for free white inhabitants plus three-fifths of the slaves.

This was no more than the logical step, but for some reason now the northern consciences began to balk. Of course, this balking was prodded by the universal expectation that southern slave-state population would continue in the future to expand, and at a much faster pace than the North; thus, periodic revision would mean accelerating southern predominance in the national government. But now the arguments of the beleaguered northerners could only be very weak indeed. The only thing they could say was that the Congress, in its wisdom, should be free to set its own representation (e.g., Sherman, Gouverneur Morris), and this was clearly unsatisfactory. And Morris' remonstrance was highly unbearable to the demagoguery of James Madison, for here was Morris urging representation by population, yet trying defiantly to weaken future representation of the southern-western population! Madison frankly declared that Morris must have "determined the human character by the points of the compass."

The Randolph-Williamson census plan was subject to two amendments from the Right. The ultra-slavery forces, headed by Pierce Butler and Charles Cotesworth Pinckney, demanded *equal* representation for slaves and free men, a proposal beaten down on July 11 by 3-7. The only states in favor were Delaware, South Carolina, and Georgia. New York's Lansing and Yates had left the convention for good the previous night, in disgust at the agreement for proportional representation in the House, and charged it was a nationalist conspiracy they would have nothing to do with. This was one of the great fateful errors at the convention, for while they were there, the New Yorkers had much to gain and nothing to lose by staying in the convention. They could have used their state's vote to weaken the Constitution's power as much as possible and then refuse to sign it at the end. The loss of New York deprived the liberal Antifederalists of what little precious vote they had at the convention.

The next move from the Right was John Rutledge's motion to put wealth back in as a factor in representation along with number, a motion frankly designed by Rutledge to suppress the potential rise of the western states. Rutledge's plan lost by a tie vote of 5-5 (South Carolina and Georgia being joined by Massachusetts, Pennsylvania, and Delaware; staunchly opposed were Connecticut, New Jersey, Maryland, Virginia, and North Carolina).

The convention then agreed, by a margin of only 6-4, that a periodic census should be made of the free inhabitants; then came the vital three-fifths clause for slaves, and on this fateful vote the three-fifths clause was defeated by 4-6. For this clause were all the southern states except South Carolina, holding out for parity, and including Connecticut, were willing to compromise; opposed were all the northern states

174

and Maryland. It now looked as if the convention would fall apart on both issues of representation in the Senate and the House.

The next day Gouverneur Morris softened the blow of representation by population and wealth by requesting that direct taxation (e.g., land and poll taxes) be in proportion to a state's representation. This apparent softening, however, also meant that the poorer and soon more populous western states would be reluctant to claim their full representation because it would subject them to greater taxation. At this point William R. Davie of North Carolina bitterly attacked the elimination of the three-fifths clause and threatened a walkout if slaves were not to be represented by at least three-fifths in the Congress. Davie proposed a light slap at the slave states by imposing direct taxation in proportion to a state's representation, in order to win back the three-fifths clause. The new climate of opinion, led by Ellsworth of Connecticut, managed to reverse the convention's decision, and on July 12 it approved the three-fifths rule, including the direct-taxation clause. The vote for the whole clause, including the three-fifths rule, was now 6-2-2 (Pennsylvania and Maryland's vote switched from no to yes, and South Carolina and Massachusetts from no to divided).

Now that the South had won on the three-fifths clause, there was no need to insert a wealth clause for representation; indeed, the coming western slave states were expected to be relatively poor. The large-state nationalists like Randolph, Madison, and Wilson had always opposed anything but population as the standard for representation, and the convention unanimously agreed to drop wealth (only Delaware was divided) and return to the original Virginia Plan of apportionment by population only (including three-fifths of slaves) and updated by periodic censuses. Gouverneur Morris, resisting to the end the elimination of wealth as a factor in representation, threatened breakup of the convention and a separate northern confederation. Above all, the basis of mere population led Morris to adopt the "vicious principle of equality" of voting in the Senate to protect the supposedly eventual smaller population of the North against southern and western discrimination.

Attention returned to the problem of the Senate, on whether to accept the previous vote of equality of votes in that branch. With Luther Martin of Maryland and Jonathan Dayton of New Jersey adamantly insisting on equality, the provision was counterattacked bitterly by Wilson, Madison, King, and Pinckney. King reflected the large-state nationalists' vehemence in urging this offense to "justice" and declared that "he preferred the doing of nothing, to an allowance of an equal vote to all the States," and Wilson and Madison maintained similar views. Madison also raised the point that states' equality would benefit the relatively smaller-state, non-slave North as against the slave South.

Finally, on July 16 the convention voted on the Senate problem; in a very close vote, equality of state voting in the Senate was approved by 5-4-1. Voting for state equality: Connecticut, New Jersey, Delaware, Maryland, North Carolina; opposed: Pennsylvania, Virginia, South Carolina, Georgia; Massachusetts was divided, Gerry and Caleb Strong for, King and Nathaniel Gorham, no. The Connecticut Compromise was barely approved.

Thus were the climactic struggles over representation in the federal government decided, and state equality in the Senate was the very first vote in which the original Virginia Plan was significantly attacked. The large-state nationalists were incensed by *this single* rebuff, and some wanted to walk out and form their own nationalistic constitution, but they finally decided to stay in the convention. It was now time to turn from the problems of representation in the central government to the question of the substantive powers of that government.[9]

---

[9][Editor's footnote] Farrand, *The Records of the Federal Convention*, vol. 1, pp. 177–78, 245, 261, 297–99, 301–06, 324, 423–26, 437, 471, 483–91, 504, 527–33, 552–66, 604; Max Farrand, *The Records of the Federal Convention*, vol. 2 (New Haven, CT: Yale University Press, 1911), p. 7.

17

Strengthening the Executive and Judiciary

The Virginia Plan Report gave Congress the power to "legislate in all cases to which the separate States are incompetent; or in which the harmony of the United States may be interrupted by the exercise of individual Legislation." This vague grant of the broadest of powers to the central government was now attacked by Rutledge and Butler of South Carolina who urged that it be returned to a committee for a specific enumeration—and therefore limitation—of powers. For such enumeration the states decided on a tie vote of 5-5, with Connecticut, Maryland, South Carolina, Georgia, and surprisingly Virginia voting for enumeration, and Massachusetts, Pennsylvania, Delaware, North Carolina, and surprisingly New Jersey holding out for unlimited power. Hence the re-committal lost; the pressure of New York could have broken the tie in favor of enumeration. Delaware's Gunning Bedford, an ardent nationalist now that his state had achieved great representation in the Senate, moved to insert an even broader and wider grant of national powers "to legislate in all cases for the general interests of the Union." Even Randolph warned that the general government would then violate laws and aggrandize power, but the convention approved the clause by 6-4.

Next came the clause empowering Congress to veto all state laws *it* believed were unconstitutional or in violation of national treaties. The struggle over this clause was basically minor, however; for while the fanatical James Madison, as usual, considered the veto power "essential," Roger Sherman, Gouverneur Morris, and even Luther Martin preferred accepting national supremacy in the more softer guise of national judicial supremacy. Thus Sherman "thought it unnecessary, as the Courts of the States would not consider as valid any law contravening the Authority of the Union," and Morris pointed out that "a law that ought to be negatived will be set aside in the Judiciary departmt. and if that security should fail; may be repealed by a Nationl. law." The congressional veto power was removed by a vote of 7-3 (only Massachusetts, Virginia, and North Carolina insisting on it), and Martin then moved and the convention accepted a clause that all constitutional congressional acts and treaties would have to be treated as "the supreme law" by the states and state courts.

Turning to the executive, the nationalists drove to strengthen still further the independent and dominant executive power. A limitation to a single term was replaced by allowing two terms; next, Dr. James McClurg of Virginia moved to replace seven years by a life term "during good behavior." Gouverneur Morris was undoubtedly overjoyed at this proposal and Madison, favoring above all the idea of an independently powerful executive, countered George Mason's perceptive and cogent fears of a national monarchy with a clever but empty paradox: a weak executive would lead to revolution and hence to monarchy. The proposal for a lifetime executive was defeated by the close vote of 4-6 (Voting for was Pennsylvania, New Jersey, Delaware, and Virginia).

The nationalists next turned to take the power to appoint the Supreme Court from the Senate (as it was represented from the Committee of the Whole) and force it into the executive. James Wilson and Gouverneur Morris urged this change but it was opposed by Luther Martin. The motion lost by 2-6 (Massachusetts and Pennsylvania voting yes, Georgia being absent). The nationalists were successful, however, in retaining the power of Congress to appoint inferior federal courts, despite the articulated attacks of Luther Martin and Pierce Butler; Randolph and George Mason led the defense. One clause of the committee report provided for a national guarantee to "a Republican Constitution & its existing laws" to each state. James Wilson explained that the clause was simply designed for the federal government's suppressing of insurrections and rebellions within the states, a clause backed by Randolph and Mason, and changed by Wilson to guarantee "a Republican Form of Government" and to protect each state from "foreign and domestic Violence." Luther Martin vainly upheld the liberal view; he "was for leaving the States to suppress Rebellions themselves."

The convention was not finished with the executive, and through the remainder of July the ultra-nationalists, led by Madison, Wilson, and Gouverneur Morris, tried desperately to amend the Virginia Plan Report by freeing the executive power from subordination to Congress and allowing it to become an independent and separate power. Again the nationalists used democratic demagoguery to advance some form of popular election of the president, independently chosen by special electors, when their real aim was to erect a powerful executive remote from and uncontrolled by the mass of the people. Thus, the power pyramid of the nation would flow from the top—the president—down to the broad mass of the country. After discussion, the convention finally decided to leave the executive clause as it had been originally reprinted from committee: chosen for seven years and ineligible for a second term.

The nationalists also tried to change the committee plan by restoring the old idea of a joint executive-judicial veto of congressional measures. The idea was to add judicial and executive vetoes on the democratically elected legislatures. The oligarchical judge should not only be able to nullify unconstitutional laws, explained James Wilson and Madison, to his power should be added the right to veto any laws they deemed unwise. Madison professed no worry about excessive power in the executive or judiciary; only the legislature is to be feared. Thus, the elected legislature "was the real source of danger to the American Constitutions." Nathaniel Gorham, Luther Martin, and Elbridge Gerry seriously objected that the judge's rule would then confuse the authority and constitutionality of the legislature and judiciary and give the latter redoubled power. Madison, with his love of paradox, straightforwardly assured that a blending of executive and judiciary was necessary to *really* keep them separate. And he held up the ultras' favorite model of Great Britain as the example to follow. The nationalist attempt, however, to give the judiciary a vote in the veto power was turned down by 3-4-2 (Yes: Connecticut, Maryland, Virginia; No: Massachusetts, Delaware, North Carolina, South Carolina; Divided: Pennsylvania, Georgia).

There was one more crucially important point to settle in this phase of the convention's work: the procedure for ratification of the Constitution then in progress. The moderates and anti-nationalists made a desperate attempt to return to legality and submit the new Constitution to the state legislatures. Ellsworth, Gerry, and William Paterson led the fight for this motion. In his reply Gouverneur Morris made clear that the main reason for referring the Constitution to popular state conventions rather than the legislatures was to evade the unanimity requirement of the Articles. By transcending the Articles altogether, Morris and the nationalists were making the revolutionary proposal of launching the Constitution by less than unanimous agreement of the states. The motion for legality failed by 3-7, with only Connecticut, Delaware, and Maryland voting aye.

The basics of the Virginia Resolution had now been voted upon and the arch-nationalists had pushed through virtually every element of the reported Virginia Plan. Only the small-state victory on equal voting in the Senate, and the pro-states' rights decision to have senators chosen by their respective state legislatures marred the record of the large-state nationalists' triumph; their only defeats were on attempts to make their Virginia Plan even more centralist and powerful. It is true that the nationalists' cherished veto of state laws had been eliminated, but its substance was retained by enlarging on the rule of federal laws and the federal judiciary.[10]

---

[10][Editor's footnote] Ibid., pp. 27–29, 33, 47–48, 74, 133.

18

The Preliminary Draft

The next phase of the convention now began. The basic attributes of the Constitution had been lain down. Now the convention selected a Committee of Detail, a five-man committee to actually draft a constitution based on the principles agreed upon during the convention sessions. Of the five now uniquely powerful men, only one—Oliver Ellsworth—was somewhat critical of nationalism, while the four—John Rutledge, Edmund Randolph, Nathaniel Gorham, and James Wilson—were dedicated nationalists, but only James Wilson was a true fanatic. The convention adjourned from July 26 to August 6 to allow the committee to prepare a draft constitution. The draft was prepared by Edmund Randolph, revised by James Wilson, and then submitted to the convention on August 6.

The draft committee, however, did not confine itself to the resolutions passed by the convention. Instead it injected parts of the various plans put before the convention, from the various state constitutions and the Articles of Confederation. In the process the committee cordially watered down much of the overt nationalism of the convention's resolutions. Particularly important was transforming the general all-inclusive grant of power to Congress into specifically enumerated powers. Of course, such an enumeration of power in essence removed the mantle of ultimate sovereignty from the Congress. Among the powers specifically granted to Congress: to lay and allocate "Taxes, Duties, Imposts and Excises," to regulate commerce with foreign nations and among the states, to coin money and regulate the value of foreign coins, to establish post offices, to borrow money and emit paper money

("Bills of Credit"), to make wars, raise armies and navies, to call up the militia "in order to execute the Laws of the Union, (to) enforce treaties, (to) suppress Insurrections, and repel invasions," and very fatefully "make all Laws that shall be necessary and proper" for executing the government's power.

Another new element in the draft largely absent from previous debates was the placing of specific restrictions on the powers of Congress. Thus, Congress was prohibited from levying any tax on exports or imposts on importation of slaves (at the behest of the southern members), or any other direct taxes not proportional to the free population plus three-fifths of slaves. It could also only pass a navigation act with consent of two-thirds of each house of Congress (again a southern demand). Furthermore, the central government was restrained from intervening in a state to protect it against domestic violence or to subdue rebellion unless requested to do so by the state legislature. The jurisdiction of the Supreme Court was also spelled out and made more specific, thus delineating its power.

Instead of the states being subjected to the vague absolute rule of the central government, the draft document imposed specific restrictions on state power. The prohibitions on state actions were designed to assume to the central government a monopoly of certain critical functions: coinage of money, making treaties, emitting paper money, legal tender laws, imposing tariffs, building a standing army and navy in peacetime, and making war.

The draft constitution, consisting of a preamble and twenty-three articles, opened with a clear and straightforward preamble: "We the people of the States of ... do ordain, declare, and establish the following Constitution for the Government of Ourselves and our Posterity." Apart from the abovementioned resolutions and changes, there were a few basic alterations. New provisions required the citizens of each state to receive all the privileges and immunities of other states, and each state was to give full faith to the acts and records of the others. New states were to be admitted on the same terms as the original states but would have to gain the consent of two-thirds of each house of Congress.

From August 7 through September 10, the convention debated the draft Constitution in detail. The first fight came over the sensible provision that the qualifications in each state for voting for the House of Representatives should be the same as its qualifications for voting for the lower house of the state legislatures. In short, the eligibility of suffrage would be up to each state. Unsurprisingly, Gouverneur Morris was not satisfied, and he moved to restrict the right of suffrage to landowners. In addition to excess democracy, Morris wanted to reduce the states' power over Congress. To this charge of aristocracy, Morris countered with the classic method of the right-wing paradox: the current plan is *really* aristocratic because the people in a democratic House would sell their votes to the rich. John Dickinson backed Morris' plan as a "necessary defence agst. the dangerous influence of those multitudes without property & without principle." In his speech James Madison, of course, cleverly combined both of these arguments. Ellsworth and Mason attacked these points, as did even so rabid a nationalist as Wilson. Ellsworth cogently asked, in effect, why landowners? "Ought not every man who pays a tax to vote for the representative who is to levy & dispose of his money? Shall the wealthy merchants and manufacturers, who will bear a full share of the public burdens be not allowed a voice in the imposition of them?" The Morris proposal for restricted suffrage lost by 1-7-1. Delaware was the only state that approved while Maryland was divided.

The next battle was again a reactionary move on the part of Gouverneur Morris. The draft had requested that a senator be a U.S. citizen for at least four years before their election. Morris urged raising the requirement to fourteen. Madison and Franklin, to their credit, turned liberal on this subject and pleaded eloquently on the importance of foreigners who loved liberty in waging the American Revolution. Randolph was also critical of the proposal, as was Ellsworth, and poor Wilson, a man born in Scotland, was particularly against it. He eloquently denounced the "degrading discrimination, now proposed." He was strongly backed by the foreign-born Hamilton, who had returned to the convention at just the right time. But rabid reaction on this point held sway, Colonel Mason longed to restrict the Senate to the nation-born, and Pierce Butler and Charles Pinckney of South Carolina hinted of the "peculiar danger" of "foreign attachments." But the most passionate was Gouverneur Morris himself. Calling of all things from "reason" to "moderation," while assuming the darkest prejudices, Morris lashed out bitterly at the rationalist libertarian philosophers prominent among the intellectuals of the age: "As to those philosophical gentlemen, those Citizens of the World, as they called themselves, He owned he did not wish to see any of them in our public Councils. He would not trust them. The men who can shake off their attachments to their own Country can never love any other. These attachments are the wholesome prejudices which uphold all Governments." Gouverneur Morris had indeed touched the chords of bigotry in the members of the convention; the citizen eligibility requirement was raised to nine years for a senator and from three to seven years for a representative.

While the draft Constitution had not imposed suffrage requirements on the states, it did authorize Congress to establish property qualifications for its members. While Madison and others wanted the Constitution to fix property qualifications directly, Benjamin Franklin, opportunist, was by far the most liberal, and shrewdly declared that "if honesty was often the companion of wealth, and if poverty was exposed to peculiar temptation, it was not less true that the possession of property increased the desire for more property—Some of the greatest rogues he was ever acquainted with, were the richest rogues." From the Right Gouverneur Morris wanted to allow the legislature to set not only property qualifications, but all qualifications for its members. However, on August 10 the entire clause was struck out by a vote of 7-3, with only New Hampshire, Massachusetts, and Georgia assenting to the congressional power to set its property qualifications. The lack of suffrage uniformity among the states and strong political opposition were enough to strike out this highly conservative clause of the draft Constitution.

Another liberalizing change was to modify the draft requirement of an oath upon all state and national offices to support the Constitution; an "affirmation," a clause necessary for such sects as the Quakers, was unanimously approved as a possible alternative to an oath. Charles Pinckney also moved to prohibit all religious tests for any federal office. Again, this important victory for religious freedom was overwhelmingly approved, with only North Carolina against and Maryland divided.

On the organization of Congress, the ultra-nationalists tried desperately once more to restore judicial veto power over Congress (led by Madison) and absolute executive veto (led by Morris), but after much travail the two-thirds power to override an executive veto was retained. A long squabble came over the compromise provision to grant to the House the right to originate money bills not amendable by the upper house: an old Anglo-American tradition to preserve the control of money in the hands of the directly elected representatives of the people. However, the clause was changed to allow the Senate to amend money bills, which effectively evaded the point of the whole provision.

The nationalists went along surprisingly and readily with the shift from an unlimited grant to enumerated grants of power to the central government. Probably the reason for this "restrictive" anomaly was the broad list of enumerated powers of Congress and the poverty of specific restrictions on that power. Congress would look restricted when in reality it would have a broad legislative scope over the country. Congress was, first and foremost, granted the power to tax, although direct and poll taxes were required to be proportioned to population (including three-fifths of slaves). There was no opposition to this power, to the commercial power, or to the bulk of the other granted powers. Indeed, the Convention added to Congress' power the establishment of "Post-Offices" along which it could monopolize the postal service.

Congress' proposed broad military powers occasioned much debate. The nationalists tried to narrow Congress' power to make war into a more concentrated, and therefore a more controllable, form: Pinckney to the Senate only, Butler to the president himself. While these were defeated, Madison cunningly moved to alter congressional power: "make war" became "declare war," which left a broad, dangerous power for the president, who was grandiosely designated in the draft as the "commander in chief" of the U.S. army and navy, and of all the state militias. For now, the president might *make* war even if only Congress could formally *declare* it. If Congress had the power to "declare" war, then it was no more than a lapse to vest the power to make peace in Congress too. Instead, the draft Constitution placed this power in the oligarchical Senate alone; while Gerry and Butler urged the placing in Congress, this attempt was defeated unanimously.

The liberals tried valiantly to limit this vast and unlimited scope for national military actions, and Elbridge Gerry and Luther Martin proposed a maximum limit of a few thousand on any national peacetime army. But the proposal was rejected unanimously and scornfully by the convention. However, the power to call up and command the state militias met more heated and sustained opposition. Here rested with the American tradition of anti-militias and of opposition to centralized power. The liberals in that tradition were opposed to any standing army and to any central government control. But the attempt of Ellsworth, Sherman, and Dickinson to restrict central power met sharp defeat.

The nationalists, for their part, tried to bring back the idea of unlimited central government power to intervene in a state's troubles without request by the state legislature. The nationalists wanted absolute power to intervene. The nationalists were repelled, however, by an opposition led by Gerry and Luther Martin and the "subdue rebellion clause" was eliminated altogether.

Not content with the vast enumeration of powers, the nationalists proposed adding more, and Madison and Pinckney succeeded in inserting grants to Congress that included the power to rule absolutely an enclave of federal government that could be totally apart from the states. They failed to include the power to grant corporate charters or to establish a government university.

One successful attempt was made in the convention to remove a grant of congressional power, and the attempt came from none other than the arch-nationalist Gouverneur Morris. Morris' distrust of recent state paper money transcended both his own previous advocacy and his dedication to ultra-nationalism. Morris wanted to remove the grant of power to Congress to borrow money and to emit paper money. He received support, especially from John Langdon of New Hampshire and George Read of Delaware. George Mason and John Francis Mercer of Maryland defended the clause, but the power to "emit bills on the credit of the U. States" (i.e. paper money) was successfully struck from the Constitution, and only Maryland and New Jersey voted against the change.[11]

Considering the importance of the public debt question at the end of the war, not much was said about the public debt at the convention. During the 1780s many states had begun to assume their citizens' shares of the national debt, but the result was to aggravate further the problem of the war-born state debts, especially in such high debt states as Massachusetts. The heavy burden of state debts gave both the state taxpayers and their public creditors an incentive to favor federal

---

[11]In any interpretation in good faith of the Constitution, it should have been crystal clear from this exercise that Congress had and has no constitutional power to emit paper money!

assumption, especially of their debts. In this way, the tax burdens could be foisted on the taxpayers of the other more prudent states. South Carolina, another heavily indebted state, led a drive in the convention to impose the national assumption of state debts. Rutledge, Pinckney, and King of Massachusetts managed to refer the whole issue to a "Grand Committee."

The Grand Committee quickly proposed that Congress be empowered to assume the debts of the old Confederation Congress, as well as the war debts of the U.S. and of the several states. Gerry and Gouverneur Morris then insisted that Congress be *forced* to pay the debts, and the convention agreed. But Mason and Butler raised the issue of why security speculators should benefit from such a generous windfall. Finally, all states except Pennsylvania voted for a Randolph proposal which conceded the windfall to the speculators and obliged Congress to assume all debts previously assumed by the U.S. Congress. As for the *state* debts, Hamilton and Madison argued that it would be more expedient, and raise less political opposition, to postpone decision of this controversial issue and to push the assumption even later as an administrative measure.

One crucial indirect consequence of this decision was a proposal by Roger Sherman that the congressional tax power be intimately and expressly connected with paying the national debt. In the final committee appointed at the end of August, this was vaguely adopted by inserting the congressional taxing power "to pay the debts and provide for the common defence and general welfare of the United States." In this way, the famous "general welfare" clause slipped through, unheralded, into the Constitution and was later misdirected and blown up to allow Congress to levy any tax whatsoever as long as it might be used to promote the vague "general welfare."

While the powers of Congress were enumerated, these grants were added by a vague and portent *supremacy* clause. Originally an antinationalist clause to replace the congressional veto power over the states, the draft Constitution greatly strengthened the supremacy clause by putting acts of Congress and U.S. treaties above state constitutions as well as state laws, and specifically over state as well as federal judges. John Rutledge then was unanimously able to add the U.S. Constitution, as interpreted by inferior or superior courts, a third supreme law over state and state courts. Still not satisfied, Pinckney, Wilson, and

Madison tried to insert as well a congressional veto power over all state laws by a two-thirds vote of each house. Opposed were Mason, Rutledge, and Sherman. This proposal lost by the closest vote, 5-6 (Yes: New Hampshire, Pennsylvania, Delaware, Maryland, Virginia; No: Massachusetts, Connecticut, New Jersey, North Carolina, South Carolina, Georgia).

In contrast to the trampling grants of power, albeit specifically enumerated, to Congress, the specific restraints on Congress proposed in the draft were but few. However, this was still a decided improvement over the total power and complete absence of restraint in the Virginia Plan Report. Most of these were prohibitions on certain invasions of individual liberty. For example, the crisis of "treason," usually loose and totally vague, was restrained in the Constitution. Furthermore, Congress was forbidden to pass bills of attainder or *ex post facto* laws and to suspend the right of *habeas corpus*, although this right was weakened by allowing its suspension "when in cases of rebellion or invasion the public safety may require it." This fateful weakening was put through by Gouverneur Morris. No discriminatory legislation was allowed to benefit one port of a state over another, and ships from one state to another could not be forced to pay duties. The libertarian *ex post facto* and bills of attainder prohibitions were moved by Elbridge Gerry and James McClurg of Maryland, and there was little disagreement about either. The vote on this prohibition was 7-3-1 (against were Connecticut, New Jersey, Pennsylvania; North Carolina was divided).

It is crucial to note that the enthusiasm at the convention for restraints and prohibitions on the states was far more severe than for Congress. This reveals the basic desire to cripple the states and bring them under the aegis of the central government. For example, the states were to be prevented from making treaties without the consent of Congress, from maintaining any peacetime army or navy, making war, granting titles of nobility (as was the central government also prevented from doing so), levying tariffs, emitting paper money, and issuing legal tender laws. States were also prohibited from passing any bills of attainder or *ex post facto* laws, and in general jury trials were required in criminal cases. The libertarian fervor which prevented invasions of freedom by the states was scarcely matched by any equivalent enthusiasm for limiting the potential actions of the central government.

Wilson and Sherman moved to make the prohibitions on state issue of paper money and paper legal tender laws absolute even with the consent of Congress. Sherman exulted that this was a "favorable crisis for crushing paper money," and this prohibition was made absolute by 8-1-1 (only Virginia voted no and Maryland was divided). The protection of individual contracts from the states was moved by Rufus King and supported by Wilson and Madison; Gouverneur Morris objected in the name of majority rule and he and Mason thought this was "going too far." But the protection finally prevailed.

One of the most important debates of the session was waged over the procedure for admitting new states into the Union. The basic provision in the draft Constitution was that new states must "be admitted on the same terms with the original states." But this provision scarcely suited the aim of the conservative easterners to keep perpetual domination over the growing West. Gouverneur Morris, leader of this group, moved quickly to eliminate this requirement for equality of treatment. And despite the opposition of Madison and Mason, Morris' motion was overwhelmingly approved in the seaboard-dominated convention by a vote of 9-2; only Maryland and Virginia objected to this blatant disregard for western equality.

The next debate was over Morris' proposal to require the consent of any existing state, as well as of Congress, for the admission of any new state out of its present territory. The large states made the general guarantee of their current territory a major sticking point and threatened to leave the convention if their demands were not met. They were led by Morris and Wilson with Luther Martin and Daniel Carroll of Maryland leading the opposition. Here again was a recurrence of the old struggle between the large landed and the small landless states, a recurrence prompted by the revolutionary new-state movements brewing in the West, as well independent Vermont. Martin, backed by John Dickinson, eloquently urged the uniformity of allowing all the people of the frontier lands, of western Virginia, North Carolina, Georgia, and Maine (which belonged to Massachusetts), to continue without the consent of their state governments. Martin, too, warned that the small landless states would walk out if they were required to guarantee the western territories to the large landed states. But only three landless and small states—New Jersey, Delaware, and Maryland—took the point of freedom for the western settler; the easterners had won the right to consider every new admission on completely arbitrary terms and to keep the westerners *de novo* enthralled if they so desired. There could be no clearer indication that, for the ardent nationalists of Pennsylvania and Virginia, the declaration of state's rights applied only to situations where the large states could discriminate; lest the large landed states be directly threatened, these nationalists revealed quickly enough that their real desire was for power, and not for an abstract ideology of nationalism divorced from a power struggle for land.

A slight hitch developed over Vermont, for it was clear that New York would hardly consent to the admission of Vermont, which it claimed for itself, into the United States. This was taken care of in an amendment by Morris himself which stated that any new state within the "jurisdiction" rather than within the "limits" of an existing state did not need the consent of that state, and Vermont was evidently not under New York's effective jurisdiction.

The draft Constitution had vested a great deal of power in the Senate: especially the power to make treaties, appoint judges and ambassadors, establish courts, and settle disputes between states. The nationalists, who wished to establish the single executive's power above the power of all other branches or subdivisions of government, chose to transfer all this power to the presidency. Led by Morris, Madison, and Gorham, the convention agreed to at least eliminate the Senate's judiciary functions.

The draft Constitution had agreed that the single executive, the president, would be elected for a single term by the Congress, but again the nationalists put a desire to overturn the previous convention decision to eliminate this dependency of the president in the representative legislature. The joint problem arose in *how* the legislature would do the electing: should the houses of Congress vote separately or jointly? The large state delegates of course preferred a joint ballot that would deprive the small states and Senate of much influence in the decision, and this view prevailed by a vote of 7-4. Then the nationalists worked for a powerful and independent presidency: their indomitable leader Gouverneur Morris urged again a president chosen by a body of popularly elected electors. The Morris motion was first defeated by 6-5, and this important decision was postponed.

In theory, an executive is supposed to be a mere enforcer of the laws, in effect, an agent of the legislature only. But the nationalists proceeded to alter this concept and exult the executive in a highly important textual change. Whenever the draft had stated that the president "may recommend" measures to the Congress, the convention changed "may" to "shall," which provided a ready conduit to the president for wielding effective *law-making* powers, while the legislature was essentially reduced to a ratification agency of laws proposed by the president. In another fateful change, the president was given the power to create a bureaucracy within the executive by filling all offices not otherwise provided for in the Constitution, *in addition* to those later created by laws. The convention, led by Gouverneur Morris, also rejected a motion by Dickinson and Randolph to allow Congress to give the states the power to fill some federal offices. Thus, the central government was left in an unchecked domination over federal offices. On the other hand, Roger Sherman was able to win the concession that the president would only be commander in chief of the state militias when they were directly in the service of the U.S. government.[12]

---

[12][Editor's footnote] Farrand, *The Records of the Federal Convention*, vol. 2, pp. 163–68, 202, 237–38, 244, 261, 439, 454.

19

The Corrupt Bargain
and the Preservation of Slavery

The most important battle of the August days of the Constitutional Convention was waged, as had been the battle over the three-fifths clause, between the North and South and had at its heart the institution of slavery. One of the small number of restrictions on Congress in the draft Constitution was a prohibition of any tax on exports, or of any tax or prohibition on the "migration or importation of such persons as the several States shall think proper to admit"; in short, there was to be no restrictions on the slave trade. Furthermore, no navigation act could be passed except by a two-thirds vote in each house of Congress: a hallmark of the southern distrust of the northern merchants, one of whose many goals in the drive for a Constitution was to privilege themselves through a navigation act that would cripple the competition of foreign shippers in the southern foreign trade. All of these provisions were friendly to the South: two (the export tax and navigation clauses) were designed to preserve freedom of southern trade against northern attempts to seize privileges or revenues from the South; one (on the importation of slaves) was designed to preserve the traffic in slaves.

Already, Gouverneur Morris in early August had made an unsuccessful attempt to rescind the three-fifths clause decided upon in July, and Mason and the South were joined by Massachusetts and Connecticut in opposing the prohibition of exploiting the (as existing) minority South through export taxation. Then, on August 21, the slavery issue burst forth once more. Luther Martin of Maryland began proceedings by demonstrating that he was interested in individual liberty as well as states' rights. Martin flatly proposed a prohibition or a tax on the importation of any slaves, for the encouragement of slavery embodied in the three-fifths clause "was inconsistent with the principles of the revolution and dishonorable to the American character." John Rutledge replied in an interesting and revealing manner: in defending the slave trade, Rutledge insisted that "Religion & humanity had nothing to do with this question—Interest alone is the governing principle with Nations." In short, moral principle was to be turned over in favor of vested economic interest; or, rather, vested economic interest was to be elevated to the status of "moral" principle overriding all other considerations. Charles Pinckney used slightly different tactics and upheld empirical evidence and custom over moral principle: "If slavery be wrong, it is justified by the example of all the world. ... In all ages one half of mankind have been slaves." Pinckney, of course, was speaking from the vantage point of the slave-owning "half" rather than the enslaved. His second cousin, Charles Cotesworth Pinckney, added flatly that "S. Carolina & Georgia cannot do without slaves" (i.e., the slave-*owners*, not the *enslaved* inhabitants, of these states could not make do). Pinckney also used a primitive Keynesian multiplier analysis to "demonstrate" the benefits of slavery and slave importation for the whole country: "The more slaves, the more produce to employ the carrying trade; The more consumption also, and the more of this, the more revenue for the common treasury." Both Pinckney, Rutledge, and Abraham Baldwin of Georgia threatened dissolution of the convention if it should interfere in any way with the slave trade.[13]

One interesting aspect of the decision was George Mason's eloquent speech denouncing the slave trade and even slavery itself. He insisted that only South Carolina and Georgia still permitted slave imports and denounced the immorality, tyranny, and sins of slavery. Mason denounced northern merchants who had engaged in this traffic and urged that Congress have the power to prevent the slave trade. Charles Cotesworth Pinckney and Oliver Ellsworth of Connecticut, in reply, staunchly pointed to the reason for Virginia's eloquence in attacking the slave trade. Since the Virginians, despite the eloquence and depth of Mason's attack, were not after all proposing to proceed

---

[13] [Editor's footnote] For more on South Carolina and Georgia's views regarding the slave trade, see *Conceived in Liberty*, vol. 4, pp. 1293–94; pp. 179–80.

against slavery itself, Ellsworth and Pinckney saw in the Virginians' stand the new makings of a vested economic interest of this aim: slave breeding. As Ellsworth trenchantly pointed out:

> If it [slavery] was to be considered in a moral light we ought to go farther and free those already in the Country.—As slaves also multiply so fast in Virginia & Maryland that it is cheaper to raise than import them, whilst in the sickly rice swamps [further South] foreign supplies are necessary, if we go no farther than is urged, we shall be unjust towards S. Carolina and Georgia.

Similarly, Pinckney stated "as to Virginia she will gain by stopping the importations. Her slaves will rise in value, & she has more than she wants."

Both Ellsworth and his Connecticut colleague Roger Sherman tried to justify their acceptance of the slave trade by lightly and complacently opining that all the states would eventually abolish slavery themselves "by degrees." Sherman expressed his opinion that such an issue should not obstruct the business of forming a new Constitution. John Dickinson attacked the slave trade as "inadmissible on every principle of honor & safety," and James Wilson wryly observed that if defenders of the right of the slave trade were maintaining that South Carolina and Georgia would probably soon abolish it themselves, then there was no reason for them to stay out of a Union that might prohibit that trade.

In the midst of this critical rift, however, Gouverneur Morris, who had been one of the loudest talkers against slavery and had deemed it as "a nefarious institution" and "the curse of heaven," now proposed a "bargain": the slave trade, export tax, and navigation act clauses should all be recommitted to a special committee, and "these things may form a bargain." In short, Morris realized that the benefits of special privilege to northern merchants *in* a navigation act would undoubtedly outweigh in the minds of northern delegates the attraction of an abstract principle.

The export tax and slave trade clauses were then referred to a special committee, one member from each state, by a vote of 7-3. Those who held out against Morris' corrupt bargain were New Hampshire, Pennsylvania, and Delaware (Massachusetts was absent). On committal of the restrictive clauses in the navigation act, only Connecticut and

New Jersey voted nay. In the course of the debate on this committal, Nathaniel Gorham of Massachusetts said very revealingly: "He desired it to be remembered that the Eastern States had no motive to Union but a commercial one."

Two days later, on August 24, the grand committee returned with its dearly agreed upon bargain: (1) the importation of slaves could not be prohibited until 1800, but Congress could tax such imports at a rate no higher than the average duty on imported goods (the latter concern had already been hinted at by Rutledge and Charles Cotesworth Pinckney); (2) the two-thirds requirement on navigation acts was dropped. The northern (especially New England) merchants had the power to impose navigation acts, and the slave trade was to be tightly insulated for over a decade.

The first move on the committee report was Charles Cotesworth Pinckney's amendment, which proposed to extend the term of an inviolate slave trade from 1800 to 1808—thus providing the slavers a twenty-year grace. Most significantly, Gorham of Massachusetts, who was the delegate most anxious to impose a navigation law, seconded Pinckney's motion. Over the strenuous objections of James Madison, the twenty-year term was approved by 7-4 (only New Jersey, Pennsylvania, Delaware, and Virginia voted no). Not only Maryland but all of shipping-oriented New England voted cozily with the hardened slave states of the Deep South. After the maximum duty on imported slaves was changed to ten dollars per person, the slave-trade clause of the bargain was passed by the identical 7-4 vote.

At this point, on August 29, Charles Pinckney dramatically moved to scuttle the bargain with the North by proposing to restore the two-thirds requirement, not only for navigation acts, but for any law "for the purpose of regulating the commerce of the U.S. with foreign powers." Pinckney eloquently denounced "oppressive regulations" that would be imposed by a tyranny of a majority of the North's commercial interests. The liberal Luther Martin eagerly seconded the motion, and George Mason backed the proposal as protecting the rights of the southern minority. The North of course opposed Pinckney's proposal on behalf of freedom of trade. The shocked George Clymer of Pennsylvania protested that "the Northern & middle States will be ruined, if not enabled to defend themselves against foreign regulations." Gouverneur Morris indignantly protested, in the usual argument from paradox of the ultras, that navigation acts would *really* benefit the South. First, subsidies to American ships will multiply them and eventually make the shipping trade cheaper than at present—i.e., the southerners should sacrifice the current and foreseeable economy for a purportedly improved one in some distant and indefinite future. Second, only a navigation act subsidizing American shippers and seamen could build an American navy "essential to security, particularly of the S. States," from some unspecified menace. The fact that the liberal opposition remained unconvinced by these specious arguments did not of course allay the enthusiasm of Morris and the other nationalists for the navigation acts.

The other ultra-nationalists of course objected to any such restriction in national power. James Wilson fumed at the problems of the minority and called for unchecked majority rule. Madison, picking up the sophistry of the proto-Keynesian multiplier from Charles Cotesworth Pinckney, maintained the nationalist paradox: the navigation subsidies would *really* benefit the South by increasing the wealth of the East and hence the consumption of southern products, and therefore all this would be a "national benefit." As in all such multiplier paradoxes, the contra-"multiplier" effect of not spending the money seized to pay the subsidy, or the effect of coercively diverting trade from its most efficient and profitable channels, was conveniently overlooked. For his part, the blunt Nathaniel Gorham of Massachusetts was far more candid: to Gorham, the substance was simple and the threat explicit: "If the Government is to be so fettered as to be unable to relieve the Eastern States what motive can they have to join in it."

Most illuminating were the statements of those southerners who were willing to betray the interests of the traders and the consensus of their sector, and indeed of the consensus of the country, for the sake of the corrupt bargain to save the slave trade. Pierce Butler announced his distaste of navigation acts, but he frankly opposed the motion of his South Carolina colleague in order to "[conciliate] the affections" of the eastern states. And John Rutledge warned that a navigation act was necessary for New England's desire to secure the West Indies trade. After all, declared Rutledge, taking the grand view, "we are laying the foundation for a great empire." But it was Charles Cotesworth Pinckney, one of the architects of the bargain, who delivered the fullest rebuttal to his cousin's motion against navigation acts. He admitted that "it was the true interest of the S. States to have no regulation of commerce." But the eastern states (New England) had lost much commerce since the Revolution, and "considering ... their liberal conduct towards the views of South Carolina" on importing slaves "he thought it proper that no fetters should be imposed in the power of making commercial regulations." Charles Cotesworth Pinckney ended in a remarkably oleaginous note: prejudiced against the New Englanders before the convention, he now found them good fellows indeed: "as liberal and candid as any men whatever."

With this arrival of the compact by the leadership of the Deep South, the entire bargain was truly sealed. The bargain essentially benefited New England ship-owners and the southern slave owners at the expense of consumers and other beneficiaries of the freedom of trade. Charles Pinckney's motion was then voted out of order by a vote of 7-4, and the scuttling of the navigation act clause was then approved unanimously. This scuttling was later reaffirmed again in a desperate attempt to restore the clause by George Mason. It was not, apparently, enough for the northerners to sell their anti-slave principles for the sake of a strong national government and navigation subsidy to eastern ship-owners. In the spirit of happy harmony and good fellowship now permeating the convention, the assembled notables helped fasten far more securely the chains of black slaves in America. The draft Constitution had simply provided that any slave escaping to another state should be extradited to the original state. Pierce Butler of South Carolina moved to add to this clause a fugitive slave (and servant) law, a motion that passed the convention not only unanimously but without one iota of debate. This infamous clause expressly provided that even if slavery had been abolished in the state to which the slave may flee, it must deliver up the slave on demand of his master.

Slavery was now driven into the heart of the Constitution: in the three-fifths clause, in the protection of slave importation for twenty years, in the fugitive slave clause, and even in the congressional power to suppress insurrections within the states. The fact that the words "slave" and "slavery" do not appear explicitly in the Constitution does not change unduly this judgement. Indeed, the habitual use of such terms as "other persons," "such person," or "Person held to ... labor," instead of "slave," were simply shamefaced evasions by men who knew that they were betraying anti-slave principles dominant in their constituencies. To Luther Martin, therefore, the American Constitution was a grave betrayal of the idea of equal rights set forth in the Declaration of Independence. The Revolution, Martin strikingly declared, was grounded in defense of the natural, God-given rights possessed by all mankind, but the Constitution was an "*insult to that God* … who views with equal eye the poor *African slave* and his *American master*" [italics in original].[14]

Another deep failing of the Constitution from the standpoint of liberty was the failure to include a bill of rights—a prohibition against governmental interference with individual rights. All of the revolutionary state constitutions had included these cherished provisions, and on August 20 Charles Pinckney proposed clauses that amounted to a bill of rights, to a list of prohibitions on national government interference with individual freedom. Pinckney urged that the freedom of the press be "inviolably preserved," and that soldiers may not be quartered in homes in peacetime without the owners' consent. During the final act of the convention in mid-September, Elbridge Gerry and Hugh Williamson of North Carolina urged the requirement of jury trials in civil cases as well as criminal, Gerry warning of the "necessity of Juries to guard agst. corrupt judges." This prompted George Mason, the author of the great Virginia Bill of Rights, backed by Gerry, to move for a committee to propose a bill of rights for the Constitution. But Gorham and Sherman protested that Congress "may be safely trusted," and the convention, so feeble was its devotion to liberty, voted unanimously against any bill of rights. Pinckney and Gerry soon returned to the attack, moving to insert a clause "that the liberty of the Press should be inviolably observed." Sherman scornfully asserted that the power was "unnecessary" since Congress had no power over the press, and the convention then voted the freedom of the press clause down by a vote of 4-7 (it was backed by Massachusetts, Maryland, Virginia, and South Carolina).[15]

---

[14]Lynd, "The Abolitionist Critique of the United States Constitution," pp. 238–39. On the bargain over slavery, also see Merrill Jensen, *The Making of the American Constitution* (Princeton, NJ: D. Van Nostrand Co., 1964), pp. 90–94.

[15][Editor's footnote] Farrand, *The Records of the Federal Convention*, vol. 2, pp. 183, 221, 364–74, 449–53, 524, 587, 617.

20

The Ratification
and Amendment Process

A particularly vital aspect of the Constitution was the procedure to be set up for its ratification. The draft proposed that the Constitution be submitted to Congress and then to special conventions, so that state legislatures could be circumvented. More importantly, it imposed a revolution in the country's polity because it proposed that only a certain number of states would need to ratify to put the Constitution into effect—a strong violation of the Confederation's unanimity principle.

The draft left blank the number of states needed to ratify the Constitution, and James Wilson began discussion of ratification by proposing that only seven state conventions had to ratify. Wilson brusquely dismissed existing law or rights and employed an irrelevant metaphor: "The House on fire must be extinguished, without a scrupulous regard to ordinary rights." Madison supported this view, though he suggested that the number might be raised to eight or nine states. Daniel Carroll of Maryland demanded unanimity: "unanimity being necessary to dissolve the existing confederacy which had been unanimously established." Finally, Randolph's proposal of nine was adopted by a vote of 8-3, the three holdouts being Virginia, North Carolina, and South Carolina. Rufus King also moved to clarify that the Constitution would only apply to the states ratifying it. Obviously it could not be imposed on the other states, short of open war.

What of the state conventions? Even Gouverneur Morris relented from the ultra-nationalist program and moved to allow every state to ratify whichever way it wished. Madison insisted that the special convention would be the most likely to ratify, and King became yet another delegate to hint of dissolution if the draft was changed. For his part, Luther Martin led the pro-state-legislature opposition. But state conventions were retained and the nine-state convention clause of the Constitution was voted by all states except Maryland, whose nay vote was led by Martin and Carroll.

Finally, there was the question of submitting the Constitution to Congress for approval. Charles Pinckney and Gouverneur Morris now brusquely moved to end the need for congressional approval; instead, the Constitution would be submitted to state conventions regardless, the idea being to ram the Constitution through the conventions before the people could have second thoughts. Or, as Morris put it, any delay would allow the state government leaders to "intrigue & turn the popular current against it." In other words, deliberation and modification were not needed anymore as all of the important discussion had occurred by the wise men at the convention. Luther Martin, staunchly opposed to this critical nationalist scheme, was certainly more accurate. It is true, he maintained, that "after a while the people would be agst. it. [the Constitution] but for a different reason … he believed they would not ratify it unless hurried into it by surprize." Elbridge Gerry backed Martin in opposition. This particular proposal was defeated, but the essence of the plan was approved, and the approval of Congress was no longer required in the ratification clause. Gerry and Mason moved to postpone the whole clause, and Mason bitterly denounced the Constitution, declaring that he would "sooner chop off his right hand than put it to the Constitution as it now stands" and hinted at a later constitutional convention to redo many defeated parts. Randolph concurred and suggested that state conventions be free to propose amendments to be submitted to another convention. Without this the people would only have a chance to ratify or reject a document handed to them as a whole *fait accompli*; on the other hand, the Randolph proposal would actually allow the people to participate in the constitution-making process. Morris agreed and sarcastically argued that he looked forward to another convention, but one that would erect a much tighter central government, a convention "that will have the firmness to provide a vigorous Government, which we are afraid to do." However, postponement was defeated by 3-8 (in favor: New

Jersey, Maryland, North Carolina), and the new ratification clause was approved by 10-1 (only Maryland opposing).

In mid-September, Elbridge Gerry renewed the attack. He picked up a most unexpected ally in Alexander Hamilton, who had returned to the convention in Philadelphia to take part in the final debates. Hamilton argued that not only should Congress have the power to approve the Constitution, but that the state legislatures should also turn the Constitution over to their respective conventions. Randolph, one of the main framers of the Constitution, insisted that he could not agree to it if the ratification clause were not changed—specifically for his plan of a second convention after the state decisions were recorded.

The Hamilton Plan, supported by Gerry, was bitterly attacked by his old fellow ultra-nationalist James Wilson. Wilson declared that it would be unsafe to give the Constitution to Congress because with New York, Rhode Island, and Maryland reflecting strong disapproval of the proposed constitution, a nine-state requirement would barely succeed. King, Rutledge, and George Clymer of Pennsylvania backed Wilson, and the Hamilton-Gerry attempt lost on several votes, the last one being unanimous. Congressional approval was eliminated from the ratification of the Constitution.

In mid-September, Virginia Governor Edmund Randolph, who was at this time now a moderate, made a desperate attempt to revive his cogent plan for a second convention that would consider state convention amendments to the Constitution. It was a poignant moment as this marked the beginning of the end of the convention. Randolph warned that he could not sign the Constitution unless his proposal was adopted. Earlier, Randolph had spelled out his objections to the developing Constitution and believed that the government would "end in Tyranny." Randolph particularly objected to: the unlimited power for a standing army, the broad necessary and proper clause, the lack of restraint on power to pass navigation acts, and generally, an excessive power in the federal government. George Mason seconded the motion, heavily noting that the dangerous power of the central government would end in tyranny. Warning too that he could not sign the Constitution without this amendment, Mason cogently declared "this Constitution had been formed without the knowledge or idea of the people. A second Convention will know more of the sense of the people, and be able to provide a system more consonant to it. It was improper to say to the people, take this or nothing." Elbridge Gerry, a highly prominent delegate involved in the hammering out of the Constitution, backed up Randolph and Mason; he too could not sign unless a second constitutional convention was held. Gerry particularly objected to the vague and broad power of Congress in the necessary and proper clause, to its unlimited power to raise navies and armies, and to no requirement for trial by jury in civil cases. Charles Pinckney, however, replied that the Constitution would then not be agreed upon; "Conventions," he rather absurdly declared, "are serious things, and ought not to be repeated." And despite the poignant warnings of such moderates and luminaries of the convention as Randolph, Mason, and Gerry, the convention in its penultimate act rejected Randolph's motion unanimously.

A final question was the provision for future amendments to the Constitution. The draft provided for amendments to be proposed by two-thirds of the states, which would compel Congress to call a convention to consider them. This initiative in the states and in a special convention pleased the liberals and moderates, but did not satisfy the nationalists who wanted all the power in the central government. Fearful of any amending power in the states, Madison and Hamilton, now back on the ultra-nationalist track, moved to make amending the Constitution far more difficult by placing the imprimatur under the aegis of Congress. Congress could propose amendments by a two-thirds vote of each house, or upon application of two-thirds of the states, and they would then be ratified by three-fourths of state legislatures or state conventions. Crucially, Congress had full authority to either propose amendments or call for state conventions. The convention agreed to this proposal by a vote of 9-1. In mid-September, now, however, the unmoved moderates tried again. Roger Sherman declared his warning that amendments might literally destroy a minority of states, and George Mason warned that the congressional control of amendments would deprive the people of liberating amendments, "if the Government should become oppressive, as he verily believed would be the case." Gouverneur Morris moved to mollify the moderates, he and Gerry proposing to *compel* Congress to require a new convention upon application by two-thirds of the states. The proposal passed unanimously. But the ultimate power remained with Congress, for although the nationalists were forced to make concessions, they had achieved their aim of transferring control of the amending process from the states to Congress. The states were left with a passive role: they must await the submission of amendments to them. They had lost their power to propose amendments, and they have never used their right to request a constitutional convention.[16]

As early as the August decision, the convention had made a special and rare resolution upon any future amendment process. At the behest of John Rutledge, to the Madison-Hamilton resolution was added a provision that no amendments before 1808 could be made that would affect the slave-importation clause. Here was yet another strengthening of slavery in the American Constitution, a clause cheerfully agreed to almost unanimously at the convention.

Now, in the September session, the moderates and states-righters tried to add further clauses to the Constitution that would be beyond amendment, i.e., never changeable by the people of future generations. Sherman moved that no state without its consent might ever be disturbed in the absolute use of its internal police power or be deprived of its equal suffrage in the Senate. The motion was defeated by 3-8 (Connecticut, New Jersey, and Delaware approving), but Morris, in seeing the restlessness of the small states, proposed the equality of States in the Senate clause, and it passed unanimously without debate. In this offhand way, the framers of 1787 laid their dead hand upon all future generations of Americans, arrogantly dictating to them that they could virtually never choose to change the structure of voting in the Senate without the consent of *every* state.[17]

---

[16]Jensen, *The Making of the American Constitution*, p. 102.

[17][Editor's footnote] Farrand, *The Records of the Federal Convention*, vol. 2, pp. 469, 478–79, 629–32.

21

The Election of the President

All the articles of the draft plan having been considered by the convention, the amended draft was referred on August 31 to a grand Committee of Unfinished Parts. In the committee, the nationalists, not content with their plethora of victories, launched several important offensive strikes and secured crucial victories. It was confirmed that the Senate was allowed to amend money bills originating in the House, and the vital treaty-making and appropriations powers were transferred from the Senate to the president, although the sop was there to the small states that the Senate must approve all appointments, and two-thirds must ratify treaties. The general welfare clause was added to the power to tax, a clause of ambiguous meaning at the time, which much later became a vehicle for unchecked expansion of the federal government's powers. Most significantly, Madison and Morris were able to alter the convention's decision for Congress to choose the president and provide for an independent executive chosen by electors, who in turn were chosen directly by the legislatures of the various states. It was assumed, however, that the Senate, by having the ultimate power to choose among the candidates if none received an electoral majority, would really be exercising the decisive electing power. For it was believed that many candidates would be voted for by the electors. Furthermore, the president's term was reduced from seven to four years, he was made eligible for indefinite reelection, and he was required to have been an American citizen for fourteen years before becoming president. A major advocate of the new plan was Morris, who emphasized the "indispensable necessity" of an independent and powerful executive. Randolph and Rutledge inserted that Congress should elect, and Mason, Wilson, and Dickinson wanted the more popular House rather than the more oligarchical Senate to have the ultimate decision to choose the president. From the Right, Madison tried to bypass Congress almost completely by allowing any candidate with one-third of the electoral vote to become president, but this suggestion was overwhelmingly defeated.

The committee report was presented back to the convention on September 4 and the day following. The major struggle was waged over the suddenly new model of selecting the president. Rutledge attacked the president's reeligibility and denounced the Senate's new ultimate decision-making role as creating "a real & dangerous Aristocracy" to go alongside the quasi-monarchic development of the executive office. Wilson and Randolph, however, led the attempt to give the entire Congress, rather than the Senate, the ultimate power of choice by a vote of 3-7-1 (Pennsylvania, Virginia, South Carolina for, and New Hampshire divided).

While Wilson, Mason, and others continued to attack the "dangerous" and "inadmissible" aristocracy this placed in the Senate, Hamilton predictably urged the ultra-nationalist Madison idea of bypassing Congress by electing the man with the highest number of electoral votes. Finally, the question was resolved by Roger Sherman, who suggested that the House hold the ultimate power of choice, but one vote *per state* rather than per congressman. This obviously sensible compromise—taking the power out of the oligarchical Senate but giving the small states equal voting in the House for their particular vote—was voted for overwhelmingly with only Delaware in opposition. The clause was also clarified to provide that a majority of states in the House be required to elect a president.

One concession that the committee had made to the anti-nationalists was to transfer the power to impeach the president and other appointed officers from the House and the Supreme Court—appointed by the president—to the independent Senate. The committee had very narrowly limited the grounds for impeachment, treason, and bribery. George Mason made a critical point in checking the executive power: that "maladministration" be added to the grounds for impeachment. Such a clause could have made the president and the rest of the executive truly dependent on the representative body, the Congress; but

Madison persuaded Mason and the convention to substitute the still formidably narrow "other high crimes & misdemeanors agst. the State." From the other side, Madison and Pinckney tried to free the executive from the Congress altogether by putting the impeachment power back in the Supreme Court, but even Gouverneur Morris objected to a small corruptible Supreme Court having such power, and this proposal was defeated.

The committee's transfer of the critical appointment power from the Senate to the president produced opposition by the moderates; Mason expressly urged that appointments were too dangerous a power to treat to a president, and that it instead should be given to an executive council. On the ultra-right, Wilson proposed that the Senate be stripped even of its power to ratify presidential appointments. The Constitution, indeed, had further strengthened the presidential appointment power, allowing him the sole right to make lengthy appointments during the recesses of the Senate. The convention, at nationalist behest, had earlier changed the power to override the presidential veto to three-fourths of each house, but now, over bitter objections, the convention narrowly returned to the two-thirds clause.

As to the treaty-making power, which the committee had given to the president while leaving the ratification power to two-thirds of the Senate, the debate in the convention was brief but illuminating. The nationalists, who wanted to strip Congress of as much treaty power as possible, were here split on North-South lines. The South bitterly remembered the Jay-Gardoqui Treaty, and any further treaties might also be expected to benefit northern merchants and shippers, perhaps at the expense of southern planters or western settlers. The two-thirds clause was then a concession to southern interests. Thus, Wilson argued for a simple majority of both houses in order to ratify, while even Madison, on the other hand, proposed that two-thirds of the Senate be empowered to make treaties on its own without consent of the president, for he argued cogently that a war-time president would have so much power that he might well balk at making peace. He was seconded by Pierce Butler of South Carolina, who defended the proposal as "a necessary security against ambitious & corrupt Presidents."

For the ultra-nationalists, Gouverneur Morris spelled it out: a simple majority is necessary for peace treaties, otherwise Congress would not be willing to make war to gain the fisheries and the Mississippi

River, "the two great objects of the Union." Here was a clear-cut indication of the neglected role that the power for aggressive war and any adventurous foreign policy played in the drive for the new Constitution. Thus, as in the struggle over the navigation acts, export taxes, the power to admit new states, and the protection of the slave trade, northern nationalists showed themselves to be a bit more motivated for absolute central power than were the southerners, who were continually checked by their economic interests. For their part, Gerry and Sherman predictably urged an even greater majority than two-thirds as needed for the treaty power. The convention quickly concluded the issue by retaining the committee provisions.

On September 8, the convention chose a Committee of Style to draw up the final draft of the Constitution. Of the five members in the committee, four: Hamilton, Madison, Gouverneur Morris, and King were ultra-nationalist, and only one—William Samuel Johnson of Connecticut—was a moderate. The committee's stylistic revision, submitted to the convention, was ultimately the sole work of Morris, who, by slyly substituting a semicolon for a comma, tried to erect an unambiguously independent, and therefore very broad, general welfare clause. The Convention, however, returned the vital comma. Morris also added a grandiose preamble, which, however, was partially based on the preamble clause of the Articles of Confederation, and in any case conferred no substantive powers whatever. On September 15, the final revised draft of the Constitution was submitted to the convention and passed unanimously in essentially the same form. A last-minute, unanimously approved change on the seventeenth revised the number of representatives to one for every 30,000 instead of every 40,000 people. This made the House a bit more democratic and closer to the people. Then, after some quibbling about the form of signatures of the Constitution, and the entrusting of the secret records of the convention to George Washington, the Constitutional Convention ended on September 17. The nationalists had succeeded, and the new Constitution was ready to be sprung upon an unsuspecting country.[18]

---

[18][Editor's footnote] Ibid., pp. 500, 513, 541, 548–50, 638.

The Nationalists Triumph: The Constitution Ratified

22

Congress and the First Step

The Constitution was unquestionably a high-nationalist document, creating what Madison once referred to as a "high mounted government." Not only were the essential lines of the nationalistic Virginia Plan Report carried out in the Constitution, but the later changes made were preponderantly in a nationalist direction. Of the fundamental changes, only the equality of states in the Senate and their election by state legislatures, the former bitterly protested by the determined large state nationalists, was a concession to the opposition. In contrast, on the nationalist side congressional selection of the president was changed to chosen by popular election, admission of new states was made purely arbitrary, and the amendment power was transferred from the states to the Congress. While it is true that the general congressional veto over state laws and the vague broad grant of powers in the original Virginia Plan were whittled down to a list of enumerated powers, enough loopholes existed in the enumerated list: the national supremacy clause; the dominance of the federal judiciary; the virtually unlimited power to tax, raise armies and navies, make war, and regulate commerce; the necessary and proper clause; and the powerful general welfare loophole; all allowed the virtually absolute supremacy of the central government. While libertarian restraints were placed on state powers, no bill of rights existed to check the federal government. And

211

slavery, albeit not explicitly named in the document, was cemented into American society by the nationalists' twenty-year guarantee of the slave trade, in the three-fifths clause "representing" slaves in Congress, and in the compulsory fugitive slave clause. The northern nationalists were willing, if shamefacedly, to agree in exchange for the right to regulate commerce and thus grant themselves commercial privileges, while the southern nationalists were willing to concede regulation of commerce in confident expectation of an early slave-state preponderance in Congress for the South and Southwest. Both wings of nationalists looked forward to a central government that could pursue an aggressive foreign policy, either on behalf of commercial interests to pry open the West Indies trade, or on behalf of interests in the western lands to push Britain out of the Northwest or Spain out of the southwestern Mississippi.

The first step in the ratification of the Constitution was for the delegates to sign, but here the new plan ran into trouble from the start. Of the fifty-five delegates who had attended the convention, fourteen had left before the end, most of them in disgust at the nationalism of the developing Constitution. John Lansing and Robert Yates of New York, and Luther Martin of Maryland, the only major delegates who could be considered hardcore liberals, were prominent among these withdrawals. No one could vote or sign from New York since it lacked a quorum for the last half of the convention, but Alexander Hamilton had the presumption to sign as an individual. At the last, three prominent delegates in attendance refused to sign: Edmund Randolph, Elbridge Gerry, and George Mason, all moderates. One delegate, William Blount of North Carolina, was only persuaded to sign by the convention's adopting of the fiction that the delegates signed as "states" rather than "individuals."

The fullest explanation of the opposition came from George Mason: the calamitous absence of a bill of rights; inadequate representation in the House; a great deal of power in the oligarchical Senate; the absolute supremacy of the national over the state judiciaries, thereby "enabling the rich to oppress and ruin the poor"; the absence of a Council of Revision to check the presidential power; the ease of passing commercial navigation laws that could ruin the South for the benefit of northern and eastern shippers; the vague and enormous power implicitly given to the government; and the compromise over the slave trade.

Whether or not the Constitution can be seen as a nationalist document may be gauged from the attitude of the wildest ultra-nationalist of them all, Alexander Hamilton. While Hamilton was disappointed at not having a pure and naked American version of a British monarchy, he saw no choice but to support the Constitution wholeheartedly. "Is it possible to deliberate," he added, "between anarchy and convulsion on one side, and the chances of good to be expected from this plan on the other?" In a somewhat similar vein, arch-nationalist James Madison was not content with the score of victories he secured and was upset at not getting the full nationalist loaf, particularly the federal veto over state legislation. But like a dutiful Federalist, he too would work hard for ratification in the coming months.

The upshot was that only thirty-eight of the original fifty-five delegates signed the Constitution, though they could unite a quorum of eleven states; and if we consider that the total number of delegates chosen was seventy-four, this meant that barely half of the delegates originally chosen signed the Constitution. When looking toward the prospects for ratification, the behavior of the delegates made clear that the big hurdle states for the Constitution would be Rhode Island, which did not even send delegates to the convention, Massachusetts, where only two of the four delegates had signed; New York, not even represented in the later parts of the convention; North Carolina, the majority of whose people were opposed to the Constitution; and Virginia, the bulk of whose eminent men were now opposed to the Constitution. With reasonable luck for the Antifederalists, all five of these might well have rejected the Constitution.

The first step for the Constitution was the old Confederation Congress, to which the convention submitted their document. Congress *should* have been furious, for not only did the convention violate its explicit instructions, but it created a revolutionary new scheme of government that violated the basic principles of the Articles and did not even require the approval of Congress. Any self-respecting Congress would not only have not transmitted the Constitution to the states, but it would have denounced the new Constitution in the severest terms.

The Constitution reached Congress on September 20, and Congress quickly proposed to consider this crucial issue. Inadvertently taking the lead of the Antifederalist forces (for now the country was to be divided between the nationalists—or "Federalists," as they fraudulently called themselves for tactical effect—and the "Antifederalists"), was Richard Henry Lee of Virginia, still one of the nation's leading liberals. Lee bitterly denounced the nationalists as a "coalition of Monarchy Men, Military Men, Aristocrats, and Drones whose noise, imprudence & zeal exceeds all belief." The Federalist cause was spearheaded by conservative delegates who were members of Congress; leading them were Madison, Gorham, and King.

Richard Henry Lee vainly proposed various sharp amendments to the Constitution along the lines of his friend George Mason. The changes included a Council of Revision, trials by jury in civil cases, and an increase in the majority required to pass laws. Above all, he eloquently urged a bill of rights, for history had proven that "the most express declarations and reservations are necessary to protect the just rights and liberty of Mankind from the silent, powerful and ever active conspiracy of those who govern."

The liberals, led by Lee, Nathan Dane of Massachusetts, and Melancton Smith of New York, proposed that Congress submit this illegal document to the respective state governors and legislatures. The nationalists, on the other hand, urged that Congress submit the Constitution to state conventions with its approval. In order to achieve unanimity in Congress, a compromise resolution was passed without dissent on September 28, swiftly transmitting the Constitution to state legislatures and their conventions without approving or endorsing the plan, *but* mendaciously using the word "unanimously" to give the appearance of congressional approval of the document, when in reality it referred to just the transmission of the document. In addition, it must be noted that Rhode Island, strongly opposed to the Constitution, had no delegates on the congressional floor. With this abdication of responsibility, the Constitution was past its first hurdle. Its fate was now up to the several states.[1]

---

[1][Editor's footnote] Miller, *Alexander Hamilton and the Growth of the New Nation*, pp. 182–83; McDonald, *E Pluribus Unum*, pp. 306–07; Burnett, *The Continental Congress*, pp. 694–702.

23

Federalist Control
of the Mail and Newspapers

The Federalists shrewdly decided to strike hard and swift and drive the Constitution rapidly through the states. The Federalist leaders were a small and cohesive group concentrated in the cities of the eastern seaboard, knew each other, were often tied into the same merchant business interests, and had united with each other and hammered out their ideas over the months of the convention and the years before. Furthermore, their constituency was also largely concentrated in the seaboard and among the commercial towns, and consequently they would command the bulk of the educated, wealthy, intelligent, and mobile. In contrast, the Antifederalist forces, caught by surprise, were scattered, local, composed mainly of the subsistence farmer of the interior, geographically spread out, relatively poor and ignorant, uneducated, and extremely difficult to mobilize for the brief but intense upcoming struggle. This applies not to the Antifederalist *leadership*, who were often as wealthy and educated as their opponents, but to their mass base, the constituency whom they depended on for votes.

Another great problem for the Antifederalist cause was that their wealthy and eminent leaders were largely not nearly as vehemently or as radically opposed to nationalism as their committed followers. Hence, they often proved willing to betray their cause. Furthermore, to mobilize the masses rapidly requires passionate radicalism, and the moderateness of their leadership and their willingness to accept a modified Constitution greatly weakened their strength and the logical force their opposition arguments could have.

In such a titanic struggle, especially for the Antifederalists whose constituency was scattered, poor, and uneducated, rapid dissemination of information and agitation throughout the country was absolutely essential. This vulnerability was viciously exploited by the Federalists, who used their control of the expensive U.S. postal monopoly to delay greatly the mainly Antifederal newspapers as well as letters to and from leading Antifederalists. The postmasters were mainly Federalists: Postmaster General Ebenezer Hazard was a Federalist, and the New York Postmaster Sebastian Bauman was a close friend of Hamilton. And the Federalist Pennsylvania Postmaster openly refused to mail an important address by the Antifederalists at the Pennsylvania convention. Thus, while letters between nationalists of Virginia and New York regularly took six to fourteen days to arrive, mail between Antifederalist leaders in the two states often took six to ten weeks to get through. The handful of Antifederalist papers often failed to arrive at all, particularly in New England, New York, and Pennsylvania, and those that did come through had particular items cut out by the postal authorities.[2] Even George Washington was outraged at the wholesale blocking of Antifederalist mail and was later to fire Ebenezer Hazard for taking the trouble to abandon stagecoaches in delivering the mail and returning to the far more inefficient method of post-riders during this period.

Even more important than postal control in the ratification struggle was the Federalist stranglehold on the nations' press—the vital medium of information and propaganda. The press was overwhelmingly Federal; for one reason, the press was urban, and the urban force, from wealthy merchants to lowly artisans, was solidly nationalist. Furthermore, the remainder of the printers who were inclined to be Antifederalist or even to publish both sides of the coin were subjected to intense and ruthless economic pressure by subscribers and business advertisers. In Boston, the Antifederalist *American Herald* lost subscribers and was forced to move out of the city; in New York City, the *Morning Post* yielded to pressure and stopped printing Antifederalist articles; and *The Pennsylvania Herald* was forced to stop covering the Pennsylvania convention by a boycott of subscribers. Federalist press control meant

---

[2]Spaulding, *New York in the Critical Period,* pp. 259–61. [Editor's remarks] Leonard D. White, *The Federalists: A Study in Administrative History* (New York: The Macmillan Company, 1956), pp. 181–82.

not only the spreading of their own propaganda and the suppression of opposition articles, it also meant that the Federalists were free to dictate the news at will, a freedom which they proceeded to exploit to the hilt. All over the country, outright lies were spread freely, such as the claim that Patrick Henry or Governor George Clinton was for the Constitution or that almost all New Yorkers favored ratification. The press systematically denied that any opposition to the Constitution existed, and as a result many Antifederalists throughout the country were not only disheartened but felt themselves to be a minority and isolated from all other Americans. Throughout the country only five newspapers printed Antifederalist material: the (Boston) *American Herald*, the *New York Journal*, the (Philadelphia) *Independent Gazette*, the (Philadelphia) *Freeman's Journal*, and the (Richmond) *Va. Independent Chronicle*.[3] The *New York Journal*, an Antifederalist island in a sea of Federalist propaganda, had been the organ of the New York Sons of Liberty, and its fearlessly radical publisher Thomas Greenleaf was a veteran of the Revolutionary cause. He was to be one of the first newspaper editors to launch an attack on the Washington administration.

To the press, postal service, superior organization, and wealth, the Federalists added in the furiously intense propaganda battle their far greater prestige and leadership. The prominent and influential men favored the Constitution in virtually every state, and the gamut was run from social ridicule to social flattery of the Antifederalist leadership. This treatment was especially effective with the Antifederalist leadership because these wealthy and socially attuned were susceptible to the kind of pressure to conform to become one of America's Great Men. The enormously prestigious George Washington, in particular, was used to sway opinion, and the inevitable occurrence that Washington was slated to be the first president carried a great deal of weight.

Against and despite all this, the Antifederalists had one crucial asset: the basic support of the probable majority of the American people. More specifically, the Antifederalists had overwhelming majorities in Rhode Island, New York, North Carolina, and South Carolina, and lesser majorities in Massachusetts, New Hampshire, and Virginia; in short, popular majorities in seven of the thirteen states. In contrast, the

---

[3]Main, *The Antifederalists,* pp. 28, 250–52. [Editor's remarks] White, *The Federalists,* p. 193.

Federalists enjoyed enormous majorities in New Jersey, Delaware, and Georgia, and lesser majorities in Connecticut, Maryland, and Pennsylvania. If justice had prevailed, the Constitution would have been ratified in only six states, four of them in the middle-states area.

But this would not be enough. It must be remembered that the people were not called upon to ratify the Constitution directly, or even in their broad town meetings. While the conventions had a superficially popular air, two grave elements of distrust of the popular will entered into the convention proceedings. Both stemmed from the fact that suffrage, as well as representation, was determined by the states to be the same as for the existing state legislatures. While property qualifications were low and suffrage broadly based, this still meant the disenfranchisement of the poorest strata of the population, which increased support for the Constitution. Only New York took the monumental step of permitting universal manhood suffrage in the vote for the Constitution. The other factor was the allocation of delegates; representation in the legislatures was often weighted in favor of the old seaboard and against the newer interior sectors, and hence, once again, in favor of the Constitution. A notable example was South Carolina, where the strongly Federalist eastern lowland had 143 seats in the lower house, while the west had only ninety-three. However, if population figures from 1790 are any guide, in reality the east should have only had fifty seats and the west 186![4]

---

[4][Editor's footnote] Shortly after Rothbard wrote this volume, Charles Roll analyzed the apportionment in state conventions during the ratification struggle. Roll found that malapportionment did aid the Federalists in several key states—notably South Carolina. His findings also confirm Rothbard's analysis of individual state preferences for the Constitution. Charles W. Roll, "We, Some of the People: Apportionment in the Thirteen State Conventions Ratifying the Constitution," *The Journal of American History* (June 1969): 21–40.

24

Little Delaware
and New Jersey Ratify

The Federalist strategy was to drive the Constitution through as quickly as possible and concentrate on building momentum by getting rapid approval in the states in which they had a comfortable majority. The two leaders of the small-state bloc, Delaware and New Jersey, were two of the earliest ratifiers and ratified *unanimously*. This bloc fought the large-state nationalists at the convention, not to whittle down the basic nationalist program, but to ensure small-state equality in running that program. The achievement of equality in the Senate satisfied their qualms. Both of these states, especially Delaware, were in the Philadelphia commercial ambit and hence acquired the overwhelmingly pro-Constitution attitude of the commercial men there. Delaware was the first state to ratify; its Assembly received the Constitution on October 4, called for elections to a state convention on November 26, and the convention ratified on December 7 by a vote of 30-0. Only scattered hints have been noted of any opposition in the state of Delaware.

On December 18, New Jersey's ratification followed soon after by a vote of 38-0. The almost unanimous support in the state, even including the large body of farmers, was received by the peculiar economic condition of New Jersey. The state had accumulated a heavy debt and was securing the debt by levying crippling taxes on land. The Constitution would undoubtedly assume much of all the state debts by the central government, which would finance most of its revenue from imposts and western land sales—and New Jersey had no foreign trade or western land. Thus, New Jersey's public creditors would welcome national assumption, and its farmers would exult over the lower tax

219

burden. West Jersey's commercial dependence on Philadelphia was also a contributing factor. Despite this overwhelming support for the Constitution and the unanimous vote, there were mumblings against the newly powerful central government led by Abraham Clark of Essex County, who had refused to attend the Philadelphia Convention. It is possible that given a decent period of time, some Antifederalist opposition could have developed in New Jersey, but in any case, the Constitution still would have been easily ratified.[5]

---

[5] [Editor's footnote] Main, *The Antifederalists*, pp. 193–95; McDonald, *We the People*, pp. 116–29.

25

The Battle for Pennsylvania

Delaware and New Jersey were absurdly easy, but the same would not be true of the premier Delaware Valley state, Pennsylvania. Here, after all, the radical Constitutionalists, particularly from the center and western rural interior of the state, promised to be a formidable foe. The Federalists, however, were in luck: the conservative Republican Party of Pennsylvania was in the final upward phase of its in-and-out battle with the radicals. The conservatives had finally triumphed in the commercial and wealthy southeastern part of the state in the fall 1786 elections and had succeeded in re-chartering the Bank of North America.

With a majority of 40-28 in the 1786–1787 Assembly, the conservatives acted with ruthless and indecent haste. The Assembly had decided to organize on September 29, but then the conservative George Clymer proposed on September 28 that a ratifying convention be called *on the same day* that Congress decided to transmit the Constitution, and hence obviously before the Assembly could have received it. Furthermore, the elections for the convention were called for the absurdly early date of November 2, weeks even before the noncontroversial elections in Delaware. The convention was to open on November 21.

Here was clearly an illegal call for a convention—a call made before the Constitution was even received. The radicals fought valiantly to refer the matter to the forthcoming Assembly and attacked the hasty and virtually illegal move, but they lost by a vote of 43-19. Finally, the desperate radicals walked out of the House as this blocked the quorum needed to set the date and conditions for the convention elections. At this point, a monstrous act occurred that added force to the common

Federalist tactic of fraud in the ratification contest. A Federalist Philadelphia mob (for all urban centers were heavily Federalist) seized two of the radical defectors—James McCalmont of Cumberland and Jacob Miley of Dauphin (from the mountainous interior)—and dragged them into the Assembly to make a compulsory quorum. The convention election was called, and the radical minority published an address that formed the basis for the Pennsylvania Antifederalist position in the battle that followed, and they flooded the press with the address before public assemblies.

The leading Antifederalist articles in the press were probably written by Samuel Bryan as "Centinel," and John Nicholson, comptroller general of the state. On the other side, the Federalists used their dominance of the press to the full, and their authoritative essays were written by two young Philadelphians: the lexicographer, teacher, and editor Noah Webster, and the opportunist Tench Coxe, soon to be the powerful author of Alexander Hamilton's financial plans. Federalist control of the newspapers throughout the state, in fact, was such that only the eastern readers were informed of the Antifederalist writings, and the easterners were almost all Federalists anyway. In Philadelphia the overwhelmingly more numerous Federalist army was led by the eminent James Wilson and Dr. Benjamin Rush. The ugly Philadelphia mob threat loomed once again on election night when it surrounded the house of a leading radical, Alexander Boyd. Seven noted Constitutionalists lived in his house. The mob surrounded the house, pelted it with stones, and threatened to hang them. The high-minded conservatives did nothing to prevent the incident or to apprehend the offenders, nor did Philadelphia newspapers mention the incident.

The old Constitutionalist Party split under the strain of the battle as the moderates in the party broke away to support the Constitution. Thus, a furious struggle occurred in the interior radical Cumberland County as the wealthier and more commercial valley citizens led by General John Armstrong battled the more numerous mountain men headed by one of the great Antifederalist leaders, Robert Whitehill.

The Federalists themselves worried and estimated the odds in Pennsylvania as almost even, and indeed the October Assembly elections gave the Republicans a majority of only three over the radicals (34-31). Yet by the convention elections in early November, the Federalists proceeded to crush the opposition by electing a majority of 46-23, the same vote by which the convention eventually ratified the Constitu-tion. Undeniably, the superior Federalist organization and propaganda machine, taking advantage of the brief time for debate, accounted for the dramatic shift. More time would undoubtedly have brought greater Antifederalist strength. Thus, in the state elections of the following fall, Antifederalists swept Northumberland County in the North and Huntingdon, Washington, and Franklin counties in the West, which sent a 2:1 majority of Federalist delegates to the convention. If the lat-ter vote had had time to be reflected in the voting, there would have been a significant change in the composition at the convention, mak-ing the ratifying margin a much lower 40-29, or perhaps even a bit narrower.

The Federalist forces at the convention enjoyed virtual unanimity in the southeastern counties, which were composed of urban Philadelphia and the surrounding area of commercial farmers sending their produce to the city. The urban wing of the radicals, which had in any case lost Philadelphia and surrounding counties in the fall elections of 1786, broke away to support the Constitution. Only a handful of radical leaders of Philadelphia, such as George and Samuel Bryan; Benjamin Workman, a teacher at the University of Pennsylvania; and the scientist David Rittenhouse; dared to oppose the Constitution. The Philadel-phia artisans, as in the other large cities of America, yearned for a strong national government that would grant them tariff privileges against British competition, while the commercial farmers wanted an aggres-sive national foreign policy and other national measures that would encourage exports. So overwhelming was the Federalist margin in the city of Philadelphia that the Federalist candidates for the convention all received almost 1,200 votes, while the radical candidates, who were only moderately opposed to the Constitution, averaged less than 150 votes. And this occurred despite the fact that the revered Benjamin Franklin, who helped frame the Constitution, was deliberately put at the head of the radical ticket. Overall, of the total number of delegates from the southeast counties, thirty-one were Federalist and only one was Antifederalist: the eminent radical John Whitehill.

All of the Antifederalist delegates came from the back counties of the state, the so-called "west," but here the vote, as we have seen above, was by no means unanimous. More specifically, the northern counties elected eleven Federalists and no Antifederalists, while the central and western counties elected twenty-two Antifederalists and four Federalists. Much of the Federalist support in the interior would be accounted for by the urban areas: Bethlehem and Easton in the northeast and Pittsburgh in the far west. Analysis shows that the key to the division of force in Pennsylvania over the Constitution was sectional-economic; specifically, commercial *versus* non-commercial. Or, as George Bryan put it: "the counties nearest the navigation were in favor of it generally; those more remote, in opposition." In the towns, the merchants and the artisans tended to be unanimously Federalist, supported by the commercial farmer; the Antifederalist mass base was the subsistence farmer of the interior. Since there were no artisans or laborers at the convention, these groups cheerfully voted for merchants and the wealthy as delegates, and the result was that the Federalist delegates were far more propertied than the Antifederalists. Thus, of the merchants, lawyers, large manufacturers, and large landowners at the Pennsylvania convention, twenty-one were Federalist and four Antifederal. Of the farmer delegates, six were Federal and eleven Antifederal. Of the eighteen delegates classified by Professor Main as "wealthy" and "well-to-do," fifteen were Federalist, three Antifederalist. Also, all the college-educated delegates were Federalist.[6]

One of the most important aspects of the proposed Constitution was its authorization for a permanent national standing army, a striking contrast to the simple reserve constituting the state militia. The standing army was a particular objection of the Antifederalists, who, in the liberal antimilitary tradition, believed such an army to be inimical to the liberty of the American people. In contrast, the ex-Continental Army officers, particularly the higher officers, yearned for the power, the pelf, and the prestige that would come to *them* once again, and this time *permanently*, should there be a standing army. The leading and most aristocratic ex-army officers were cohesively organized in the ultra-reactionary and militaristic Society of the Cincinnati, which looked for a European-type army established, preferably led by a hereditary officer caste. The ex-Continental Army officers and particularly their upper strata in the convention, eagerly welcomed and fought for the proposed Constitution as their long-awaited conduit to

---

[6]Main, *The Antifederalists*, pp. 189–93, 289. [Editor's remarks] Brunhouse, *The Counter-Revolution in Pennsylvania*, pp. 200–07, 325.

a caste status in a standing army. Elbridge Gerry, indeed, feared the power of the Cincinnati, and this was one of the reasons why Gerry (and George Mason) opposed the popular election of the president at the convention:

> The ignorance of the people would put it in the power of some one set of men dispersed through the Union and acting in concert to delude them into any appointment. ... such a Society of men existed in the Order of the Cincinnati. They were respectable, United, and influential.[7]

The ex-officer and Cincinnati support of the Constitution played a definite role in Pennsylvania. Ten delegates to the state convention were members of the Cincinnati, and all were Federalists; furthermore, of the ex-army officers among the delegates above the rank of captain, sixteen out of seventeen were Federalists. This, of course, combined nicely with the bulk of the wealthy and educated being in favor of the Constitution.

Professor Benton has done a study of the men of the ex-Continental Army officers in Pennsylvania. Of the top generals in the state, all—Arthur St. Clair, Richard Butler, Josiah Harmar, Anthony Wayne, Lewis Nicola—were all Cincinnatians, and Nicola and Wayne were such ultra-Federalists that they wanted George Washington to become King. More importantly, Benton analyzed a sample list of forty-four ex-Continental Army officers above the rank of major (comprising 41 percent of the total number), and fifty-five state militia officers of the same ranks (13 percent of the total number). Together, this comprised 19 percent of the total number of officers. Of the forty-four Continental officers, every single one was a Federalist, and thirty-two were members of the Cincinnati; in contrast, of the fifty-five high militia officers, only twenty-three were Federalist, thirty-two were Antifederalist, and only three chose to join the Cincinnati. Here is a clear contrast between the arch-federalism of the Continental officers and the absence of this trend among the far less militarily inclined officers of the state militia

---

[7]Charles A. Beard, *An Economic Interpretation of the Constitution of the United States* (New York: Macmillan, 1961), pp. 38–40. [Editor's remarks] For more on the Society of the Cincinnati, see Rothbard, *Conceived in Liberty*, vol. 4, pp. 1518–26; pp. 404–12.

who were, furthermore, much less likely to acquire leading roles in a federal standing army.[8]

Despite the fact that the outcome of the convention was a foregone conclusion, the Antifederalists, led by the eminent radicals Robert Whitehill, William Findley, and John Smilie, put up a valiant struggle. The lengthy debate lasted from November 21 until December 15, the Federalists being unsurprisingly led by James Wilson. The Antifederalists denounced the Constitution as illegally eliminating the federation of sovereign states on behalf of a consolidated, tyrannical, and aristocratic national government; this absolute national power being funded by an unrestricted taxing power, the creation of a national standing army, supremacy clause, the necessary and proper clause, and the absence of a bill of rights. John Smilie trenchantly declared that "in a free Government there never will be Need of standing Armies, for it depends on the Confidence of the People. If it does not so depend, it is not free. ... The [Constitutional] Convention knew this was not a free government; otherwise, they would not have asked the powers of the purse and sword [taxes and standing armies]." Smilie and Robert Whitehill effectively rebutted Wilson's paradoxical sophistry that a bill of rights was unnecessary because the people retain all their liberties anyway, and dangerous because the very delineation of rights might restrict these and other unaccounted for rights. Said Smilie:

> So loosely, so inaccurately are the powers which are enumerated in this constitution defined, that it will be impossible ... to ascertain the limits of authority, and to declare when government has degenerated into oppression. In that event the contest will arise between the people and the rulers: "You have exceeded the powers of your office, you have oppressed us," will be the language of the suffering citizen. The answer of the government will be short—"We have not exceeded our power; you have no test by which you can prove it."... It will be impracticable to stop the progress of tyranny. ... At present there is no security

---

[8]William A. Benton, "Pennsylvania Revolutionary Officers and the Federal Constitution," *Pennsylvania History* (October 1964): 419–35. Benton's broader interpretation of these facts differ considerably from the above; he rather naïvely attributes the pro-Constitution outlook of the army officers to their superior insight and broader outlook.

even for the rights of conscience ... every principle of a bill of rights, every stipulation for the most sacred and invaluable privileges of man, are left at the mercy of government.

Robert Whitehill added: "I will agree that a bill of rights may be a dangerous instrument, but it is to the view and projects of the aspiring ruler, and not the liberties of the citizen." Whitehill also eloquently summed up the liberal views of the Antifederalists on the menacing nature of political power: "Sir, we know that it is the nature of power to seek its own augmentation, and thus the loss of liberty is the necessary consequence of a loose or extravagant delegation of authority. National freedom has been, and will be the sacrifice of ambition and power, and it is our duty to employ the present opportunity in stipulating such restrictions as are best calculated to protect us from oppression and slavery."

Of the Federalists, only the enthusiastic Benjamin Rush was indecent enough to let slip the admission that the Constitution was a national government that ultimately eliminated the states. The other Federalists knew that it was not polite to admit in public, and their public position was to subtly deny that a national government was intended or implied in the Constitution. Wilson, however, was franker than the Federalist leaders in the other states, and while not going so far as to proclaim national government and suppression of the states, hailed the Constitution as eliminating the sovereignty of the states. Wilson then demagogically masked his cause in the mantle of "The People"; only The People were sovereign, he opined, and this was established in the Constitution. Where this led was clearly in the direction of plebiscitary tyranny, as Wilson declared: "The Supreme Power must be vested somewhere, but where so naturally as in the Supreme Head chosen by the free Suffrages of the People mediately or immediately." In short, The People became mystically transmitted into the president.

William Findley astutely replied that Wilson's argument—setting up The People against the states—was a straw man: of course sovereignty of the states ultimately depended upon the people of the various states. And Smilie quoted from the Pennsylvania Constitution: "That all power [is] originally inherent in, and consequently derived from the people."

At the end of the debate the Antifederalists tried at the very least to impose a list of fifteen amendments—basically a bill of rights—as a price of ratifying the Constitution, and to induce the convention to adjourn to give the public time to study the Constitution and the proposed amendments. This was the first suggestion of Antifederalists of insisting upon amendments to check the central government if the Constitution could not be defeated at the convention. The Federalists, however, had no time for this. They brushed the proposal aside and ratified the Constitution on December 12 by 46-23. The Federalists, with their characteristic hostility to keeping the public accurately informed, moved from the start to keep the record of the convention debates from the public. Alexander J. Dallas, editor of *The Pennsylvania Herald*, was prevented by Federalist pressure from printing the complete records in the paper. Full records were also kept by one Thomas Lloyd, an ardent Federalist; Lloyd was purportedly bribed by Federalist delegates at the convention to scuttle his original plan to publish the complete debates and was instructed to publish only the edifying speeches of the two Federalist leaders James Wilson and Thomas McKean.

The dauntless radicals refused to give up the fight, and the Antifederal delegates prepared a lengthy *Address of the Minority* to explain their position in Pennsylvania and other states. The Federalists postal authorities did their best to ban the *Address* from the mail. The *Address* repeated and elaborated the charge that the Constitution established a consolidated national government of absolute power; it particularly elaborated an incisive libertarian analysis of the dangers of national militarism:

> The absolute unqualified command that Congress have over the militia may be made instrumental to the destruction of all liberty, both public and private; whether of a personal, civil or religious nature.
>
> First, the personal liberty of every man probably from sixteen to sixty years of age, may be destroyed by the power Congress have in organizing and governing of the militia. As militia they may be subjected to fines to any amount, levied in a military manner; they may be subjected to corporal punishments of the most disgraceful and humiliating kind; and to death itself, by the sentence of a court martial. ...

Secondly, the rights of conscience may be violated, as there is no exemption of those persons who are conscientiously scrupulous of bearing arms. ... This is the more remarkable, because even when the distresses of the late war, and the evident disaffection of many citizens of that description ... the rights of conscience were held sacred. ...

Thirdly, the absolute command of Congress over the militia may be destructive of public liberty ... The militia of Pennsylvania may be marched to New England or Virginia to quell an insurrection occasioned by the most galling oppression, and aided by the standing army, they will no doubt be successful in subduing their liberty and independency ... Thus may the militia be made the instruments of crushing the last efforts of expiring liberty, of riveting the chains of despotism on their fellow-citizens, and on one another. This power can be exercised not only without violating the constitution, but in strict conformity with it; it is calculated for this express purpose ...

The address concluded with a trenchant analysis of the new centralized dispensation:

The standing army must be numerous, and as a further support, it will be the policy of this government to multiply officers in every department: judges, collectors, tax-gatherers, excisemen and the whole host of revenue officers, will swarm over the land, devouring the hard earnings of the industrious. Like the locusts of old, impoverishing and desolating all before them. ... its establishment will annihilate the state governments, and produce one consolidated government that will eventually and speedily issue in the supremacy of despotism.

The Antifederalists, furthermore, bitter at the haste of ratification, stepped up a campaign to get the legislature to repudiate the actions of the convention. As Samuel Bryan, Benjamin Workman, and William Findley waged the attack in the press, the Antifederals of Franklin County also urged this course upon the legislature, and during the month of March 1788, over 5,000 people signed petitions to the legislature to repudiate the Constitution. John Smilie was accused by the Federalists of inciting people to armed rebellion against the Constitution in western Fayette County and Pittsburgh. At the end of December 1787, in radical Cumberland County the Federalists in the town of Carlisle tried to hold a public celebration and bonfire in honor of ratification, but a radical mob intervened to give battle. The mob threw a copy of the hated Constitution into the fire and shouted "Damnation to the 46 members, and long live the virtuous 23." The next day, as the Federalists celebrated, the radicals paraded and burned effigies of James Wilson and Chief Justice McKean. At the behest of the vindictive McKean, seven of the leading rioters were arrested; finally, in late February 1788, the government agreed to release the prisoners and close the proceedings. Nearly 1,500 men paraded to the jail in celebration and hailed the liberation of their radical comrades.

The fiery Antifederalist agitation resulted in the last effort of radicals in Pennsylvania: the Harrisburg convention of September 1788. While George Bryan had developed the idea of such a convention by February, the movement for a convention began in Cumberland County, where a meeting called a county convention to insist on amendments to the Constitution. The radical convention met at Harrisburg on September 3, with thirty-three representatives from all but five scattered counties in the state, and led by Bryan, Whitehill, and Smilie. But by this point enough states had ratified for the Constitution to take effect, and all thought of overturning ratification had disappeared. The radicals mildly confined themselves to petitioning for amendments that would restrict the powers of the central government. In doing so, they overrode a young farmer of Fayette County, a brilliant associate of Smiley, Albert Gallatin, future Secretary of the Treasury under President Thomas Jefferson, who urged Pennsylvania to push for amendments at a second constitutional convention. It was young Gallatin's first appearance in the political scene. The radicals, however, failed even to induce the Pennsylvania legislature to seriously propose amendments to the Constitution.[9]

---

[9][Editor's footnote] Main, *The Antifederalists,* pp. 147, 250; Brunhouse, *The Counter-Revolution in Pennsylvania,* pp. 208–15; *Pennsylvania and the Federal Constitution, 1787–1788,* eds. John McMaster and Frederick Stone (Lancaster: The Historical Society of Pennsylvania, 1888), pp. 14–15, 250, 255–56, 161, 480, 557–58; R. Carter Pittman, "Jasper Yeates's Notes on the Pennsylvania Ratifying Convention, 1787," *The William and Mary Quarterly* (April 1965): 308.

26

Georgia and Connecticut Follow

Pennsylvania had been difficult, but the next state to ratify was as simple as Delaware and New Jersey. Sentiment for the Constitution in Georgia did not quite approach unanimity as in the former states, but it was nonetheless overwhelming. That the plantation landlords enthusiastically welcomed the Constitution was not surprising since conditions resembled neighboring South Carolina. Furthermore, much of the nearer interior settlers lived along the Savannah River, and that meant they were bound to Savannah in a commercial nexus. But what of the western backcountry? Why did it not, as did the other backcountry areas, oppose the Constitution? The answer is the acute danger of war with the Creek Indians. The Creeks, led by the brilliant young Alexander McGillivray, pursued a strategy of defending their hunting grounds from continual settler encroachments and constantly harassed and drove off settlers invading Creek territory. For their part, the Georgians of the backcountry pursued a course that was typical of American frontiersmen. After first taking upon themselves to invade and settle Indian lands, and their finding that they could not cope with meeting the responsibility for their own actions, the settlers yelled for state—or in the case of scarcely settled Georgia—national aid. Let other people, the taxpayers of other regions or even other states, be forced to come to their rescue! Hence, while Thomas Gibbons led a substantial minority of Antifederalists in Savannah and there were isolated rumblings of discontent after the Georgia convention, that convention, meeting on December 25, ratified the Constitution unanimously on January 2 by a vote of 26-0.

Ratifying soon after was Connecticut, the first of the New England states. Again, the Federalists in control of the state acted very quickly and held elections in November for the state convention. Again, the Federalists had complete control of the press and consequently propagandized them. At first the Federalists had been worried, but the direct and immediate impact of Shays' Rebellion, which spilled over into northern Connecticut, turned the great majority of the state into the Federalist camp. In addition to the press, all the prominent people in Connecticut, as usual, were concentrated in the commercial centers and thus strongly favored the Constitution. The commercial areas included the coastal towns, Fairfield County in the southwest, and the Connecticut and other river valleys. The propaganda for the Constitution was led by Roger Sherman and Oliver Ellsworth. Religion generally played no prominent part in the ratification struggle, but an outstanding exception was the vote of the congregational clergy in Connecticut. In a state where the congregated clergy retained much of its old-time power and influence, the Connecticut clergy pushed strongly for ratification.

This combination was simply too much, and Antifederalism was largely confined to the rural northern interior of the state. Captain Hugh Ledlie of Hartford, an ardent Antifederalist and former Son of Liberty for eastern Connecticut, lamented the Federalist control and their high-handed domination of the convention. Moreover, a scattered movement of the largely unknown, uneducated, and poor, such as the Antifederalists, is peculiarly dependent on the direction and drive of its leaders precisely because articulate leadership of such movements is so rare. And in Connecticut there was foreshadowed the method by which the Federalists would finally be able to win: betrayal by the Antifederal leadership. Such betrayal was particularly responsible in thwarting the popular will, which had expressed itself directly on the *single* issue of ratification by electing delegates to the state conventions. And yet, after being elected specifically on an Antifederal delegation, Joseph Hopkins of Waterbury and William Williams of Lebanon, leaders of the Antifederalist cause during the convention debates, turned renegade and voted for the Constitution. In the case of Connecticut, the Constitution probably would have been ratified even without the betrayal, but the margin would have been narrower than the final vote by the convention (128-40) that met at Hartford and ratified on January 9.

The convention's delegates were elected in a broad popular ballot by the separate towns. While many of the northern towns that had been arch-nationalist voted for the Constitution, the Antifederals also came largely from that area. As in Pennsylvania, a detailed analysis of the convention delegates shows that the wealthy and influential were overwhelmingly Federalist. While the farmers were more evenly divided, of the merchants, lawyers, and large landowners at the convention, fifty-six were Federalist and five Antifederalist; of the farmers, eleven were Federalist and eight Antifederal. In terms of the well-educated, twenty-two out of twenty-three delegates were Federalists. Virtually all the state dignitaries, judges, congressmen, state senators, and high army officers, were Federalist.

Five states had now ratified the Constitution. With the exception of Pennsylvania, all of these were small states, and they comprised five of the six states where the Federalists enjoyed a popular majority (the other was Maryland). The situation now facing the Federalists was enormously more difficult. If justice had prevailed, only Maryland of the remaining states would have ratified, and the Constitution would have been totally destroyed.[10]

---

[10][Editor's footnote] Main, *The Antifederalists*, pp. 109, 195–200, 289–90; McDonald, *We the People*, pp. 129–48.

27

The Setback in New Hampshire

The Federal cause received its first setback in the little state of New Hampshire. General John Sullivan, the president of New Hampshire and an active Federalist, called a special session of the legislature for December to arrange an early convention. A quorum failed to appear, but the legislature continued illegally in session anyway. After an attempt by the Federalists to weight the apportionment in the convention in favor of the Federalist towns around Portsmouth was rejected by the legislature, the Federalists used another device to obtain a quorum for the state convention. To make it inexpensive for the towns to send delegates, the legislature decided to hold the convention at the state capital of Exeter in mid-February, just after adjournment of the legislature session, thus allowing the legislators to readily be selected as delegates. Since the legislature that called the convention lacked a legal quorum, the conventions of 1788 were illegal as well, and thus New Hampshire has never legally entered the Union.[11]

The calling of the convention for mid-February 1788 allowed some time for thought, and although the Federalists exerted their usual dominance of the press, they were shocked to find an overwhelming majority of the convention opposed to the Constitution. Indeed, out of 107 delegates, only thirty supported the Constitution. The Federal strongholds were the commercial areas of the states, particularly the large towns of the southeast around Portsmouth and Daven, and also

---

[11]Ibid., p. 237. [Editor's remarks] Ibid., pp. 235–38; Main, *The Antifederalists*, pp. 210–12, 221–22.

the towns on the Connecticut River in the West. At the February convention, the remainder of the towns in the interior and the North were almost totally opposed to ratification.

The Antifederalists were ably led by Joshua Atherton, an eminent lawyer from the interior town of Amherst and one of the few Antifederalist leaders in the U.S. who centered his attack on the Constitution for its sanctioning of the evil of slavery. Although out-argued, the Federalists now began to use their plentiful stock of leading politicos in the state. In particular, Samuel Livermore, Chief Justice of the New Hampshire Supreme Court, represented the Compton area in the North and exercised an enormous influence in his area. Livermore persuaded a bloc of northern delegates to betray their instructions to vote against the Constitution, but since they could not vote for the Constitution against their express instructions, they arranged with the Federalists to adjourn the convention to June 18 in order to give the powerful Federalist machine enough time to change delegates' minds. The adjournment squeaked through by 56-51; a shift of only three would have defeated adjournment, and the convention would then have undoubtedly gone on to repudiate the Constitution.

Still, the New Hampshire failure to ratify was a severe setback to Federalist leaders and to Federalist ammunition throughout the country. Federalist New York City was shocked, and Nicholas Gilman wrote that "Much is to be apprehended from this unfortunate check to the tide of our political prosperity. ... this unfortunate affair will at least give a temporary spring to the opposition and I fear its effects in other States." George Washington was afraid that the mystical popularity of the Constitution was damaged since the Constitution was not as popular "as they had been taught to believe." Massachusetts loomed very large as the crucial state; a Massachusetts ratification would not only give a great victory, but it would also be a turning point in the drive for the Constitution. Defeat in Massachusetts, the next battleground, would of course crush the Constitution then and there.

28

The Battle for Massachusetts

As the epochal struggle for Massachusetts began, it was clear that the majority of the people of the state opposed the Constitution. Furthermore, in contrast to Pennsylvania where the Federalists had the important advantage of recently acquired control of the state government, the story in Massachusetts was almost the reverse. For in 1787, in reaction to the harsh measures taken to suppress Shays' Rebellion, the people had swept the ultra-conservative Governor James Bowdoin out of office and reelected the highly popular John Hancock. Hancock, a dedicated opportunist who might be described as slightly left of center, certainly gave no comfort to the Federalist cause. It was clear that the Federalists would need every item in their large bag of tricks to win, if indeed they could possibly do so.

The Federalist forces were concentrated in the commercial eastern seaboard cities and towns, and the surrounding areas of commercial farms and fishermen serving them. The seaboard merchants and shippers were desperately anxious for a strong national government and the (all-seaboard) delegates had been some of the leading nationalist forces at the Constitutional Convention. It was the Massachusetts merchants and shippers who were most anxious to grab the export trade from their more efficient British competitors by means of national navigation acts, and who were particularly anxious to force open the West Indies trade and the northern fisheries by aggressive pressure upon Britain and the other European countries. The artisan masses of the urban towns were also allies of the eastern merchants, as they yearned for protection from British imports, as well as the commercial river towns along the Connecticut River in the West. The Federalists were led by Caleb Strong of Northampton in the Connecticut Valley, and Theodore Sedgwick of Stockbridge. In contrast, the remainder of the interior of Massachusetts strongly opposed the Constitution. Similarly, in Maine the maritime towns along the northeast seacoast tended to support the Constitution while the interior areas tended to be opposed.

In contrast to many of the other states, by no means were all of the eminent leaders of the state in the Federalist camp. Indeed, the struggle began with a formidable army of leaders, especially those inclined to liberalism, on the Antifederalist side. As Governor Hancock remained silent, such eminent liberal leaders of the state joined heartily in the Antifederalist cause: Samuel Adams, James Warren, Nathan Dane, James Winthrop of the founding Massachusetts family, Benjamin Austin, and of course Elbridge Gerry.

The Federalists tried desperately to push a convention through by December, and while the Senate approved, the House insisted that there be time for discussion, so the date was fixed for January 9. While more precious time was given to the Antifederalists, the Federalists as usual were predominantly in control of the press, especially in the early days, and very little of the Antifederal side could be published in the press *before* the convention elections in early December. Federalist control of the press was viciously abetted by the fanatically pro-Federalist printers of Boston who agreed not to publish any articles or pamphlets on the Constitution without knowing the writer's name. The Federalist George Richards Minot observed in his journal that by this means, "The press was kept under the most shameful license. … all freedom of writing was taken away, as ye mechanicks had been worked up to such a degree of rage, that it was unsafe to be known to oppose it [the Constitution], in Boston."[12] But Elbridge Gerry's statement attacking the Constitution was published and had an electric effect in stimulating Antifederalist sentiment. A particularly intense publication for the Antifederal cause was James Winthrop, an entrepreneur and former librarian at Harvard. Writing as "Agrippa," Winthrop argued the liberal case against the Constitution as a cripple on the freedom of enterprise. He argued that Congress' unlimited power over trade, taxes, and com-

---

[12]Ibid., p. 209*n.*

mercial regulations would gravely injure the commerce and prosperity of Massachusetts.[13]

In the election struggle, the Federalists stooped readily to the depths of chicanery. An example was Berkshire County in the extreme western area of the state. In the town of Stockbridge, the Federalists published a report shortly before the election that John Bacon, a popular Antifederalist leader of the town, had been converted to Federalism by Theodore Sedgwick. Bacon had no time to circulate his denial, and the Federalist candidate won. Illegal means were pursued by the Federalists throughout Berkshire County. In Great Barrington, former-Judge William Whitney, a Shaysite leader, stumped against the Constitution and was elected despite election fraud. But the town refused to allow the election and pushed through a pro-Constitution delegate. And in Sheffield the town officials pushed through John Ashley, a supporter of the Constitution, by pure fraud over the Shaysite Antifederalist candidate. Overall, the Federalist George Richards Minot privately admitted that the Federalists were obliged "to *pack* a Convention whose sense would be different from that of the people," and systematically used "*Bad* measures in a *good* cause."

Despite the massive Federalist fraud and trickery, when the convention opened, the delegates opposed the Constitution by a clear majority. Estimates of the size of the Antifederalist majority, out of the 360 delegates, range from twenty to forty, or around 10 percent. And this is true despite the fact that over fifty towns did not bother to send delegates, and the bulk of them were interior towns that probably would have been Antifederalist. The delegates were generally not formally instructed by the towns that elected them, but the position of the candidates at the convention was well-known, and they were elected on that basis. The Antifederalists, however, suffered in the convention from a crisis of leadership, for their eminent, able, and influential leaders—the Gerrys, the Danes, the Winthrops, et al.—came from the eastern seaboard towns. And being in a small minority in that region they could not possibly get elected to the convention. Elbridge Gerry, for example, was defeated as a delegate for the convention. Sam Adams was one of the few eastern leaders to be elected, but he remained largely

---

[13]Dorfman, *The Economic Mind in American Civilization*, p. 276.

silent at the convention, possibly disheartened over the recent death of his son. Hence, the Antifederalists at the convention were essentially rank-and-files, including around twenty Shaysites from the interior, who were no match against the superior Federalist leadership and articulation. The famous convention speech of Amos Singletary of Sutton, in Worcester County in western Massachusetts, came as a veritable *cri de coeur*:

> These lawyers, and men of learning, and moneyed men, that talk so finely and gloss over matters so smoothly, to make us, poor illiterate people, swallow down the pill, expect to get into Congress themselves; they expect to be the managers of this Constitution, and get all the power and all the money into their own hands, and then they will swallow up all us little folks, like the great leviathan. …

The first thing that the Federalists did was to empower the selection of their own man, George Richards Minot, as secretary for the convention, for purposes of chicanery. As a result, Federalist speeches were recorded and published for mass consumption while Antifederalist speeches somehow went unnoticed. To gain time for their tactic of confusing and out-maneuvering the opposition, the Federalists induced the convention to take their time and describe each clause of the Constitution separately. In debates, the able and well-to-do Federalists bewildered and completely out-maneuvered the passionate but inarticulate opposition. A favored tactic was to tar the opposition as anarchists at their slightest resistance to unchecked government power. In his private journal, Minot ruefully admitted how the process worked:

> The most serious principles in government were argued away to nothing, by able casuists, & the mouths of the opponents being shut, they were ashamed to say that they were not convinced. Annual elections, rotation in office, qualifications of officers, standing armies, & declarations of rights, were all shewn to be too trivial to be insisted upon. And it was demonstrated that to withhold any powers of taxation, or of any other kind from government, lest they should abuse them, was an unreasonable principle of jealousy which would prevent any government at all.

Thus, to answer Singletary, the Federalists trotted out an obscure farmer delegate, Jonathan Smith. Opining that the choice was either the Constitution or "anarchy" and the "wild beasts," Smith's naïveté was surely too excessive to be true:

> But I don't think the worse of the Constitution because law-yers, and men of learning, and moneyed men, are fond of it. I don't suspect that they want to get into Congress and abuse their power. I am not of such a jealous make. They that are honest men themselves are not apt to suspect other people.

Aided by Minot's selective reporting, the Federalists stepped up their propaganda barrage during the convention and put pressure on the Antifederalist delegates. One of the Federalist pamphlets was par-ticularly illuminating in pushing the logic of the Federalist power to its proper conclusions. This was *Thoughts Upon the Political Situation* by Jonathan Jackson, a British lawyer and member of the powerful "Essex clique." This faction was a group of a dozen or so prominent merchants and lawyers, most of whom had been born and lived in Essex County, although some had moved to Boston during and after the Revolution. This faction constituted the extreme right-wing of the Federalist ranks in Massachusetts. Jackson supported the Constitution, but he attacked it for not going far enough "in restrictions upon the people, and towards a union of the whole." To Jackson, the federal House should have been much smaller and elected by a series of intermediate electoral colleges, and the Senate should also be chosen by electoral colleges. This would make the elected officials as remote as possible from the people and popular choice, and to enhance this effect, the president should have sole and unimpeded power of appointment and should be appointed for a life term.

Expounding the social philosophy of the Essex clique as the ground-work for his proposals, Jonathan Jackson asserted that society was "one large family ... a perfect whole, in which the general harmony may be preserved, each one learning his proper place and keeping to it." Of course, the proper place in the seats of power belonged to the aristocratic elite. As Professor Fischer shows, "without possessing any extended notion of egalitarianism, the Essex gentlemen were collectiv-ists. They spoke in mystical terms of the 'general will'—*not* the will of the majority but the 'interests of the whole.'"[14] Needless to say, the interpreters of the general will, the social family, and the interest of the whole were to be the ruling elite. Professor Fischer continues: "The Essexmen had no fear of an enlarged economic role for government, as long as it was administered by 'the natural leaders of society.' They favored bounties, tariffs, rebates, drawbacks, licenses, subsidies, and also prohibitions, inspection, and all manner of restrictions."[15] Jackson and his fellow Essexmen scorned checks and balances, and Fisher Ames, an Essexman delegate to the Massachusetts convention, later described constitutional restraints on popular power as "Cobweb ties for lions."

Jackson saw that the fundamental problem of such absolute aristocratic rule was to instill and maintain the confidence of the ruled people in their rulers. The way to do it was through mass education in the public school system. As one Essexman put it: "The people must be *taught* to confide in and reverence their rulers." This is best done in the schools; as Jackson explained: "it is necessary to pay great attention to the education of the youth; teaching them their just rights, at the same time they are taught proper subordination." But not only the schools; the military was also an important institution for inculcating the proper civic spirit, i.e., the willingness to obey authority. Jackson's pamphlet therefore advocated universal military training explicitly as a way of indoctrinating in the masses that noble "discipline of the mind—subordination ... Mankind are abundantly happier," opined our philosopher, "when obliged to confirm strictly to rules." The right churches were also important in teaching how to respect the government. In the words of one Essexman, churches propagated the "knowledge and practice of our moral duties, which comprehend all the social and civil obligations of man to man, and of the citizen to the state." Another vital method of education was the press, but, alas, the press was not Federalist enough for Jackson and the Essexmen. For on the market, writers and pamphleteers are obliged to cater to the mass of customers. Only a formal and truly independent subscriber could do,

---

[14]David H. Fischer, "The Myth of the Essex Junto," *The William and Mary Quarterly* (April 1964): 201–02. [Editor's remarks] Ibid., p. 215.

[15]Ibid., p. 204*n*.

and this, wrote Jackson, could only be accomplished by a state-owned newspaper established "at the publick expense."

But the Federalists did not win their way in the convention solely by debates, either in the public print or in the convention itself. The key to their eventual victory was a wholesale shift of position by the top Antifederal leadership in and out of the convention. And the key to inducing their sudden "conversions" was "influence." There was, for example, the case of Nathaniel Barrell, a wealthy citizen of the seaboard town of York in Maine, and one of the leaders of the Antifederalist cause in the convention. Barrell's wealthy father-in-law, an influential judge, put intense pressure upon him, and there are hints by the knowledgeable in the town of persuasion by letters "and other matters." So Barrell came to his particular "conversion." Oliver Phelps, an Antifederal delegate for Berkshire County, was induced to withdraw from the convention. The Federalists stated that his withdrawal was due to his view that resistance was futile and his belief that his fellow Berkshire delegates would support the Constitution, which was patently false if judged by the actual votes. The real reason was subtle influence by the man he owed money to—Samuel Osgood—and his partner in land speculation, Federalist leader Nathaniel Gorham.

Outright bribery was another Federalist technique. The bulk of the Antifederal delegates were poor and would be hard put to decline money. The state had paid their way to the convention, but the Treasurer told them that there were no funds available for the return trip. At this point, several Federalists graciously stepped in to help. Writes one: "We have circulated, If the Constitution is adopted, there will be no difficulty respecting the Pay—If it *is not* they must look to the Treasurer for it."

But the critically important "conversions" were two: Sam Adams and Governor Hancock. Adams, though instinctively liberal, had grown old, weary, and (their usual concurrent) conservative over the years, but his liberal instincts reasserted themselves when he drew back from the extreme nationalism embodied in the Constitution. To Adams, the proposed national government smacked strongly of the British system, against which he had led a revolution decades before. But one thing in the world could influence Adams more than anything else—more even than consideration of principle—the wishes of his old-time constituency, the city of Boston. The mechanics and tradesmen of Boston had always been Sam Adams' mass base, and these he could not deny. Knowing this, the Federalist path was clearly discernible, and it was not difficult for the Federalists to mobilize mass support in a Boston that overwhelmingly favored the Constitution. In contrast to the old Tories, the Federalists were not shy about courting and welcoming mass support for their own benefit. Old colleagues of Adams were mobilized, and two days before the start of the Massachusetts convention they organized a mass meeting of artisans and tradesmen symbolically held at the Green Dragon Inn, the home of Adams' cherished revolutionary movement of years before. The meeting thundered its unanimous support of the Constitution in resolutions drafted by Paul Revere and others. To Adams, this was conclusive; he felt that he simply could not go against their wishes. When hearing of the meeting, Adams is said to have declared "Well, if they must have it, they must have it." Sam Adams reluctantly swung to support the Constitution.

Even more important was the conversion of John Hancock, governor of the state and also president of the convention. Like Adams, Hancock was basically opposed to the Constitution, but also like Adams, the governor had a crucial weakness that the crafty Federalists could exploit. Like virtually all politicians, Hancock's weakness was one of character: a vain and ambitious opportunist, Hancock had decided not to announce his position publicly until he could see which way the wind was blowing. As the Federalists suspected he would, John Hancock quite literally "sold out." The price was a Federalist promise to support him for the vice-presidency, or, if Virginia should not ratify—which the Federalists convinced him was going to happen—for the exulted and eminently prestigious position of president of the United States. At the very least, the Federalists would support him for reelection as governor. John Hancock could not possibly resist such a temptation.

Hancock's miraculous conversion quickly propelled the shift of about a score of delegates who had pledged themselves to oppose the Constitution. These turncoats were the wealthiest and most eminent Antifederalists at the convention and the leaders of the opposition, most of them coming from the eastern part of the state near the coast. They included Sam Adams; John Winthrop, a wealthy merchant of Boston; Samuel Holten, a wealthy doctor from Danvers; Charles Jarvis, a Boston doctor; William Symmes, a lawyer from Andover; the

Reverend Charles Turner of Scituate; Nathaniel Barrell of York; John Sprague, an anti-Shaysite lawyer from the Lancaster; and a ship-owner of Harpswell, Captain Isaac Shaw. Bereft of the few able and wealthy leaders at the convention, the Antifederalists had suffered a blow from which they could not recover. And outside the convention, such eminent eastern Antifederalist leaders as Nathan Dane, Silas Lee, and Samuel Osgood had shifted to favor the Constitution.

Despite their success at subduing the opposition, the Federalists also realized that they would not be able to induce enough Antifederalists to betray their constituents without sugarcoating the pill. The coating consisted of restrictive amendments that the Massachusetts convention would strongly *recommend* to the central government, but not *insert* before ratification. Thus, the route that the Pennsylvania Federalists, in the driver's seat, scornfully rejected—urging amendments along with ratification—was now seized upon by the astute Federalists as the way by which renegade Antifederalists could appease their conscience and constituency and approve the Constitution. Massachusetts set the pattern: from then on out, every ratifying state except Maryland (where there was firm majority support for the Constitution) took the same route. The amendments included jury trials in civil cases, prohibitions on congressional direct taxes and erection of monopolies, and a clause reserving powers not delegated by the Constitution to the separate states. To include this clause in a bill of rights was surely the definite Antifederal answer to the James Wilson argument that a bill of rights would be taken to exclude popular liberties that had not been expressly enumerated. The Antifederalists placed a great deal of importance on this clause as making the national government one of enumerated powers, but failed to realize that the clause would be reduced to a tautology by shrewd politicians, lawyers, and judges stretching the loopholes in the various enumerated clauses as far as they desired. These amendments, even the fuller amendments of the eventual Bill of Rights, were no real substitutes for rejecting the Constitution outright as far as liberty was concerned.

The amendment sop was very cunningly arranged by the Federalists. After drawing up the amendments themselves in secret, the Federalists slipped them to Hancock, who, as part of his political deal, presented them to the convention as his own, along with support of ratification. The result was a total bombshell, followed rapidly by the rash of defections by eminent men in the Antifederal ranks, led by Sam Adams in seconding Hancock's motion. Utilizing the shock and surprise, the Federalists drove through adoption of the Constitution on February 16 by a slim vote of 187-168. The victory was the consequence of the induced betrayal of the voters who elected them—and of the majority of the citizens of the state—by twenty to thirty of the Antifederalist leaders at the convention. Most of these defections were not the rank-and-file delegates but the relatively wealthy and prominent leaders from eastern towns.

The sectional-economic conflict in Massachusetts over the Constitution was certainly clear: on the one hand, the commercial east coast and Connecticut River towns; on the other hand, the rest of the state. Of 160 towns in the former region, 131 favored the Constitution; of the 195 in the latter area, only fifty-six favored, and the others opposed. All the towns of the lower Connecticut River favored ratification, while in Maine, the coastal towns supported the Constitution by 22-5, while the interior opposed it 17-2. The old Shaysite areas were almost uniformly Antifederal and the anti-Shaysite areas Federalist. Of ninety-seven Shaysite towns, ninety opposed the Constitution; of ninety-seven towns that expressed anti-Shaysite views, eighty-five supported the Constitution.

Almost all the wealthy men—the propertied, the merchants, and the educated—in the state were Federalist as well as the artisans of the eastern areas, while the great bulk of landless and poor farmers formed the mass base of the Antifederal opposition. This class division was admitted by both sides of the struggle. A very large majority of merchants, builders, large manufacturers, ship-owners, lawyers, college graduates, high army officers, and members of the Society of the Cincinnati were Federalists. Even within the same counties, the Federalist towns were wealthier than the Antifederal. At the convention, the title "esquire" was held by seventy-five Federalists and fourteen Antifederalists, while plain "mister" was used by thirty-four Federalists and eighty-nine Antifederalists. Overall, the largely upper strata delegates voted 107-34 for ratification, while the lower strata voted 126-61 in opposition. It must be remembered, however, that the poorer Boston artisans were happy to vote for their upper Bostonians to represent them in favor of the Constitution.

Boston's mechanics wildly celebrated the news of ratification in Massachusetts and happily threw an effigy of the "Old Constitution" into a bonfire. The Federalists fulfilled the least important part of their bargain by supporting Hancock for reelection in 1788. For their part, the Antifederalists confirmed their command of the majority of the voters of the state by retaining control of the Massachusetts House throughout the year. Sam Adams, however, was crushed during 1788 in his attempt at political advancement while running for U.S. Congress for Suffolk County against the brilliant young reactionary lawyer of the Essex clique, Fisher Ames. While Adams worried about a centralized despotism and called for libertarian amendments to the Constitution, Ames, on the other hand, denounced crippling amendments and derided Adams' cherished "Spirit of 75" as old fashioned and outdated. While Adams got few votes in Suffolk County, the Federalists performed the feat of carrying Boston heavily for Ames by using all the old Adamsesque techniques of mobilizing mechanics in conventions and town meetings and handing out rum to the voters. While his old mechanic supporters were repudiating him for being basically against the Constitution, the Antifederalists understandably spurned him for betraying the cause. As a result, even Hancock was not able to drive through the selection of Adams as Lieutenant Governor in 1788; the Antifederalists voted for James Warren, and this split in the Left permitted the Federalists to elect Benjamin Lincoln to the post. It was only in the following year that Hancock was able to squeeze Adams in as his Lieutenant Governor. The two aging veterans of the Revolution were now united again at the last. But this time it was too late.

Massachusetts was indeed the turning point. Six states had now ratified the Constitution, including Pennsylvania and Massachusetts, and Maryland would be an easy win. By mid-February 1788, the goal of formal adoption of the Constitution by nine states was definitely in sight.[16]

---

[16][Editor's footnote] Main, *The Antifederalists*, pp. 200–10, 257; McDonald, *We the People*, pp. 182–202; Taylor, *Western Massachusetts in the Revolution*, pp. 168–77; Miller, *Sam Adams*, pp. 374–89; *The Debates in the Several State Conventions, on the Adoption of the Federal Constitution*, vol. 2, ed. Jonathan Elliot (Philadelphia: J.B. Lippincott Company, 1836), p. 103.

29

Rhode Island Holds Out

Almost on cue, now the Constitution received its first positive and emphatic setback. Predictably it came from Rogues' Island. Little Rhode Island had been the only state that had staunchly, though by a close margin, refused to send delegates to the Constitution Convention. Now, in March 1788 the Rhode Island Assembly refused to call a state convention, and instead, by a heavy majority, it very democratically decided to turn this momentous decision over to the people in the various towns of the state. The Assembly thus overrode the absurd decision of the Federalist minority that the state was somehow duty-bound to hold a convention even if the majority were opposed.

The Federalists had quickly squashed an attempt in Massachusetts to turn the voting over to the towns, and now they boycotted the vote in most of the towns of Rhode Island. Hence, the vote of twenty-eight towns against the Constitution as against two in favor (Bristol and Little Compton) is quite misleading. The fact that almost no one voted in the two big port towns of Providence and Newport shows that both places were overwhelmingly Federal. Professor Main, correcting for the towns with an abysmally low total vote, estimates the true reflection of town sentiment in Rhode Island as twenty-three or twenty-four opposed to the Constitution, seven or six in favor (including the two main commercial centers of Providence and Newport, the bay towns of Bristol, Little Compton, Warren, and Jamestown, and Westerly on the old Narragansett coast). Once again the struggle over the Constitution was commercial-navigational versus rural-interior. Of the fourteen Rhode Island towns on the coast or bay, half were for and half were against the Constitution (and the two large ports were in favor); of the sixteen inland towns every single one was Antifederalist. The slave-plantation owners of the Narragansett lands also tended to be much less inimical to the Constitution than the rest of the interior.[17]

---

[17] [Editor's footnote] Main, *The Antifederalists,* pp. 212–13.

30

Maryland and South Carolina Ratify

It is not surprising that the next state to ratify should be Maryland, where the Constitution commanded a comfortable popular majority. But the proceedings were curious. The Federalists were actually quite worried, for some of the great men and leading oligarchs of the state were opposed to the Constitution, and they could have wielded great influence. They included Samuel Chase and former governors William Paca and Thomas Johnson, who had all refused to become delegates to the Constitution Convention; the present Governor William Smallwood; John Francis Mercer; and especially Attorney General Luther Martin; who had led the liberal bloc at the convention and bitterly attacked the Constitution afterward.

Federalist fears seemed to be justified at the time, when under the dominance of Samuel Chase, the House forced the Maryland legislature to postpone the convention until April 21. George Washington wrote forceful letters in the state, despairing that if Maryland refused to ratify or even adjourned its convention, the Constitution would not be ratified in Virginia. But while the Federalists organized and propagandized with their usual fervor, the Antifederals proved strangely silent: none of them except Luther Martin wrote against the Constitution, and few Antifederal candidates bothered to run in the election. The Antifederal camp was also hurt by the defections of Johnson and later of Paca. The people of Maryland were accustomed to following the lead of the local oligarchs, and hence great activity by the leaders on one side and apathy or defection on the other could only have one result. The Maryland convention was overwhelmingly Federalist, and the Federalist delegates treated Chase, Martin, and the other important opponents with pure contempt and refused even to speak at all in favor of the Constitution. The convention quickly ratified the Constitution, without even bothering to recommend amendments by a lopsided vote of 63-11 on April 26. What Antifederal votes that existed were concentrated in the upper Chesapeake Bay counties, but Maryland is one state where no professed economic or sectional explanation of the voting (whether the very different ones by Beard, Main, or McDonald) is at all convincing. However, Main's observation that, in a sense, Maryland, situated as it was between the Chesapeake and Potomac, *had* no non-commercial interior is valuable.

The aftermath of the ratification struggle in Maryland was a heated election contest for members of the U.S. Congress from Baltimore. In one respect, Maryland was consistent with the voting pattern in other states: the urban centers of Annapolis and Baltimore were heavily pro-Constitution, even though the countryside around Baltimore provided the bulk of the voters in opposition. Dr. James McHenry, one of the leaders in the fight for ratification at the convention and who ran against Samuel Chase for Congress, accused Chase of being "anti-mechanic" for voting against the Constitution. Chase was also bitterly attacked by Robert Smith, one of Baltimore's wealthiest merchants. Chase's election meetings were drowned out by mobs of hecklers and attacked by groups with bludgeons, and the Chase ticket predictably lost the election.

South Carolina was a touchy proposition indeed. The people were overwhelmingly opposed to the Constitution, but, on the other hand, the seaboard planter districts were grotesquely overrepresented in the state legislature and hence in the convention, and the seaboard was the great area of Federalist strength. As in the other states of the Union, the seaboard was joined by all classes, high and low, in the major port city of Charleston in favor of the Constitution. In contrast, the backcountry farmer region where the bulk of the people lived was overwhelmingly against the Constitution.

The crucial vote came early in January 1788, on the question of whether the South Carolina House should call a state convention. James Lincoln eloquently led the backcountry forces in opposition, and he was joined by Rawlins Lowndes, leader of a small Antifederal group of wealthy lowland planters, and the brilliant Judge Aedanus

Burke, the great opponent of the Society of the Cincinnati. The vote in favor of holding the convention could not have been closer: 76-75. Thus, despite the handicap of poor representation, the Antifederal forces came within one vote of blocking the Constitution then and there; a shift of one man might have well stopped ratification in its tracks. Without both Carolinas (North Carolina, would, like Rhode Island, refuse to ratify), Virginia would surely not have joined, and the Constitution scheme would have been defeated. But the House did approve the convention, and the South Carolina Antifederalists were never to come that close again. The convention was called for May 12.

The voting in the House reflected an overwhelming sectional split: from the eastern seaboard (Charlestown and the large planters, preponderantly slave parishes), virtually every vote favored a convention; from the west backcountry parishes, only two delegates failed to be opposed. The only intra-sectional division occurred in the "border" parishes between the two areas; *their* representatives voted against a convention by a narrow margin.

Yet, despite the closeness of the vote, when the convention met at Charleston, the delegates were split by about 125-100 in favor of the Constitution. The reasons for this shift in strength are by now familiar. First, Federalist domination of the press, and hence of propaganda outlets, all of which were located in Charleston and subject to severe pressure in that zealously Federal city. A second familiar factor was the lack of leadership, cohesion, and organization on the part of the Antifederal forces scattered throughout the vast backcountry as contrasted to the energy, cohesion, and supreme organization of the geographically concentrated Federalists. The greater wealth and influence of the Federalist leadership helped account for the great advantage in organization.

At the convention the Antifederalists found themselves deprived of the vital leadership of Rawlins Lowndes, who didn't attend because he saw the effort futile. With the able leaders in their camp, the Federalist pressure was able to swing twenty to twenty-five Antifederalist delegates to their camp. The wining and dining of the up-country delegates by the social Charleston aristocracy and the chilling news of Maryland's ratification combined to change these Antifederal votes, and South Carolina ratified the Constitution on May 23 by the large margin of 149-73.

An analysis of a more pivotal vote on adjournment two days earlier (defeated by 135-89) shows that the coastal parishes voted 111-9 against adjournment and for the Constitution. Of the nine holdouts against this virtual unanimity, four came from a "border" parish. Apart from a Federalist pocket around the Savannah and Edisto district, the backcountry voted 72-9 against the Constitution. Of the Antifederal renegades on the final vote, half came from the swing "border" region.

It should be noted that the areas that sent Antifederal delegates contained 80 percent of the white population of South Carolina, while three-fourths of the slaves lived in the federal parishes. Once again, the Federalists included the bulk of the wealthy, the lawyers, the large slave-owning planters, the top army officers, the leading ministers, the merchants, the educated, and the powerful, joined by the artisans and mechanics of Charleston. The Antifederalist masses were almost all small farmers.

After the vote of South Carolina on ratification, Judge Burke penned a moving description of the sorrowful reaction of the backcountry:

> In some places the people had a Coffin painted black, which borne in funeral procession, was solemnly buried, as an emblem of the dissolution and internment of publick Liberty. … They feel that they are the very men, who, as mere Militia, half-armed and half-clothed have fought and defeated the British regulars in sundry encounters. They think that after having disputed and gained the Laurel under the banners of Liberty, now, that they are likely to be robbed both of the honour and the fruits of it, by a Revolution purposely contrived for it.[18]

Eight states had now ratified; the Constitution saga was now driving toward a climax. The month of June would prove crucial for three state conventions: New Hampshire, Virginia, and New York would be held during that time.

---

[18]Main, *The Antifederalists*, pp. 133–34. Also see Ibid., pp. 215–20. [Editor's remarks] Ibid., pp. 107, 213–14; Allan Nevins, *The American States During and After the Revolution, 1775–1789* (New York: Macmillan, 1924), pp. 320–21.

31

New Hampshire Follows

The first of the state conventions to make its decision was New Hampshire. Between the adjournment in February and the resumption in June, Federalist votes and propaganda had been executed to the maximum. The energetic Federalist-controlled press naturally excluded Antifederalist material, and personal influence by prominent men did its work, with Judge Samuel Livermore succeeding in converting many of the northern towns. Also, the Connecticut River towns were strong in their adherence to the Constitution, both they and the north were influenced by the ratification in Connecticut from which many of their citizens had migrated from. This influence was spurned by a propaganda campaign directed from the Connecticut River towns in Connecticut toward ex-citizens living in New Hampshire. A major feature of this campaign involved whipping up fears of foreign invasion from Canada against New Hampshire's northern frontier. The upshot was that thirteen towns on the Connecticut River voted for the Constitution and only three against, while the northern towns now supported the Constitution by a margin of 11-3. The most important change, however, was the defection from the Antifederal cause of many towns in the previously solid interior of the state. Influential in all these defections was the powerful example provided by the ratification in Massachusetts. After all, New Hampshire's two nearby neighbors had now both ratified the Constitution. Personal deals, patronage, promised amendments, and bribery dispensed by the political leaders of the state also played a role. As Joshua Atherton bitterly wrote, "I believe it will be conceded by all, they did not carry their Point by Force of argument and Discussion; but by other Means, which were it not for the Depravity of the humane Heart, would be viewed with the warmest Sentiments of Disapprobation." The result of all their influence is that New Hampshire ratified the Constitution on June 21 by the slim margin of 57-47.

Of the delegates to the New Hampshire convention, the wealthy, the educated, the merchants, and the prominent were almost all Federalist; the majority of farmers were Antifederal. Thus, of eight merchant delegates, all were Federalist, as were five of the seven large landowners and five of seven ministers; on the other hand, the farmers split 19-15 against the Constitution.

Nine states had ratified, and the Constitution could now go into effect. But no Union could hope to get underway without Virginia and New York, so the drama of ratification now reached its climax as it was do or die in these two states.

32

The Battle for Virginia

The Virginia contest was definitely close. For once, here was a state where ability, wealth, influence, and leadership were evenly distributed on both sides. Thus, James Madison ruefully learned that most of the judges and the bar opposed the Constitution. More important was the fact that the Antifederal forces were led by men of immense prestige and ability: Patrick Henry, George Mason, Richard Henry Lee, Benjamin Harrison, and Governor Edmund Randolph. On the Federal side were James Madison, Edmund Pendleton, George Wythe, Henry Lee, and above all the enormously prestigious George Washington. For Washington, the stakes were high because without Virginia's ratification, there was no chance that he could become the nation's first president. In France, Thomas Jefferson dithered and wavered in the middle, but formally came out for the Constitution when the Massachusetts Federalists adopted the program of supplementing amendments along with ratification.

The Antifederalists, although strong in the state legislature, decided not to block the Constitution, and a convention was called for the designedly late date of June 2 to allow time to organize opposition. Moreover, Henry and Mason managed to include with the call a recommendation for a second federal convention to consider amendments. In the storm of the public debate and organization preceding the convention, the immensely popular and formidable Patrick Henry assumed the leadership of the Antifederalist forces, ably seconded by the great George Mason, whose *Objections to the Constitution* received wide circulation throughout the state. The best known Antifederal pamphlet of the ratification period was the *Letters from the Federal Farmer*, published as five letters in October 1787, and then as a pamphlet that earned wide distribution throughout the country. Protesting his devotion to the "protection of property," Richard Henry Lee added that he could "consent to no government, which … is not calculated equally to preserve the rights of all orders of men in the community." He attacked the Constitution as establishing "one consolidated government," granting Congress undiluted powers "over the purse and the sword" and lacking a bill of rights for individual liberty. However, the writer revealed himself as a moderate who was ready to scrap the Articles of Confederation and accept a system of "partial consolidation."[19]

A particularly astute article was published by a brilliant young Antifederalist lawyer Spencer Roane. Roane detected ambivalence and ambiguities in Edmund Randolph's published objections to the Constitution. To Roane the whole piece sounded like a defense. In calling for a bill of rights, Roane also coined a telling phrase about the Constitution: "A Constitution ought to be like Caesar's wife, not only good, but unsuspected, since it is the highest compact which men are capable of forming, and involves the dearest rights of life, liberty and property."

Patrick Henry was much fiercer than Lee and hinted at disunion rather than to subscribe to the Constitution. Between them, Henry, Mason, and Lee championed Antifederalist opinion throughout the state in defiance of the nine states that had ratified. Furthermore, the New York Antifederalists had organized a Federal Republican Committee in New York City, from which the doughty old radical and Son of Liberty General John Lamb was able to connect with Antifederals in New Hampshire and Virginia. But in the meanwhile, Governor Randolph, while claiming to be Antifederalist, had secretly begun his course of betrayal and sellout of a cause which he himself had helped launch by refusing to sign the Constitution. When Governor Clinton of New York, the great leader of Antifederalism in his state, wrote in early May to Randolph to propose coordination of strategy to insist on a bill-of-rights amendment prior to ratification, Randolph suppressed the letter at the Virginia convention, and this killed chances

---

[19][Editor's footnote] Beginning in the 1970s, some historians have argued that *Letters from the Federal Farmer* was written by Melancton Smith of New York. The true authorship is uncertain.

of cooperation between the liberals of the two great states. It was an act properly and trenchantly denounced by George Mason as "duplicity." One can suspect that the reason for Randolph's defection was as simple as the reason of Governor Hancock for *his*: whereas the Federalists promised Hancock the presidency or vice-presidency, they lured Randolph with some prominent position in the new government. The only difference, of course, is that in the case of Randolph they followed through, and President Washington rewarded his old friend with the position of Attorney General.

The Federalists, for their part, were beginning to realize with great reluctance that there would be no chance of ratifying without the corollary adoption—as in Massachusetts, but far more solemnly—of a set of bill-of-rights amendments to the Constitution. There was, of course, a vast gulf between such a concession to the Antifederalists strategy of insisting on a bill of rights *prior to* any ratification. The Federalists, however, did seem to realize initially the zeal of many leading Antifederalists for broad and total opposition to the Constitution.[20]

The key to the voting in Virginia was the geographical-economic structure of Virginia society. Virginia's sectional division was not, as in the case of such other states as Massachusetts or South Carolina, a simple case of the coastal east versus the western interior. Instead, its navigational area comprised not only the seacoast but also the peninsula and valleys formed by the Potomac, Rappahannock, York, and James Rivers. It was along these river valleys, navigable a long way inland, that the great slave-owning plantations—the great Virginia oligarchy—were formed. This condition was particularly intense in the Northern Neck, where a large and long-lasting monopoly land-grant system had imposed a quasi-feudal community of particularly large plantations with tenants and slaves. It has, furthermore, been a great

---

[20][Editor's footnote] McDonald, *E Pluribus Unum*, pp. 339–40; Malone, *Jefferson and the Rights of Man*, p. 172; Elliot, *The Debates in the Several State Conventions*, vol. 3, pp. 279, 282, 287, 291; Spaulding, *New York in the Critical Period*, pp. 221, 258, 261; *Essays on the Constitution of the United States*, ed. Paul Leicester Ford (Brooklyn, NY: Historical Printing Club, 1892), p. 392; Robert Allen Rutland, *George Mason: Reluctant Statesman* (New York: Holt, Rinehart and Winston, 1961), pp. 93–103; Irving Brant, *James Madison: Father of the Constitution, 1787–1800* (New York: The Bobbs-Merrill Company, 1950), p. 163.

mistake of historians to regard the great southern planters as non- or anti-commerce. While it is true that there were no great urban ports in the states, the southern planters were very conscious of their dependency on the export staple of tobacco and their intimate tie-in with the southern trade. Furthermore, the navigable rivers permitted boats to dock directly at the planters' wharves.

A contrasting sector was the large area south of the James River and back of the actual coast, "Southside Virginia." Not located near navigable streams, the Southside was a prosperous area of small middling-sized farmers with a small number of slaves apiece, rather than of vast plantations. Removed from navigation and commerce, the Southside also had far more equality in distribution of land, slaves, and property.

As in the other states of the Union, the commercial sections tended to be Federalist and conservative, and the non-commercial Antifederalist and liberal. In Virginia, these two sections tended to offset each other east of the Blue Ridge Mountains, generally giving the western areas a balance of power. The West, for its part, comprised three basic sectors: the Shenandoah Valley, the "Alleghany" region further west constituting modern-day West Virginia, and the Kentucky settlements in the southwest. The Valley consisted of a wide distribution of smaller farmers than the Southlands, but on the other hand, its farmers shipped a large agricultural supply down the Potomac to Alexandria and across land to Maryland, and were thus tied strongly into the commercial world. Kentucky was preoccupied with the problem of the Mississippi and the Alleghany country, now West Virginia, with the problem of the Northwest frontier.

In the Virginia election, the Federalists predictably swept the river valleys, and the Antifederalists, the Southside by about roughly the same overwhelming majorities. Typical of the great sentiment against the Constitution, in the Southside was the roughly 23:1 majority in Amherst County. In contrast, the Northern Neck elected nineteen Federal delegates to five opposed. The other river-valley counties largely supported the Constitution as well, with some exceptions, especially among inland counties. Altogether, the Antifederalists had east of the Blue Ridge by over a dozen delegates.

The tale would be told in the West. Kentucky, bitterly opposed to the North's attempt in the Jay-Gardoqui Treaty to abandon the Mississippi River to Spain, and still intriguing with Spain, voted almost solidly for the Antifederalists (ten delegates out of twelve). The Federalists, however, swept the Shenandoah Valley, its interests tied into the Potomac River, by at least as great a margin as in the river-valley strongholds, capturing every single delegate from the Shenandoah. How tied in they were may be gauged by the fact that many of the Valley delegates were active in projects for imposing navigation on the Potomac River.

This left the odds about even, with the balance ready to be tipped by the frontier settlements of the seven counties of the Allegheny area. In the past, this land of small non-commercial slave-less farmers had overwhelmingly supported the Southside liberals on Virginia and Confederate issues. In a sense, this remarkable turnaround of the Allegheny counties was the main factor that tipped the scale in this tight contest over the Constitution, for the thirteen Allegheny delegates ended by voting almost unanimously for the Constitution. What, then, was the factor that overrode the natural tendency of the western Virginians to support liberalism and Antifederalism? The reason was their frontier concern over the British retention of the Northwest forts along their western border, and it was their desire to see a strong national government adopt an aggressive foreign political and economic policy that would drive the British out of the Northwest that led the Alleghenians to succumb to Federalism.

There was little class difference, in the case of Virginia, between the Federal and Antifederal delegates. Not only were the current leaders of the state rather equally divided, but the wealth advantage of the eastern river counties was offset by the particularly modest means of the Federal delegates from the West. As in the other states, the Antifederal counties tended understandably and proudly to pick as delegates the wealthiest and most prominent members of their locality who could often match the Federalists. However, it is significant to note that more of the delegates who owned at least fifty slaves were Federal (twenty-six out of forty-one), more Federalists held state and federal securities (twice as many), and Federalists were roughly two-thirds of the state's richest men. Overall though, the split in Virginia was sectional (commercial versus non-commercial) rather than economic class in the conventional sense.

The delegates probably entered the Virginia convention about equally divided, with perhaps a very slight Federal majority, but in such a close contest there were a handful of waverers from the West and elsewhere who could tip the balance either way. Yet, despite this equality at the convention, it is generally conceded that a comfortable majority of Virginians, even of eligible Virginia voters, opposed the Constitution. The proportion has been estimated as 60 percent or more Antifederal. The overrepresentation of eastern counties, of course, helped outweigh the popular majority, but the Virginia legislature with the same representation would still remain Antifederal throughout 1787 and 1788. The main differential, then, came from Antifederal counties whose delegates deserted the wishes of their constituents and voted to support the Constitution. Two processes were partially at work here: Antifederal voters who choose eminent local dignitaries even though they were Federalist, and delegates chosen as Antifederalist who betrayed their trust. But even in the former case, the delegates who persisted in voting contrary to the wishes of their electorate were, in a profound sense, betraying the democratic process. They were, in effect, choosing oligarchy (doing things by their own will over the voters' will), instead of democracy (representing the voters as best they could).

On the final vote, delegates from at least four Antifederal counties chose to vote against the views of their principals at home. They were the brilliant young Federalist lawyer John Marshall from Henrico County, at least two direct cases of treachery by delegates elected as Antifederalists who then shifted at the convention (Humphrey Marshall from Kentucky and William Ronald of Powhatan in the Southside), and above all, Governor Randolph of Heinrico County, who had acted to betray his supposed Antifederal allies as well as his constituency. Since a shift of four or five votes would have defeated the Constitution, the defections were particularly decisive.

Another factor influencing delegates for the Constitution was not so much important in itself as in foreshadowing an ugly blackmail threat that was to prove decisive in the conventional adoption of the Constitution. Early in the ratification struggle, news circulated that Northern Neck would secede from the state if Virginia refused to ratify—presumably into the new Union on its own. In the last analysis it becomes all too apparent that one of the major factors that tipped the scale to the Federalists—throughout the Union—was superior gall, greater intensity of belief, and a greater willingness to take extreme measures to have their way. This is not of course surprising, since the Antifederalists were generally more moderate and passive men defending the *status quo*, or half-hearted compromise measures, while the Federalists were the ideological "aggressors" in the struggle and were thus more interested in bringing about their veritable counterrevolution.[21]

The Virginia convention opened on June 2 at Richmond and was filled with visitors from the entire nation. Almost on cue, it opened on a note of high perfidy as Governor Randolph suddenly revealed himself as a Federalist and reversed his previous stand. Randolph's betrayal undoubtedly influenced many uncertain delegates. Of the top leadership, all were there except Lee, who would not attend but continued to exert an influence, and Washington, who preferred to exert pressure from the outside.

The debates at the convention were lengthy and celebrated, with the Constitution being assessed in detail at the behest of the opposition. As usual, however, the convention reporter was a Federalist who might well have suppressed news and disturbed some of the Antifederal voting. Patrick Henry, taking the lead of the Antifederal forces, was a host unto himself: tireless, fiery, ideological, hard-hitting, and superbly eloquent. Moreover, he was a gifted orator, and the Federalists knew it. It was *the* Patrick Henry, the revolutionary born again. Of the Antifederal movement, Patrick Henry was one of the few leaders who did not suffer from the enfeeblement of moderation and who had the fire and the spirit and the conviction to dare to be an "extremist." To Henry, it was immaterial that other states had ratified: "I declare," he thundered, "that if twelve states and a half had adopted it, I would with manly firmness, and in spite of an erring world, reject it." Again, in the course of arguing for a guarantee of trial by jury, Henry warned: "Old as I am, it is probable I may yet have the appellation of *rebel*," and he prophetically called for the menace of "congressional oppression" to be "crushed in embryo."

Henry centered his attack, as did the other Antifederalists, on the grave absence of a bill of rights. A consolidated national government lacking such guarantees, he charged, was a betrayal of the spirit of the American Revolution. The Federalists often scoffed at the old libertarian ideals of the Revolution as old fashioned, good for their time, but

---

[21][Editor's footnote] Main, *The Antifederalists*, pp. 28–31, 221–33, 285–86; McDonald, *We the People*, pp. 255–58.

outdated in the progressive days of 1788. Henry was not afraid to be scoffed at:

> But I am fearful I have lived long enough to become an old-fashioned fellow. Perhaps an invincible attachment to the dearest rights of man may, in these refined, enlightened days, be deemed old-fashioned; if so, I am contented to be so.

Henry keenly recognized that what they were facing was "a revolution as radical as that which separated us from Great Britain." Here was a plan, concocted in secret, for a consolidated government infringing on American liberty. Henry warned:

> Twenty-three years ago was I supposed a traitor to my country? I was then said to be the bane of sedition, because I supported the rights of my country. I may be thought suspicious when I say our privileges and rights are in danger. ... Guard with jealous attention the public liberty. Suspect every one who approaches that jewel. Unfortunately, nothing will preserve it but downright force. Whenever you give up that force, you are inevitably ruined. ... Consider what you are about to do before you part with the government. Take longer time in reckoning things; revolutions like this have happened in almost every country in Europe; similar examples are to be found in ancient Greece and ancient Rome—instances of the people losing their liberty by their own carelessness and the ambition of a few.

Henry also brilliantly perceived that the essence of the great epochal struggle between the two camps was between Liberty and Power, or, more specifically, between liberty and national empire:

> You are not to inquire how your trade may be increased, nor how you are to become a great and powerful people, but how your liberties can be secured; for liberty ought to be the direct end of your government. ... Will the abandonment of your most sacred rights [e.g., trial by jury, freedom of the press] tend to the security of your liberty? Liberty, the greatest of all earthly blessings—give us that precious jewel, and you may take every thing else! ...

Shall we imitate the example of those nations who have gone from a simple to a splendid government? Are those nations more worthy of our imitation? What can make an adequate satisfaction to them for the loss they have suffered in attaining such a government—for the loss of their liberty? If we admit this consolidated government, it will be because we like a great, splendid one. Some way or other we must be a great and mighty empire; we must have an army, and a navy ... When the American spirit was in its youth, the language of America was different: liberty, sir, was then the primary object. ... But now, sir, the American spirit, assisted by the ropes and chains of consolidation, is about to convert this country into a powerful and mighty empire. ... Such a government is incompatible with the genius of republicanism. There will be no checks, no real balances, in this government. What can avail your specious, imaginary balances, your rope-dancing, chain-rattling, ridiculous ideal checks and contrivances? But, sir, we are not feared by foreigners; we do not make nations tremble. Would this constitute happiness, or secure liberty?[22]

The field marshal of the Federalist forces at the convention was James Madison, and he, as well as Washington, were the staunchest opponents of including a bill of rights. Madison adopted the specious Wilson argument about the dangers of a bill of rights and said that they could be left unenumerated but still retained by the people. Indeed, the leading young Federalist John Marshall inadvertently revealed the sophistry and insincerity of the Federalists' presumed concern for "rights." Marshall, in attacking the idea of a bill of rights, observed that the Virginia Bill of Rights doesn't mean very much; it is "merely recommendatory." If it were otherwise, many expedient laws would clearly

---

[22]In Maryland, Antifederalist leader Luther Martin emphasized a similar theme; Martin attacked the Constitution as a design for "one great and extensive empire, calculated to aggrandize and elevate its rulers and chief officers far above the common herd of mankind, to enrich them with wealth, encircle them with honors and glory." William Appleman Williams, *The Contours of American History* (Cleveland, OH: World Publishing Company, 1961), p. 161.

[Editor's remarks] For Henry's remarks, see Elliot, *The Debates in the Several State Conventions*, vol. 3, pp. 44–46, 53–54, 546. Rothbard was an enormous fan of Patrick Henry and later wrote a neglected review of a Henry biography. Murray Rothbard, "Patriot Henry, Noble Rhetorician," *Reason* (January 1987): 53–54.

be unconstitutional. This exultation in the state's bill of explicit rights hardly showed the Federalists to be truly concerned about the *unenumerated* rights of the people! More interesting was Madison's rejection of the idea that the gravest danger to liberty has always been the accretion of power by the rulers of government. Instead, Madison, using the conservative trick of argument-by-paradox, tried to shift the blame of government despotism from the government itself to the people being governed—specifically, the people daring to have a difference of opinion. Thus:

> When the gentleman [Patrick Henry] called our recollection to the usual effects of the concession of powers, and imputed the loss of liberty generally to open tyranny, I wish he had gone on farther. Upon his review of history he would have found that the loss of liberty very often resulted from factions and divisions; from local considerations, which eternally lead to quarrels; he would have found internal dissensions to have more frequently demolished civil liberty, than a tenacious disposition in rulers to retain any stipulated powers.

In short, liberty is lost through its very exercise! Self-interested local governance is the source of oppression, and to counter this, the people should instead put their faith in one large centralized government (clearly without such self-interest) remote from their control.

Less candid than James Wilson or the Massachusetts ultras, Madison and the other Federalists adopted the lie that the proposed government was not *really* national or consolidated, but a new sort of tangled mixture, with no real locus of supremacy.

As the debate proceeded, even the reluctant Madison finally realized that the Federalists would have to agree to a bill-of-rights amendment, but *not*, of course, as a condition of ratification—only as a corollary recommendation. Finally, the dramatic vote arrived when Patrick Henry moved that the convention refer a bill of rights and other amendments to the other states as a requirement *prior* to ratification. He also assured the delegates that whatever the result, he would "be a peaceful citizen" and work for constitutional, non-violent change of the new system. The next day, June 25, Henry's motion came to a vote and lost by the slim margin of 88-80; immediately following, the motion to ratify the

Constitution passed by 89-79. A mere shift of five votes would have defeated the Constitution.

But at least the Federalists had been forced by opposition pressure to agree to appoint a committee immediately to recommend amendments, otherwise they could not have won ratification. The committee, including Henry and Mason, adopted a bill of rights patterned after the Virginia Declaration of Rights, as well as a score of other comprehensive amendments restricting federal power. These justly proposed amendments were adopted by the convention, which also instructed the Virginia delegation to the new Congress to do their utmost to attain their ratification. For the benefit of the pseudo-Wilsonian argument, the amendments included a clause reserving to the states every power or right not expressly delegated to the federal government in the Constitution. The amendments also included, in addition to a bill of rights and restrictions on taxation, the provision that any navigation law, law regulating commerce, or maintenance of a standing army, required two-thirds approval of each house of Congress. The Federalists, for their part, could quietly scoff at the whole proceeding; after all, was it not a facade that was binding on no one?

The ratification left tempers and conflict in Virginia sharpened rather than rendered. Mason and Henry talked bitterly of issuing an Antifederalist manifesto similar to the *Address* of the Pennsylvania minority. Mason denounced Randolph as a young Benedict Arnold, and relatives shared part of the breaking point between Mason and Washington, between Henry and Washington, and between Madison and Henry. The Virginia legislature remained in Antifederal control, and the Antifederalists were determined never to relax the pressure until the victors, humored by them as "Non-Emendo-Tories," were forced to fulfill their agreement for a bill of rights. They especially wanted to secure these amendments at a second constitution convention to undo the centralizing damage of the first.

Then, led by Patrick Henry, the Antifederalists determined to advance their program and crush James Madison. They furthered both goals during 1788 by electing two of their leaders, Richard Henry Lee and William Grayson, to the U.S. Senate over the bid of Madison. Then, Madison eked out a victory in the race for Congress over a brilliant young Antifederalist leader James Monroe, who had voted against ratification at the convention.[23]

And so, Virginia too had ratified; at this point, ten states were in the new Union. Of the crucial states, only New York, the great bastion of Antifederalism, stood alone and isolated. Rhode Island and possibly North Carolina were not important enough to give the Empire State much aid and comfort. To the Antifederal party struggling at the convention at Poughkeepsie in New York, the news of the double defection of New Hampshire and Virginia came as a grave blow.

---

[23][Editor's footnote] Rutland, *George Mason*, pp. 100–05.

33

The Battle for New York
and the Twilight
of the Antifederalists

New York was the toughest nut for the Federalists to crack. For here was one state where not only was the population overwhelmingly opposed to the Constitution, but the opposition was also in firm and determined control of the state government and the state political machinery. Here was a powerful governor, George Clinton, who would *not*, like Hancock and Randolph in the other critical states, yield to a sellout under pressure. Clinton had been a highly popular governor since the formation of the state, had a strong political machinery based on the mass of upstate yeomanry, and was determined to organize and defeat the Constitution.

Still, their final organization was sluggish. It was only in February 1788 that the Albany Antifederalists, guided by Clinton, formed a committee to organize the election campaign. The committee, including John Lansing and Jeremiah Van Rensselaer, organized the sending of articles to the press and joined in confidence with other committees in the state. The general headquarters for the Antifederalist campaign was in New York City, in the Federal Republican Committee; chairman was the veteran General John Lamb, leader of the New York radicals since the days of the Sons of Liberty, and other leaders in the committee were merchants Marinus Willett and Melancton Smith. The committee organized and distributed articles within the state but also to Antifederalists in other states. Clubs and committees of correspondence were set up in the backcountry, and poll-watchers mobilized for the election. But strangely, critically important attempts to coordinate the campaign with Antifederalist efforts in other states were delayed until May when it was already too late. The lack of coordination prevented the Antifederalists of different states from hammering out an agreement on what prior constitutional amendments they should insist upon.

As usual, moreover, the Federalists dominated the press, particularly in heavily Federalist New York City. While the Federals were characteristically energetic in their press propaganda, the Antifederalists countered in force as early as October 1787. But soon, behind-the-scenes Federalist pressure was able to close almost all the papers except the *New York Journal* to Antifederalist writings. However, Antifederalist material was still being published in the upstate press. The Federalists, highly concentrated in New York City and enjoying a cohesive leadership, needed no formal organization. Through pressure they were able to flood the New York press with their literature. Seeing their weakness upstate, they were able in March to form a Federal committee in the town of Albany, a stronghold of nationalist sentiment upstate.

The public pre-election debate was waged furiously in the press and in pamphlets from in and out of the state, although by this time the newspaper press was beginning to outweigh in importance the pamphlet, which had been dominant before and during the Revolution. On the one side were the liberty-minded Clintonian Antifederalists, and on the other were the centralizing Hamiltonian Federalists. The Antifederalists put their libertarian-democratic case staunchly: the rich and well-born few were trying to create a strong government in order to tax and mulct the poorer and productive many for their own power and profit. Thus, one newspaper poet wrote:

> But LIBERTY, keep thou Columbia free,
> Nor let man use us as we use the bee;
> Let not base DRONES upon our honey thrive
> And suffocate the maker in his HIVE.[24]

"Sidney," who believed that the Articles of Confederation were sufficient for New York's needs, warned of the people too quickly giving

---

[24]Spaulding, *New York in the Critical Period,* p. 215. [Editor's remarks] Ibid., pp. 205–22, 259–61; Main, *The Antifederalists,* pp. 233–38.

up their liberties, for "being once lost, [they] are not to be recovered, but with disquiet and disorder." "Brutus Junior" wrote in the *New York Journal* that the framers of the Constitution had "high aristocratic ideas and the most sovereign contempt of the common people," and were "strongly disposed in favor of monarchy"; they were proficient at intrigue and greedy for power and its privileges.

Governor Clinton himself, purportedly writing as "Cato," pressed a similar Antifederal theme: the Constitution would create a consolidated government at the expense of the localist states. But perhaps the most incisive survey of the libertarian Antifederal case came in a letter to the governor from his brilliant young nephew and future secretary DeWitt Clinton:

> From the insolence of great men, from the tyranny of the rich—from the unfeeling rapacity of the excise-man and Tax-gatherer—from the misery of despotism—from the expense of supporting standing armies, navies, placemen, sinecures, federal cities, Senators, Presidents and a long train of et ceteras Good Lord deliver us.

On the Federalist side, Hamilton led the charge against Clinton and responded to "Cato" with "Caesar," a response mostly full of *ad hominems* and even a thinly veiled threat: it would be best for New York and the country as a whole "that [Washington] should be induced to accept of the presidency of the new government, than that he should be solicited again to accept command of an army." But by far the lengthiest and most authoritative statement for the Right came in a ten-month series of articles by "Publius," in the New York *Independent Journal*. The articles were written until August 1788 and were published in book form as *The Federalist*. *The Federalist*, coauthored by Alexander Hamilton and James Madison (with a few articles by John Jay), is a remarkable document. Remarkable *not* for its influence or success at the time, which was negligible, for the essays were too high-toned to influence public sentiment. Nor were they remarkable as a comprehensive and accurate presentation of the nationalist position. The essays contained in *The Federalist* were designed not for the ages—not as an explanation of nationalist views—but as a propaganda document to allay the fears and lull the suspicions of the Antifederal forces. Consequently, these field marshals of the Federalist campaign were concerned to make the Constitution *look* like a mixed concoction of checks-and-balances and popular representation, when they really desired, *and* believed that they had, a political system of overriding national power. What *is* remarkable is the fact that historians and conservative political theorists have seized upon and canonized these campaign pieces as fountains of quasi-divine political wisdom, as hallowed texts to be revered, even as somehow a vital part of American constitutional law.

Thus, Hamilton, in *Federalist No. 32*, mendaciously tried to assure the public that the new government was only a "partial" rather than an "entire" consolidation, and that the states *really* retained most of their previous sovereignty.[25] And in *No. 9*, Hamilton did his best to confuse and blur the issue by dismissing any real distinction between "confederacy" and "consolidation." Madison, too, in *No. 39*, exhorted his readers that the Constitution established a mixture of "federal" and "national" government; in *No. 45*, trying to head off a bill of rights, he spread the myth that reserved powers under the Constitution ineluctably belong to the states. Characteristic, also, of Madison's discourses is his self-contradictory plea in *No. 40* that: (a) the framers of the Constitution did not exceed their legal powers, and (b) even if they did, it was a good and proper thing.

The later-famed *No. 10*, written by Madison, is an elaboration of his argument at the Constitutional Convention that a large republic, or a government powerful over a large area, will protect liberty far more than a small republic, or government powerful over a small area. Madison claimed that the greater diversity of interests over a large area will make it more difficult for a majority of the interests to combine and oppress a minority. It is difficult to see, however, why such a combination should be difficult. Suppose the Antifederalist argument: a larger republic, *precisely* by including under it a greater diversity of interests, will be bound, *however* it acts, to oppress *some* minority interests. The smaller the scope of government, and therefore the more homogenous its citizens, the less likely will there be oppressed communities, and the

---

[25]On Hamilton's activities in general during the ratification struggle, the comment of Charles Tillinghast, leading Antifederalist and son-in-law of General Lamb, is illuminating: "You would be surprised did you not know the Man, what an *amazing Republican* Hamilton wishes to make himself be considered. But he is known." Main, *The Antifederalists*, p. 238.

more likely will each interest have its *own* government. But the main fallacy in Madison's argument is that it is part and parcel of the anti-democratic Federalist doctrine that the danger of despotic government comes, *not* from the government, but from among the ranks (i.e., the majority) of the public. The fallacy of this by now should be evident. Even if a majority *approves* an act of tyranny, it almost never *initiates* or *elaborates* or *executes* such action; rather they are almost always passive tools in the hands of the oligarchy of rulers and their allied favorites of the state apparatus. On *such* a view of the political process, a view implicit in the Antifederal doctrine, the smaller the size and scope of a governmental unit, the better, for the closer to the people, the less oligarchic, the more susceptible to vigilance and check, the easier to put down.[26]

We might also note a neglected recurring theme in *The Federalist*: the need for the Constitution in order to promulgate an aggressive foreign policy on all sides, to make America into what Patrick Henry brilliantly saw as a great "empire." Thus, the appeal to charisma, vainglory, and national greed of Hamilton's *No. 15*:

> We may indeed with propriety be said to have reached almost the last stage of national humiliation. There is scarcely anything that can wound the pride or degrade the character of an independent nation which we do not experience. ...
>
> Have we valuable territories and important posts in the possession of a foreign power [England] which, by express stipulations, ought long since to have been surrendered? These are

---

[26]Particularly large praise is given, by Marxists as well as conservative analysts, to such statements as these in *No. 10*: "A landed interest, a manufacturing interest, a mercantile interest, a moneyed interest, with many lesser interests, grow up of necessity in civilized nations, and divide them into different classes, actuated by different sentiments and views." There is no wisdom here, but a realization of simple everyday observation and basic social philosophy. That there exists numerous economic classes and interests was not a fact that waited for Madison to come along and observe, but common knowledge to everyone. The fallacy is that specific, diverse, and antagonistic interests only exist not *in* society itself but only *in relation to* government action (i.e., as antagonistic social "castes")—in short, the very government whose scope Madison wished to maximize to enforce even-handed justice upon the factions. On the contrary then, the wider the scope and power of government, the fierce and more fanatical will be the social and economic class struggles.

still retained to the prejudice of our interests, not less than of our rights. Are we in a condition to resent or to repel the aggression? We have neither troops, nor treasury, nor [national] government. ... Are we even in a condition to remonstrate with dignity? ... Are we entitled by nature and compact to a free participation in the navigation of the Mississippi? Spain excludes us from it. Is public credit an indispensable resource in time of public danger? We seem to have abandoned its cause.[27]

Upon receiving the Constitution from Congress, Governor Clinton made what later turned out to be a grave tactical error. It was an understandable error, for throughout the country, the Federalist tactic was to rush the Constitution through, while the Antifederalists tried to delay as much as possible. Clinton therefore adopted the tactic of delay, postponing the convention as much as possible. He also hoped to be able to avoid a battle by having the Constitution fall in the other states first; a case of let-George-do-it that backfired very badly. But another consideration was that neither Clinton nor the Federalists foresaw the depth of New Yorker antagonism toward the Constitution. Both sides expected a close fight; the existing legislature itself was closely divided, and the Federalists were optimistic about the outcome of an election.

Clinton's first act was to rebuff Congress' request for a special session of the legislature to call a convention. The New York legislature met in mid-January 1788 and, at the end of the month, Egbert Benson, a lawyer from Dutchess County and a Federalist leader in the Assembly, moved to call a convention. At that point, Cornelius Schoonmaker from Ulster County included a creative resolution: that the legislature attach a preamble attacking the convention at Philadelphia for illegally exceeding its authorized power. The vote could scarcely have been closer, the Schoonmaker preamble losing by 27-25, and after that climactic vote the Assembly voted for the call to convention. But in the Senate there stood the indomitable radical Abraham Yates. Yates had previously attempted to block the Constitution, and here he would only redouble his efforts, arguing that the Philadelphia Convention

---

[27][Editor's footnote] *The Federalist Papers* have been reprinted multiple times. For the classic collection, see *The Federalist Papers*, ed. Clinton Rossiter (New York: New American Library, 1961).

was never authorized to write a new constitution. A member of the Schuyler family brusquely responded that this was old news. In fact, Yates never gave up even after the Constitution was ratified. Yates was the author in 1789 of the first (but unpublished) history of the drive for the Constitution in which he perceptively traced the nationalist movement from the time of the Revolutionary War and its method to organize a *coup d'état*:

> The meeting at Philadelphia in 1787 for the sole and express purpose of revising the Articles of Confederation, got the name of a Convention (I believe before long that of a Conspiracy would have been more Significant), [and] paid no more regard to their orders and credentials than Caesar when he passed the Rubicon. Under an Injunction of Secrecy they carried on their works of Darkness until the Constitution passed their usurping hands.[28]

Yates was surely on the mark when he wrote "they have turned a *Convention* into a *Conspiracy*, and under the Epithet *Federal* have destroyed the Confederation." In the Senate, this veteran Clintonian led the Antifederalist attempt to defeat the call, but it passed the motion by another close vote of 11-8. A shift of two votes in the New York legislature could have defeated the Constitution. Elections were set for April and the convention at Poughkeepsie for June 17.

In calling the convention, the New York legislature did a unique and remarkable thing: they deemed that for this particular and momentous election all property requirements for voting would be waived and there would for the moment be universal manhood suffrage in New York State. This democratic move seems to have increased the total vote by almost one-third. There is no evidence that the outcome of the victory was changed to any significant extent. If the Clintonians had been more astute, they would have concentrated even more on correcting the apportionment to the state legislature. As in the other states, the delegates to the convention were apportioned in the same way as the legislature and the Antifederal counties were underrepresented, while

---

[28]Staughton Lynd, who discovered the manuscript, is more seriously critical of Yates in his introduction. Staughton Lynd, "Abraham Yates' History of the Movement for the U.S. Constitution," *The William and Mary Quarterly* (April 1963): 223–45.

the Federal counties overrepresented in the legislature and the convention.

The elections for the convention were an amazing and smashing victory for the Antifederalist forces, who swept the convention delegates by 46-19. The Federalists came only from New York City and its immediate environs, Kings, Richmond, and Westchester, four counties out of the state's thirteen. The four Federal counties contained a population of 65,000, while the more Antifederal counties numbered 274,000. Thus, Federalist New York, Richmond, and Westchester, with 18 percent of the total state population, garnered 26 percent of Assembly delegates in 1790; the Antifederalist upstate counties, with 71 percent of the population, had only 57 percent of Assembly delegates (swing Long Island, with 11 percent of the population, had 17 percent of Assembly delegates). If the convention delegates had been apportioned according to population, there would have been a shift of six, making a split of 52-13 against the Constitution. If this proper apportionment had been in force, the Constitution might never have been ratified in New York, for it was actually ratified by only a razor thin three vote majority (New York City would have sent six delegates instead of nine, Albany County fifteen instead of seven).[29]

The conflict was, once again, quite starkly, commerce-navigation versus inland. Commercial New York City was the stronghold of Federalism, and in rural upstate New York there existed ardent pockets of Federalism in the commercial Hudson River towns of Albany, Hudson, and Lansingburgh towns that were swamped by the surrounding rural population in the countywide voting. In the swing county of Albany, a Federalist victory in the city of Albany was swamped by an enormous Antifederal majority in the rest of the county, giving the Antifederals an overall county majority of 2:1. Of the swing counties near New York City, Westchester went heavily Federalist, while Suffolk and Queens, counties of small farmers but close to the sea and commerce, voted Antifederal by narrow margins. The differences in voting may be seen by comparing the heart of Antifederalism, Ulster, Clinton's home county of small farmers, and New York City where all classes, merchant and mechanic alike, heavily and even fanatically favored the

---

[29]Spaulding, *New York in the Critical Period,* p. 203. [Editor's remarks] Ibid., pp. 198–204.

Constitution. In Ulster, the Antifederalist ticket amassed about 1,200 votes each, while the highest Federalist delegate received a whopping sixty-eight votes. In New York City, the Federals each averaged 2,700 votes, while Governor Clinton was the highest Antifederal candidate with only 134 votes!

When the convention met on June 17, the New York voters had elected forty-six delegates against nineteen for the Federals. Yet when the vote on the Constitution came on July 26, the voting was 30-27 in favor of ratifying. What happened in the interim? What induced this massive betrayal of the New York electorate? One critical factor was the grim news of the ratification in the supposedly Antifederal states of New Hampshire and Virginia, which came to New York in the middle of the convention. Now it was no longer a question, as it had been even as late as Virginia's struggle, of blocking or adopting the Constitution: with ten states ratifying, the Constitution would clearly be put into effect by the other states. New York was facing a dilemma far more difficult than her predecessors: should she go in or stay out of the new and inevitable Union?

But the most important impetus for the massive change in votes stemmed from the contrasting traits of the opposing camps. On the one side, the fierce fanaticism of the great bulk of nationalists that would stop at nothing to achieve their ends; on the other, a soft spread of decay in outer sections of the Antifederal forces that made them susceptible to capitulation. The fanaticism of the Federalists was reflected in *the* decisive move of the New York convention—the force that caused the surrender of a timorous minority of the Antifederal forces. That force was the blackmail threat effectively employed in Virginia: if New York did not ratify, New York City and its environs would secede from the state and join the new Union. It was this ugly and fearsome threat that led the defecting minority to turn tail and surrender. The secession threat could not have been a credible one unless the whole city were solidly and enthusiastically behind it. No one would have paid attention to the muttered threats of a Jay or a Hamilton if they knew that these oligarchs had no great mass-backing on the issue. But the city, all of it, *did* back their leaders zealously and all the way. It was the fervent mass support of the artisans that gave the unity and the strength to the Federalist blackmail.

The mechanics (not only in New York City but in Boston, Philadelphia, Charleston, and other cities as well) were not laborers in the sense of proletarians, but petty bourgeois, i.e., small businessmen and apprentice businessmen. After the Revolution, especially in the postwar depression of 1780s, the often marginal small businessmen found themselves apt to be *sub*-marginal, unable to meet the competition of more efficient imports of British manufactured goods. And like inefficient businessmen everywhere, they turned from the free market to the state apparatus to acquire special privileges—in this case a protective tariff. It was the lure of a national tariff, and a privileged market at home and in the other states, that brought the artisans *en masse* into the Federalist camp. With the onset of the depression, merchants and mechanics, who had formerly organized among themselves, formed joint committees in all the large cities to press for federal regulation of trade (for the merchants) and a tariff against European imports (for the mechanics). Nationalist propagandists had demagogically fomented the view among formerly anti-Tory artisans that anyone who opposed tariffs on British imports must be under the influence of the former enemy. As a result, even before the election when the city people were already threatening secession, the corporal's guard of the New York City Antifederalists were already beginning to cave under the tremendous pressure around them. Thus, on the eve of elections, Marinus Willett, a veteran radical who had always depended on his artisan constituency, was beginning to buckle: to think that the Constitution "might be right—since it appears to be the sense of a vast majority" [in New York City]. Indeed, of the old radical leaders of the Sons of Liberty in the city, only John Lamb remained staunchly anti-nationalist, and he was rewarded for his fidelity to the old radical cause by seeing his house threatened by a rioting mob.

Another important reason for the adamant demands of New York City was the strong possibility that it would be the capital of the new government. Already the existing headquarters for the Confederation Congress, if New York remained out of the Union, the city would be deprived of all of the subsidies, commerce, and privileges any government headquarters receives. For many New Yorkers, this was simply too much to give up.

On July 23 the fearsome massed ranks—nearly 4,000—of New York City artisans from over fifty trades marched down Broadway in celebration of New Hampshire's—and therefore nine states'—adoption of the Constitution. Even though the convention had been closely located upstate at Poughkeepsie, news of the parade could *not* help but make the downstate secession threat most believable indeed. One after the other, the slogans and the shouts of the various trades went by, and each trade celebrated the special privilege and subsidy that it expected to get out of the new polity in the making. Thus, the Skinners, Breeches Makers, and Glovers: "Americans, encourage your manufactures!"; the Peruke Makers and Hairdressers: "May we succeed in our trade and the union protect us"; the Blacksmiths: "Forge me strong, finish me neat, I soon shall moor a Federal fleet"; and the Brush Makers: "May love and unity support our trade, And keep out those who would our rights invade."[30] Other floats celebrated Alexander Hamilton, especially because of his work as the field marshal of the Federal forces at the Poughkeepsie convention. When we consider that the number of marchers constituted virtually *half* of the adult male population in New York City, the mass power and intensity of that city was evident to all.

If the New York City artisans provided the *push* that spliced off a large number of Antifederal delegates, which jumped the fire? The voters had originally elected forty-six Antifederalists and nineteen Federalists; the final convention vote of 30-27 for the Constitution was achieved by the defection of nineteen men, twelve who voted for the Constitution and seven who abstained (in contrast, in the more cohesive Federalist bloc only one abstained and none shifted into opposition). Was there anything particularly significant about the eighteen turncoats? Firstly, of the nine delegates elected from Queens and Suffolk Counties on Long Island, fully eight were disloyal, all four from Queens and four out of five from Suffolk. This shift reflected the lack of firmness of the liberalism of counties of commercial farmers closely tied to the seacoast and to commercial New York City. Moreover, the Queens Antifederalist delegate Samuel Jones, a close personal friend of Clinton, had business interests in New York City; his reneging reflected

---

[30]Staughton Lynd, "Capitalism, Democracy, and the U.S. Constitution: The Case of New York," *Science and Society* (Fall 1963): 402–03, 410. [Editor's remarks] Lynd, *The Revolution and the Common Man*, pp. 221–81; Spaulding, *New York in the Critical Period*, pp. 220–31.

a massive defection by the final vote of the whole crowd of beleaguered Antifederal merchants in the city. Thus, by the final vote, every delegate from the city and environs—New York City, Long Island, Staten Island, Westchester—supported the Constitution, with the exception of one absentee from Suffolk and the same county's redoubtable jurist, Thomas Tredwell, who had the courage to vote no.

Of the other eleven turncoats, only three were scattered through the upstate counties (Orange, Montgomery, and Ulster), while the others were highly concentrated. Of the seven delegates from Albany County, three defected. At least two of these were merchants from the city of Albany. Most significant was the defection of Dutchess County; for of the seven delegates elected as Antifederalist, no less than five disobeyed their voters. Since a mere shift of two votes would have defeated the Constitution, the Dutchess betrayal takes on the aspect of the critical change in the convention picture.

The Dutchess shift takes on far more significance when we realize that one of the defectors was none other than Melancton Smith, veteran Clintonian, one of the governor's two leaders at the convention (the other was John Lansing, who remained loyal to the end). The apostasy of Smith must have been the decisive blow in disheartening the staunch Antifederalists, including Governor Clinton, and the swinging over of his colleagues. Certainly the wholesale Dutchess defection stemmed from the powerful influence in the county of Melancton Smith.

Pursuing the problem more deeply, we find that Smith was only a *former* resident of Dutchess, and he was currently residing as a leading merchant in New York City. Indeed, he was one of the leaders of the unfortunate Lamb Committee, the bulk of whom were to go over to the enemy. Smith, then, was *really* a New York City man, though elected for Dutchess, and he was subject to all the urban pressure that subdued his colleagues.

It must never be thought that "upstate" New York was an ideological monolith. On the contrary, while the subsistence farmers were Antifederal, the giant quasi-feudal landlords of the Hudson Valley were almost uniformly Federalist, and where the landlords resided on their manorial states, they were usually able to dominate their tenants and control their voting. Thus, in Dutchess County, which went Antifederalist by a 2:1 majority—close to the average of the state—northwest

Dutchess, the stronghold of Federalism in the county, was an area of large manorial estates dominated especially by the oligarchic Beekmans and Livingstons.

The Antifederal constituency were the independent yeomen of the remainder in the county, but their leadership was a small group of middling merchants intertwined in family and business connections who conducted their affairs in the commercial river town of Poughkeepsie. Both classes had been long allied in the great fight against feudal landlordism, and the confiscation of Tory estates during the Revolution had freed southern Dutchess and converted the region into a land of small and middling farmers who voted over the years for the liberal and Clintonian Antifederalists.[31] In the campaign for delegates, one rank-and-file Antifederalist of the county, "One of Many," already protested the overrepresentation of the "little overbearing precinct of Poughkeepsie" at the Antifederal convention, and the result of this malapportionment was the Antifederal nomination of Melancton Smith. Or, as the Antifederalist complained, "What is the plain English in the nomination of Mr. Smith of New York ... Must we call in the assistance of strangers and New York merchants?" "One of Many" also gave an accurate prediction of Smith's behavior as a delegate:

> It is said (and we apprehend the information may be relied on) that Mr. Smith has grown *cool* on the question, and that he considers the adoption of the new Constitution by Massachusetts, as decisive for the continent, and that it would be as fruitless as it would be inexpedient for this State, even if there should be a majority against it, to stand out against the general sense and ardent feelings of America. If this be the case, we would oppose such a delegate even if he lived in this county.[32]

---

[31][Editor's footnote] For an analysis of some of the early confiscations and redistributions of Tory lands, which were an important corrective since the landlords never really justly owned the land, see Rothbard, *Conceived in Liberty*, vol. 4, pp. 1543–47; pp. 429–33. Confiscation of Tory lands allowed New York to keep taxes low in the 1780s, which solidified agrarian support for the Clintonians.

[32]Staughton Lynd, *Anti-Federalism in Dutchess County, New York* (Chicago: Loyola University Press, 1962), p. 16.

Of the other four turncoats from Dutchess, Gibert Livingston was a Poughkeepsie merchant in partnership with Melancton Smith's brother. He was also a member of the arch-conservative Livingston family and served as agent for a Livingston manor. To round out the picture, Gilbert Livingston was also the law partner of the high Federalist James Kent. The other Poughkeepsie defection was Zephaniah Platt, a partner of Smith in land speculation and father-in-law of Gilbert Livingston's sister. It is true that Ezra Thompson, a fourth Dutchess defection, came from the rural northeastern part of the county, but it is also true that he was (a) a brother-in-law of Smith, and (b) father-in-law of Livingston's daughter and law partner of Livingston himself. In contrast, the two delegates who remained faithful and Antifederal to the last, Jonathan Akin and Jacobus Swartwout, both came from the non-commercial small-farmer southern Dutchess, the great stronghold of Antifederalism among the electorate. Furthermore, both the Akin and Swartwout families had been highly involved in the Smith Dutchess tenant rebellion of 1766.[33]

In the last analysis, the division in New York State over the Constitution was once again essentially one of the commercial interests: merchants and artisans of New York City, commercial cities and towns on the Hudson River, landed oligarchs along the Hudson Valley, and commercial middling farmers (e.g., Long Island, near Poughkeepsie). A corollary was that of the convention delegates in the final vote, all the merchants, more than two-thirds of the large landowners, almost all of the wealthy, and virtually every college graduate voted for the Constitution.

Desertion by Melancton Smith of a motion that he himself had instructed, for a bill of rights and other rectifying amendments conditional to ratification, defeated the plan by two votes. Thus, New York ratified the Constitution unconditionally on July 26, 30-27. Despite all of this—betrayals, secession threats, ratification in other states— it is admirable just how many New York Antifederalists fought until the bitter end: to push for conditional amendments, to argue that the new government not exercise certain powers until a new convention, to argue for an escape clause that would allow New York to secede, and to

---

[33][Editor's footnote] For more on the tenant rebellion, see Rothbard, *Conceived in Liberty*, vol. 3, pp. 926–29; pp. 162–65.

just barely lose the final vote. It was because of this determination that the Federalists had to pay a higher price than usual, for the convention unanimously agreed, not only on the usual corollary amendments, but also to send a circular letter to the other states urging them to ask Congress for a second constitutional convention to adopt the various amendments proposed by the states. To Madison, Washington, and the other Federal opponents of checks on the national government, this was chilling news indeed. Madison, seconded by Washington, was one of the bitter enemies of a bill of rights and was particularly extreme in his reaction: he believed that outright rejection would have been better because New York's letter would encourage the other states that ratified to also press for amendments. For their part, the response of the Federalist New York City mob to the ratification was much less sophisticated. Their celebration took the form of ransacking the building of the great Antifederal organ, the *New York Journal*, and paying a visit to Governor Clinton's home. Fortunately, Clinton arrived at his house three days after the incident.

The New York circular letter was sent out promptly at the end of July and helped inspire the abortive Harrisburg convention in Pennsylvania. The Antifederal Virginia legislature, led by the zealous Patrick Henry, responded by resolving that Congress immediately call a national convention to adopt restrictive amendments. There still seemed to be hope that the Constitution might be whittled down and restructured. At the end of October, the New York Antifederalists, led by the turncoats who presumably wanted to redeem themselves (e.g., Marinus Willett, Melancton Smith, and Samuel Jones) formed a society to secure a second federal convention.[34]

---

[34][Editor's footnote] Spaulding, *New York in the Critical Period,* pp. 265–76, 285–87; Main, *The Antifederalists,* pp. 241–42; McDonald, *We the People,* pp. 304–05; Lynd, *Anti-Federalism in Dutchess County,* pp. 27–31, 86–88.

34

The Constitution Takes Effect

With all but two relatively obscure states—Rhode Island and North Carolina—having ratified the Constitution, the Confederation Congress was now ready to put the new federal government in place. As soon as New Hampshire became the ninth state to ratify, Congress dutifully created a committee to get the new Constitution up and running. Only the doughty Abraham Yates dissented—in a sense, the last attempt to block the Constitution as a whole. To the determined Antifederalists throughout the county, their next tack was forcefully imposed upon them by the very course of the ratification struggle: they must mobilize and put their plans into Congress in order to fulfill their pledge for restrictive amendments, preferably by calling another constitutional convention that would redress the imbalance of the first.

It was relatively easy for the old Confederation Congress to decide to hold elections and choose electors for the president the following January 7, to assemble the Electoral College to vote for a president on February 4, and to assemble the new U.S. Congress on March 4, 1789.

Attendance at, and interest in, the old Confederation Congress drifted away, and its last day with a quorum was October 10, 1788. There was a flurry of hope in January of the new year, when everyone awaited the new government, and members began to drift into the old Congress, where the faithful Charles Thomson, secretary ever since the opening of the glorious first Continental Congress, sat waiting for the old Congress to meet yet another time, and also to preserve its tenuous existence so that he could hand over the reins to the new government. When March 4 arrived, the old executive departments of Congress were passed into the new Congress for a traumatic period—the nation could not be permitted to live for a few days without the continuity of an executive bureaucracy. Poor old Thomson lounged around for several months and hopefully expected to find a place in the swollen bureaucracy of the New Order. But he found it not, and resigned his office at the end of July to sink into a life of obscurity. In a sense, the passing of Charles Thomson from the political scene paralleled the passing of the Confederation Congress: both met the end of their days humbly, passively, resignedly, and making not a peep.

The old Congress' most important problem was to decide where the site of the national capital would be. Every large city wanted the honor, and of the two leading Federalists, Hamilton wanted the site to be in New York, and Madison wanted to see it located on the Potomac. Wherever it was, the Federalists would undoubtedly be strong at that location, and the Federalists of that location would correspondingly control the levers of power in the national government. Baltimore, pushed by the southern states, was accepted in early August 1788. However, within a month Hamilton had succeeded in changing the vote to have the capital be New York City. Shrewdly, he was able to argue that since the capital site was agreed by all to be strictly temporary, there was no point in moving the Confederation Congress to another location. As a result, Madison repeated his bitter accusation that Hamilton and the New York Federalists' shrewd acceptance of the convention's circular letter was made to have the state ratify in time to retain the capital in New York City.[35]

The capital would be temporary because the nationalists had made a proviso that the Constitution empowered the Congress to receive a district no larger than one hundred square miles of land, which its governing state or states may cede to it; Congress might then treat the District as its fief—its seat of national government over which it can exclusively rule. This specter of such a protected Federal city, an enclave for supergovernment unique in the world, was one of the points of contention by the Antifederalists. But, as the new government loomed on the horizon, Maryland, at the end of December 1788, offered to cede a district that Congress might decide upon for the eventual capital.

---

[35][Editor's footnote] Spaulding, *New York in the Critical Period*, pp. 270–71.

The Constitution provided that at the meeting of the Electoral College, the person garnering the majority number of votes would be chosen president; the person with the second highest to be vice-president and presiding officer of the Senate. It was a foregone conclusion that George Washington would be the president, but the victorious Federalists had to decide on whom they would choose for the second post. Since Washington was a Virginian, the vice-president must obviously be from the North, which meant either New York or Massachusetts. New York was out of the question, for while the Federalists now grew more powerful in the state and were able to control the choice of U.S. senators, Governor Clinton was still the commanding personality. Clinton, who had abstained from the final vote at the New York Convention, was the Antifederalist candidate for vice-president and planned on pushing for restrictive amendments. Due to political gridlock, New York was to cast no electoral votes in 1789.

Massachusetts it was, then; here, there were clearly only two possibilities: Governor Hancock, who had been promised the post, and John Adams, who had returned from his term as minister to England in the spring of 1788 and chosen as a member of the House of Representatives for Massachusetts. The Federalists realized full well that Hancock was a vain, flighty opportunist whose views, such as they were, differed greatly from their own, so it was a pleasure for them to double-cross the Massachusetts governor. This left John Adams.

Adams, of course, was a hard pill for Hancock and the Federalist leaders to swallow, for they remembered all too well Adams' radical role during the Revolutionary War and the powerful Left leadership of the Adams-Lee faction in Congress. But Adams had come a long way since those days. As Hamilton wrote to the Massachusetts Federalist Theodore Sedgwick: "his further knowledge of the world seems to have corrected those jealousies which he is represented to have once been influenced by."

Adams, conservative enough in the postwar period, had indeed shifted staunchly and significantly rightward during his term in England—rightward enough to take his full place in the "high mounted" new Federalist order. Away in England from 1785 to 1788, he found there in the British imperial monarchy the model of ideal government, and his admiration for monarchical statism deepened and intensified under the shock of Shays' Rebellion. During his stay in London, Adams published in 1787–1788 his newly developed views in his *A Defense of the Constitutions of Government of the United States of America*. In this original work, Adams developed and advocated what would later be called the social philosophy of "Bonapartism"—from Napoleon's role in French politics. In the analysis of Bonapartism, Napoleon was supposed to have maintained himself in power by playing off against each other the two great power groups in France: the masses and the aristocracy. John Adams' theory was an exalted and precursory view of essentially the same process. Adams, too, saw the world as basically divided into the aristocracy and the democracy, or "the common people," and these two great classes, he believed, were permanently destined to war against each other. The fundamental task of government, for Adams, was to hold the equal balance between these two vast groups and to enforce impartial justice upon them both. Both groups should be equally represented in government, i.e., the rich in an upper house, the common man in a lower house, of the country's legislature. Where, then, shall the all-important, impartial arbiter of justice come from? He is to appear, according to Adams, in the pen of the executive, the great man who, with an absolute veto over the legislature, is to be exalted above all mere conflicting groups and classes in society and to dispense equal justice for all.

But by what mysterious process is this noble *deus ex machina* to appear and perform his great work? What is to ensure that the Great Man will really perform in this exalted way? The traditional solution to this problem, of course, was the Divine Right of Kings; the king operating as the vehicle of divine wisdom *by definition*, so that takes care of that. But John Adams, after all, as a man of the eighteenth century, couldn't accept this kind of solution. Instead, he thought he saw the answer in sheer self-interest. In a kind of parody of the theory of the free market, the king (or president) was to advance the social interest by serving his own:

> It is the true policy of the common people to place the whole executive power in one man, to make him a distinct order in the state, from whence arises an inevitable jealousy between him and the gentlemen; this forces him to become a father and protector of the common people.

Assuming, as we must, that John Adams was serious in this apologetic for executive power, the naïveté of this interesting theory is staggering. In the first place, it is by no means given that the self-interest of the dictatorial Chief Executive is to spend his days as the supreme balancing agent of impartial justice. On the contrary, as the head and will of the full-time executive bureaucracy, the Chief and his followers constitute an independent class interest of their own and will exploit the rest of the population for his and their own benefit. Secondly, in order to catapult himself into power, the Chief will undoubtedly purchase allies among either of the two classes, more profitably so among the influential aristocracy. We can only conclude that the vaunted "realism" of John Adams' conservative social theory is actually the worst naïve kind of utopian fancy, a fancy, however, that *does* perform the required function of spinning plausible apologies for executive depredation and oligarchical statism.

The chief executive, Adams believed, should have the absolute power to appoint, make war, and conclude treaties. Only with a single chief executive at the helm with the entire nation looking up to him can one "hope for uniformity, consistency, and subordination ..." In fact, Adams, as his ultimate ideal, yearned for a hereditary monarchy and aristocracy. Privately he wrote that hereditary monarchy and aristocracy are

> the only Institutions that can possibly preserve the Laws and Liberties of the People, and I am clear that America must resort to them as an Asylum against discord, Seditions and Civil War, and that at no very distant period of time. ... Our Country is not ripe for it, in many respects ... but our ship must ultimately land on that shore or be cast away.

Adams felt that the English government exemplified his ideal: it was, he wrote grandiosely, "the most stupendous fabric of human invention." Only ancient Macedonia could come close to this standard. In this admiration, derived from Montesquieu, Adams did not realize that England at the time was far less of an absolute monarchy and far more of a parliamentary oligarchy than what Adams desired.

Adams was particularly enamored of titles of nobility, and even for elective officers, Adams held titles to be absolutely necessary to maintain the dignity and honor of the federal government, and above all "to make offices and laws respected." Apparently, the real choice was between titles of nobility and anarchy: "I do not abhor Titles, nor the Pageantry of Government. If I did I should abhor Government itself—for there never was, and never will be, because there never can be, any government without Titles and Pageantry."[36] So enamored was Adams of the title, indeed, that he spent a good part of his first year as vice-president trying to persuade the Senate to adopt a system of titles.

It is apparent that Alexander Hamilton was right; John Adams had indeed learned much, and his ideological worldview had matured compared to so many years ago. He was obviously as ready as any man could be to assume the exalted post of vice-president of the United States of America.

The way the electoral system worked, then, was along the design that the vice-presidential and presidential nominees might tie, so it was obviously expedient to arrange the "throwing away" of a few votes so that the agreed upon vice-presidential choice might place second. Hamilton, however, still suspicious of Adams, secretly threw himself into this task with excessive relish, and Adams ended with thirty-four electoral votes to Washington's sixty-nine. The latter vote was unanimous except for New York, which, due to a clash between a Federalist New York Senate and Clintonian Assembly, never agreed on a choice of electors. Adams was bitterly upset at the results, for he thought he had a real chance to be the supreme arbiter of justice.

While Washington and Adams were elected in February, the Constitution could not go into effect until the opening of the new Congress, scheduled for March 4, 1789. But a quorum of the new Congress did not appear until April 6 when the electoral votes were officially counted; the presidential inauguration then took place on April 30, 1789, the effective starting date of the new government.

---

[36]Manning J. Dauer, *The Adams Federalists* (Boston: Johns Hopkins Press, 1953), p. 48*n*. [Editor's remarks] Ibid., pp. 37–54, 78–83.

35

North Carolina Postpones
and then Ratifies

There were still two beleaguered states not yet in the Union: Rhode Island and North Carolina. Of all the southern states, North Carolina was by far the least aristocratic. Only the Edenton–New Bern area of the northeast, with its ports, navigable inlets, large slave plantations, and swollen commercial farms, was typically "Federalist"; almost all of the rest of the state was non-commercial subsistence farming. Of the five North Carolina delegates at the Philadelphia Convention, the one westerner, former Governor Alexander Martin, walked out from the forming of the Constitution. Now the Federalists had to face the great burden of the people from the small farming parts of the state, men who remembered the old struggles of the Regulators and who were properly suspicious of government abuses. The North Carolina legislature overrode an attempted filibuster and called elections in March 1788 for a convention to meet at Hillsboro on July 21.

The campaign was a fierce one, with Antifederalists receiving material from Lamb's Federal Republican Committee in New York and the Federalists aided by Robert Morris' Federal propaganda headquarters in Philadelphia. Leading the Federalists were William Blount and his northeast clique, including the lawyer James Iredell, while the Antifederalists, in addition to Thomas Person, were led by Willie Jones and Timothy Bloodworth, both well-connected individuals. Bloodworth wrote that the people mostly in favor of ratification in North Carolina were "The Attorneys, Merchants, and Aristocratic part of the community." The wealthy Jones was the field marshal of the Antifederalists, and for once the Antifederal powers of organization were adequate to the task.

The North Carolina elections were overwhelmingly Antifederalist, even more so than New York, and the number of delegates was seventy-five for the Constitution, 193 opposed. The Federalists, predictably, covered the northeast, but lost four counties behind the coastal communities. The smaller farming inland counties voted extremely Antifederalist, and no other state had such an extreme area of small farms remote from transportation and navigation. The surprise was the heavy Antifederal vote in the southeast counties dominated by large slave-holding planters. The southeast, however, lacking the inlets of the northeast, was far less commercial and export-minded. In the one commercial port town of the southeast, Wilmington instead voted Federalist. The northeast towns—New Bern, Halifax, and Edington—of course supported the Constitution, as well as Wilmington in the southeast and Salisbury in the staunchly Antifederal West.

In the far west, in the Tennessee settlements, the vote was almost unanimously Antifederal. As in the case of Kentucky, the settlers had been persuaded by the Jay-Gardoqui Treaty that the great potential of the Mississippi River trade would not be safe in the hands of the northern nationalists. It is interesting, also, that while the Blount-led western land speculators voted Federalist the settlers themselves were almost totally opposed.

Since Antifederalists and Federalists, as in other states, tended to select their most prominent men as delegates, the disparity in wealth and prestige between the delegates was not nearly as great among the rank and file. In particular, Tennessee and southeastern planters swelled the ranks of wealthy Antifederal delegates, and the disparity was not significant in the distribution of land. Still, the bulk of large slave owners in North Carolina was disproportionately in favor of the Constitution.

The North Carolina convention in mid-1788 listened stolidly to the Federalist propaganda and was unimpressed. This time there was no betrayal, no sudden conversions—not even pressure—because eleven states had ratified, and the new government of the U.S. was clearly inevitable. The only concession the Antifederalists made was to insist on prior amendments, especially a bill of rights, and to adjourn, rather than reject, the Constitution outright, by a vote of 184-84 on August 2.

The North Carolina Antifederalists were enthusiastic over the New York circular letter for a second constitutional convention. But one of the secrets of the Federalists' success throughout the country was that they never took no for an answer. No sooner had the convention adjourned than did James Iredell and other Federalists distribute literature and circulate petitions for a new state convention to ratify the Constitution. Secession blackmail now reared its ugly head in yet another state, for the northeastern Federalists had threatened secession from North Carolina to join the Union, and this meant the shaving off of the commercial navigational area of the state. The Federalists began to win elections, and they managed to gain control of the state Senate. Seeing the tide turn against them on a second state convention, the Antifederalists in the House managed to have the convention postponed for many months, until November 1789.

A massive propaganda campaign was conducted throughout 1789, and Federal strength grew, particularly as Congress agreed to the bill-of-rights amendments. In the August elections, the Federalists achieved a success on the level of the Antifederalists in the prior year, and the November convention only lasted a few days. On November 21, 1789, the second North Carolina convention voted to ratify the Constitution by 194-77.[37]

---

[37] [Editor's footnote] Main, *The Antifederalists*, pp. 242–48; Spaulding, *New York in the Critical Period*, p. 269; McDonald, *We the People*, pp. 310–13.

36

The Coercion of Rhode Island

Doughty, courageous little Rhode Island was the last state left. It is generally assumed that—even by the most staunchly Antifederalist historians—Rhode Island could not conceivably have gone it alone as a separate nation. But such views are the consequence of a *mystique* of political frontiers, in which it is assumed that a mere change in political frontiers and boundaries necessarily has a profound effect in the lives of the people or the validity of a territory or region. But, in reality, political frontiers are mere excrescences, the daily lives of the people, their economic and social relations, can go on unperturbed and unchanged whether politically defined counties are large, tiny, or even non-existent. That Switzerland or Holland are small has no more prevented their people from flourishing than the large size of India has brought it prosperity. In the case of a free country of Rhode Island, its self-sufficient inland farmers would have continued to farm, and its merchants to trade with other states and countries just as before. Better than before, in fact, for this land of open trade could have gained great popularity for functioning as a free port, as a "Rogue's Island" once more of free trade and smuggling in the great Anglo-American tradition.

The Rhode Islanders realized the opportunity that awaited them. Thus, one writer in the Rhode Island press assured readers that an independent Rhode Island would not become an "Algiers" (a base for piracy), but a "St. Eustatius" (the great smuggling center of the Dutch West Indies that so aided the American Revolutionary War effort).[38]

---

[38]Ibid., p. 339*n*.

But the problem, of course, is that Rhode Island only could have been a bastion of free trade if the imperial United States had permitted it, and of course it would not. With its tariffs, its federal taxes, its commercial privileges and restrictions, its already lusty desire to grab land from others by whatever means necessary and to play a great role on the international stage, the arrogant new United States could never have permitted an independent Rhode Island almost within its borders. For this little enclave would have held up a beacon-light of freedom to all democracies and to the world at large. The United States could not countenance a republic still true to *its own* American Revolution, and true also to the glorious libertarian tradition of the independent Rhode Island of the seventeenth century.

Hardly had the new United States began, in fact, when that mighty nation began to threaten Rhode Island. Massachusetts, Connecticut, and New York were particularly alarmed at the potential flourishing of Rhode Island under a system of free trade "smuggling," and such Federalists as Fisher Ames of Massachusetts and Egbert Benson of New York led the drive from their states for the use of force to corral Rhode Island into the Union.

Little Rhode Island tried; it tried very hard. Resisting tremendous pressure from within and without, the Rhode Island legislature, for two years after the rejection of March 1788, crushed no less than four motions to call a state convention. And these defeats were brought about by such large margins as 44-12 and 40-14. Then, in September 1789, after intense pressure by Providence and Newport merchants, the legislature agreed to ask the towns for instructions, and a month later it distributed copies throughout the state of the bill-of-rights amendments recommended by Congress. The towns duly sent their instructions, and the result was that the legislature again refused to call a convention; the margin was only slightly reduced, 39-17.

Finally, however, the Assembly surrendered and voted for a convention in January 1790 by a vote of 34-29, but the doughty Senate blocked the bill by 5-4. But the sharp practice—something that had to be used in so many states to ram through the Constitution—was used again. The Senate waited until a member was absent, and then Governor John Collins—yet another governor who turned tail—broke the ensuing tie, and a convention was finally called to be held in South Kingston on March 1.

Antifederalist power had greatly eroded since the towns had repudiated the Constitution two years before. But, remarkably, the Antifederals still had a majority of a dozen or so delegates at the March convention. Finally, five days later, the Antifederals pushed through an adjournment of the convention by a vote of 41-28 until May 24 at Newport.

The climactic phase of the Rhode Island struggle was now at hand. Two titanic vectors of pressure converged on the beleaguered and heroic citizens of the Rhode Island republic. First, the United States Congress, in its first act of international aggression, threatened to place a total embargo between Rhode Island and the states of the Union. But perhaps the little state would have held out regardless. Second, when the convention reopened, it faced not a *threat* of secession by fanatical Federalists, but secession as an actual *fact*. For the main city of Providence had announced its secession from the state, to continue unless and until Rhode Island adopted the Constitution unconditionally. And, what is more, Newport and other towns threatened to do the same. Only now, facing the direct prospect of being blockaded from the sea and surrounded by a hostile power, did Rhode Island surrender—and then, remarkably and incredibly, by a margin of only two votes, 34-32. After all this time and pressure, a shift of one vote would have defeated the Constitution in Rhode Island. It truly was a last stand that just barely failed.

Even at the desperate, final Rhode Island vote, the Jackson T. Main commercial/non-commercial analysis of the ratification struggle in the United States is upheld. Every one of the Narragansett Bay towns except a divided Warwick had now become Federalist. So had the coastal towns of the southwestern Grant Lands. The commercial-navigational Bay and coastal towns had virtually become Federal, and the inland rural towns remaining had maintained their staunch Antifederalism. Clearly the commercial farmers near the Bay and coast had, as in New York, proved weak enough to provide the tiny margin of Federalist victory.

Part of the explanation for the final defection, however, is far more sinister. For in the course of the two sessions of the 1790 convention, the number of Federalist delegates from the towns rose from twenty-two to thirty-four: in short, twelve delegates betrayed the voters of their towns who had elected them to oppose the Constitution. Of these men, six defectors (who of course provided more than the margin of victory) were holders of state securities—at least two of them (Christopher Greene Jr. of Warwick and John S. Dexter of Cumberland) in large amounts. Rhode Island had been loaded with a very heavy burden of state debt and consequently high taxes after the Revolution, and then had issued large amounts of paper money largely to pay off the debt. The currency had predictably depreciated, but most of the debt had been concurrently repaid. Now, in 1790, it was fairly clear that Hamilton would push through his financial program to have the federal government assume all the old state debts. The Rhode Island state creditors saw their chance, unique among the states, to cash in twice upon the same debt. The pro-public-creditor Federalists, then, joined with enough of a corporal's guard of state-creditor Antifederals to pass a law declaring that only part of the debts had been paid because the payments had been in depreciated in paper. Thus, new debt was suddenly created, and the taxpayers of the nation were to be mulcted where the Rhode Islanders had been fleeced before.[39]

A final point on the Constitution conflict in Rhode Island: slavery was one of the bones of contention. Abolitionist Quaker sentiment was strong in Rhode Island, as was the institution of slavery, which had become powerful in the Narragansett in the South and in the coastal towns. During the 1780s, the Quakers had led a successful drive for abolition of the slave trade in the state as well as gradual abolition of slavery itself. Slavery was the source of more debate at the Rhode Island convention than any other topic; of the eight chamber members of the new Rhode Island Abolition Society, six voted against ratifying the Constitution.

---

[39]McDonald, *We the People*, pp. 345–46. Actually, however, Rhode Island turned out to be a creditor state in the final inter-state settlement of accounts, and so this particular deal did not come through. James Ferguson, "Review of Forrest McDonald, *E Pluribus Unum*," *The William and Mary Quarterly* (January 1966): 150. [Editor's remarks] McDonald, *We the People*, pp. 321–25, 342; Main, *The Antifederalists*, p. 248.

PART VI

The Nationalists Triumph:
The Constitution's Legacy

37

The Bill of Rights

The Constitution had been ratified and was going into effect, and the next great question before the country was the spate of amendments which the Federalists had reluctantly agreed to recommend at the state conventions. Would they, as Madison and the other Federalists wanted, be quietly forgotten? The Antifederalists, particularly in Virginia and New York, would not permit that to happen and the second convention movement, led by Patrick Henry and George Mason in Virginia and proposed by the New York convention circular letter, was the Antifederal goal. Already the circular letter had won approval from Virginia, North Carolina, and Rhode Island. A second convention would reopen the whole question of the Constitution and allow restrictive amendments and alterations which could severely weaken the rampant nationalism of the new government of the United States. For the same reason, a second convention was precisely what the victorious Federalists had to prevent at all costs.

The Federalists, of course, wanted no part of any amendments or reminders of their promises, and Senator Ralph Izard, wealthy Federalist planter of South Carolina, expressed their sentiments at the first session of Congress when he urged his colleagues to forget about their amendments and get down to problems of finance.

James Madison, who defeated James Monroe in the Virginia elections to the House of Representatives and assumed the leadership of the Federalists in Congress, abhorred the concept of a bill of rights. But as a shrewd political tactician, he realized that the second convention

297

movement could swell to formidable proportions. To avoid a potential crippling of the essentials of American nationalism, Madison decided that it was better to make some concessions right away and thus pull the teeth out of the drive for an overhaul of the Constitution before it really got underway. Madison also had a powerful political motive for making such concessions. Antifederalism was powerful in Virginia, as had been demonstrated in Henry's almost successful attempt to keep the hated Madison out of Congress altogether. If he was to save his political hide in his home state, Madison had to act, quickly, and in his hard-fought election campaign he had pledged to work for such amendments in Congress.

The approximately 210 amendments proposed by the states were of two basic kinds: a bill of rights for individuals and statehood reform to battle federal power. Typical of the former was trial by jury; of the latter was two-thirds requirement for passing a navigation law. The former did not alarm the Federalists nearly as much as the latter, for the former would leave intact a supreme national power, banned only in specific instances from making certain incursions on the perceived liberty of the individual. But the statehood amendments could cut aggressively into the very political and economic vitals of the national juggernaut and battle it effectively from within that power structure itself. The structural amendments would have expanded the libertarian scope of the bill of rights from personal liberties alone to the political and economic. This was too much for the Federalists to swallow.

Madison therefore decided to pass a bill of rights quickly and thus nip in the bud any drive for structural reform and a second convention. He informed Congress that the Antifederal states and a bill of rights was fortunate in that it would be possible to end this threat by granting such a bill without "endangering any part of the Constitution." If Congress refused to act, the public would be aroused, a second convention would be called, and the opposition could then force "a reconsideration of the whole structure of government." On the other hand, as he wrote to Thomas Jefferson, submission of a bill of rights would weaken the opposition by splitting the moderates away from the radicals, i.e., "the well meaning from the designing opponents, fix on the latter their true character, and give to the Government its due popularity and stability."

After Washington's inaugural speech brusquely warned that amendments must not really weaken the power of national government, Madison introduced amendments that proposed a bill of rights, based on the proposed Virginia amendments and the Virginia Declaration of Rights. Indeed he hastened to assure his intention of submitting the bill-of-rights amendments well in advance in order to forestall the next motion of Virginia's Antifederal Congressman, Dr. Theodorick Bland, from introducing a resolution for a new constitutional convention. Madison's centrist action was, predictably, opposed from Left and Right. On the Left, the Antifederal leadership understood Madison's tactic all too well. Senator William Grayson of Virginia wrote to Patrick Henry that Madison's amendments greatly overstressed personal liberty at the expense of reform of such matters as the direct-tax power and the judiciary. The whole aspect of Madison's maneuver, wrote Grayson, was "unquestionably to break the spirit of the Antifederalist party by divisions." The maneuver succeeded all too well as many in the Antifederal bloc were ready to settle for a small part of the loaf and then give in to the new Constitution. Even George Mason was almost willing to reconcile himself to the new government. In North Carolina, Madison's introduction of the bill of rights proved instrumental in changing enough Antifederal support to ratify the Constitution. On the other side, many Federalists were unconvinced of the necessity for this maneuver. In the House, Roger Sherman attacked the idea of amendments and upheld stability of government above all else. And the ultra-Federalist Fisher Ames sneered at Madison's amendment effort as based on research into personal trivia and designed to advance Madison's personal popularity. Georgia's James Jackson was *already* divinizing a constitution not quite a year old. The Constitution, he argued, must be left intact; otherwise, a patchwork flood of amendments might follow. The fact that the Constitution itself was a patchwork seemed to be lost on the Georgia congressman. Perhaps the most extreme expression in the House came from former Judge Samuel Livermore, who had pledged a key vote in ratifying the Constitution in New Hampshire. The judge was outraged about the restraints involved in prohibiting "cruel and unusual punishments" in the bill of rights. Livermore couldn't understand why necessary and salutary punishments should be prohibited merely because they were cruel.

A gallant Antifederal stand in the House was led by Aedanus Burke and Thomas Tucker of South Carolina. Burke and Tucker urged the inclusion of libertarian structural amendments, such as the prohibition of federal direct taxes, but their efforts were in vain. Tucker also tried in vain to include "expressly" before "delegated" in the Tenth Amendment, thus greatly limiting the power granted to Congress. Finally, after long and reluctant delay, the House passed seventeen restrictive amendments on August 24, 1789.

In the Senate, the libertarian Antifederalist fight was led by the two Virginia Senators, Richard Henry Lee and William Grayson. Lee and Grayson followed the Tucker-Burke path by introducing structural amendments; indeed they introduced a mixture of the amendments proposed by the Virginia convention. They also added a proposal to prohibit federal direct taxes. All of these were rejected by the Senate. The most creative and daringly democratic amendment was to bind representatives to follow the instructions of their constituents, but in all the Senate, only Lee and Grayson had the vision to support it. However, while Lee well understood the Machiavellian political reasons for the amendments, he concluded at the end that half a loaf was better than none. Lee, however, remained highly critical of the way in which his colleagues had inhibited and enfeebled the amendments. The hardline Federalists who scorned any concessions were led in the Senate by Ralph Izard of South Carolina, John Langdon of New Hampshire, and the ineffable Robert Morris of Pennsylvania.

The Senate condensed the House amendments into twelve, and a joint conference committee submitted final revisions of the twelve amendments, which were approved by the Congress on September 25. The hardcore Antifederalists were chagrined; Lee was critical, Grayson bitterly concluded that the submitted bill-of-rights amendments would do more harm than good. Patrick Henry agreed, lamenting the lack of a prohibition of direct taxes, and tried to postpone the ratification of the amendments by the Virginia House. Even the moderate Federalist Thomas Jefferson, though favoring the Bill of Rights, was disgruntled at the lack of a prohibition on government grants of monopoly and a standing army.

Patrick Henry's gallant fight against the overly soft amendments and the shrewd Madisonian strategy was able to delay Virginia's ratification until it became the last of the eleven states needed to approve. New

Jersey was the first state to ratify in late November 1789, but while nine states moved to ratify by June 1790, Virginia, the last state, took over two years after submission. In Virginia, the struggle was waged between the lower House, now controlled by the Federalists, and the Antifederalist-controlled Senate, which was finally pressured into ratifying on December 15, 1791. Massachusetts, Connecticut, and Georgia never did ratify; Georgia on the high-Federalist belief that they were unnecessary and Connecticut on the equally ultra-Federalist view that any concession would imply that the Constitution was not unflawed perfection, and would therefore give aid and comfort to Antifederalism. In Massachusetts, too, the Federalists wanted no amendments, while the Antifederals held out for stronger amendments; between the two forces, Massachusetts never ratified.

Of the twelve amendments submitted to the states, the first two were not ratified; these were minor provisions dealing with the organization of Congress. The remaining ten amendments composed nine highly significant articles guaranteeing various personal liberties against the federal government, as well as one complementary structural amendment. None of the political and economic liberties desired by the Antifederalists (prohibition of direct taxes, standing army, two-thirds requirement for laws regulating commerce, etc.) were included, but the adopted Bill of Rights was significant enough, and all of their provisions were intensely libertarian.[1]

The First Amendment provided that Congress "shall make no law" establishing religion or prohibiting its free exercise, abridging freedom of speech, press, or right of peaceful assembly or to petition the government for redress of grievances.

The Second Amendment guaranteed that "the right of the people to keep and bear Arms, shall not be infringed." While the courts have enumerated the clause to apply only to Congress, leaving the states free to invade this right, the wording makes it clear that the right "shall not be infringed," period. Since states are mentioned in the body of the Constitution and restrictions placed upon them there as well, this clause evidently also applies to the states. Indeed, the subsequent

---

[1][Editor's footnote] Jensen, *The Making of the American Constitution*, pp. 148–49, 184–86; Robert Allen Rutland, *The Birth of the Bill of Rights, 1776–1791* (Chapel Hill: University of North Carolina Press, 1955), pp. 190–218.

amendments (three to nine) apply to the states as well as to the federal government; only the First Amendment specifically restricts Congress alone. And yet the courts have emasculated the amendments in the same way, counting them as not applying to the invasions of personal liberty by the states.

The Third Amendment prohibits the quartering of troops in peace-time in a private house without the owner's consent; the Fourth guarantees the rights of the people "to be secure in their persons, houses, papers, and effects, against unreasonable searches and seizures," and only *specific* warrants, not general ones, can be issued.

The Fifth Amendment ensures grand-jury indictments for major crimes, and prohibits double jeopardy, compelling any defendant to testify against himself, depriving anyone of life, liberty, or property "without due process of law," or confiscating private property without "just compensation." The Sixth Amendment ensures the right of a defendant to a quick and public trial by an impartial jury of the locality of the crime, and to have various other rights in his trial. The Seventh guarantees the right of trial by jury in civil cases, and the Eighth prohibits excessive bail, excessive fines, and "cruel and unusual punishments."

The Ninth and Tenth Amendments were signed to give the stark rebuttal to the cynical Wilson-Madison-Hamilton argument that a bill of rights *impairs* people's rights by permitting encroachment in unenumerated rights that would supposedly belong to the people. The Tenth Amendment specifies that "the powers not delegated to the United States by the Constitution, nor prohibited by it to the States, are reserved to the States respectively, or to the people." This amendment specifies that the national government is one of strictly delegated powers, and that powers not so delegated belong to the states or to the people. In other words, the power not specifically delegated or prohibited to the federal government cannot be assumed by that government and are reserved to the states. For many years the Tenth Amendment was the great weapon of the states-rightists and other anti-nationalists in their argument that the *states* (or the people of the states) are *really* sovereign, rather than the national government.

This amendment did in truth transform the Constitution from one of supreme national power to a partially mixed polity where the liberal anti-nationalists had a constitutional argument with at least a fighting chance of acceptance. However, Madison had cunningly left out the word "expressly" before the word "delegated," so the nationalist judges were able to claim that because the word "expressly" was not there, the "delegated" can vaguely accrue through judges' elastic interpretation of the Constitution. This loophole for vague "delegated" power allowed the national courts to use such open-ended claims as general welfare, commerce, national supremacy, and necessary and proper to argue for almost any delegation of power that is not specifically prohibited to the federal government—in short, to return the Constitution basically to what it was before the Tenth Amendment was passed. The Tenth Amendment has been intensely reduced, by conventional judiciary construction, to a meaningless tautology.

Ironically, the most potentially explosive weapon of the anti-nationalists was ignored then and for the next 175 years by the public and the courts. This was the Ninth Amendment, which states: "The enumeration in the Constitution, of certain rights, shall not be construed to deny or disparage others retained by the people." With its stress on the *rights* of the people, rather than on state or federal *power* as in the Tenth Amendment, the Ninth Amendment is even more acutely the answer to the Wilsonian argument than the Tenth. The *enumeration* of rights may not be so construed as to *deny* other unenumerated rights retained by the people.

The Ninth Amendment has unfortunately (a) erroneously been held to apply *only* to the federal government and not also to the states, and (b) has been reduced to a simple paraphrase of the Tenth Amendment by the courts. But then why *have* a Ninth Amendment that simply repeats the Tenth? In truth, the Ninth Amendment is very different, and no construction can reduce it to a tautology; unlike the formulaic Tenth Amendment, the Ninth emphatically *asserts* that there *are* rights which are retained by the people and *therefore* may not be infringed upon by *any* area of government. But if there *are* unenumerated rights, this means that it is the constitutional *obligation* of the courts to find, proclaim, and protect them. Moreover, it means that it is *unconstitutional* for the courts to allow a government infringement on *any* right of the individual on the grounds that no express prohibition of that act can be found in the Constitution. The Ninth Amendment is an open invitation—nay, a command—to the people to discover and protect the unenumerated rights and never to allow governmental invasion of rights on the ground that no express prohibition can be found. In short, the Ninth Amendment expressly commands the judge to be "activist" and not "literal" *in the construction* of rights retained by the people against government encroachment.

Moreover, if it is asked what "other rights" were intended, the context of the time dictates but one answer: they meant the "natural rights" held by every human being. But a commandment that the courts are duty-bound to protect all of man's natural rights, enumerated or retained, would reduce the powerful scope of government action to such a degree as to give the last laugh to Herbert Spencer over Justice Oliver Wendell Holmes, who was in the early twentieth century to twist the strict constitutional judges of their day from holding that the Constitution endowed the individualist-libertarian social philosophy of Spencer's *Social Statics* (1851). While the taunt was directed against enabling the judges' personal preferences into Fundamental Law, the spelling out of the implications of the Ninth Amendment might well reinstate *Social Statics*, and on a far firmer legal and constitutional basis.[2]

Misconstrued as it was, the Ninth Amendment lay forgotten and made no impact whatever on American history until the year 1965. Then, suddenly, the Supreme Court, in a landmark of constitutional law, rediscovered the lost amendment and relied on it in *Griswold v. Connecticut* (1965) to prohibit the states from interfering with the individual's "basic and fundamental" right to marital privacy (in outlawing birth-control devices). The enormous implications of the decision for constitutional law and for wider liberty in the U.S. were adumbrated in the concurring opinion of the Justice Arthur Goldberg (agreed to by the Justice William Brennan and Chief Justice Earl Warren):

> The concept of liberty protects those personal rights that are fundamental, and is not confined to the specific terms of the

---

[2][Editor's footnote] Rothbard elsewhere wrote that Spencer's *Social Statics* was "the greatest single work of libertarian political philosophy ever written." Murray Rothbard, "Recommended Reading," *The Libertarian Forum* (June 1971): 5. Rothbard is referring to the famous case of *Lochner v. New York* (1905), which overturned a maximum-working-hours law on the principle that it violated freedom of contract. In his dissenting opinion, Holmes wrote that "the Fourteenth Amendment does not enact Mr. Herbert Spencer's *Social Statics*."

Bill of Rights. My conclusion that the concept of liberty is not so restricted, and that it embraces the right of marital privacy, though that right is not mentioned explicitly in the Constitution is supported both by numerous decisions of this Court, referred to in the Court's opinion, and by the language and history of the Ninth Amendment. ...

The Ninth Amendment to the Constitution may be regarded by some as a recent discovery, and may be forgotten by others, but, since 1791, it has been a basic part of the Constitution which we are sworn to uphold. To hold that a right so basic and fundamental and so deep-rooted in our society as the right of privacy in marriage may be infringed because that right is not guaranteed in so many words by the first eight amendments to the Constitution is to ignore the Ninth Amendment, and to give it no effect whatsoever. Moreover, a judicial construction that this fundamental right is not protected by the Constitution because it is not mentioned in explicit terms by one of the first eight amendments or elsewhere in the Constitution would violate the Ninth Amendment ...

Rather, as the Ninth Amendment expressly recognizes, there are fundamental personal rights such as this one, which are protected from abridgment by the Government, though not specifically mentioned in the Constitution.[3]

---

[3]Preceding the notable decision was the first treatise ever written on the Ninth Amendment, rediscovering this part of the Constitution as a particular bastion of individual liberty: Bennet B. Patterson, *The Forgotten Ninth Amendment* (Indianapolis, IN: Bobs-Merrill, 1955). Patterson accepts the thesis that Amendments two through eight apply only to the federal government. [Editor's remarks] *U.S. Reports: Griswold v. Connecticut*, 381 U.S. 479 (1965), pp. 486–87, 491, 496.

38

Was the U.S. Constitution Radical?

It was a bloodless *coup d'état* against an unresisting Confederation Congress. The original structure of the new Constitution was now complete. The Federalists, by use of propaganda, chicanery, fraud, malapportionment of delegates, blackmail threats of secession, and even coercive laws, had managed to sustain enough delegates to defy the wishes of the majority of the American people and create a new Constitution. The drive was managed by a corps of brilliant members and representatives of the financial and landed oligarchy. These wealthy merchants and large landowners were joined by the urban artisans of the large cities in their drive to create a strong overriding central government—a supreme government with its own absolute power to tax, regulate commerce, and raise armies. These powers were sought eagerly as a method of handing out special privileges to commercial groups: navigation acts to subsidize shipping, tariffs to protect inefficient artisans stampeded by national depression from foreign manufactured goods, and a strong army and navy to pursue an aggressive foreign policy designed to force the opening of West Indies ports, the Mississippi River, and the Northwest. And, to pay for all of these bounties, a central taxing power would be harnessed that could also assume and pay the public debt held by wealthy speculators. But government, by its nature, cannot supply bounties and privileges without taking them from others, and these others were to be largely the hapless bulk of the nation's citizens, the inland subsistence farmers. In western Massachusetts, taxes to pay a heavy public debt owned by wealthy men in the East had produced Shays' Rebellion. Now, a new super government was emerging and carrying out on a national scale the mercantilist principle of taxation, regulation, and special privilege for the benefit of favored groups ("the few") at the expense of the bulk of producers and consumers in the country ("the many"). And while to acquire sufficient support they had to purchase allies among the mass of the people (e.g., urban artisans), the major concentration of benefits and privileges would undoubtedly accrue to America's aristocracy.

As part of the agreed-to division of the coming spoils, the northern nationalists, though permanently abhorring slavery in a region where it was not viable and was being abolished, rather swiftly moved to protect and even encourage slavery in other regions in order to obtain support of the southern nationalists and thus the Constitution. To these nationalist leaders, abandoning the slave to his fate was a small price to pay for a strong central government to further markets for northern merchants and shippers.

Dispute has long raged among historians as to whether the Constitution was the completion, the fulfillment, of the spirit of the American Revolution, or whether it was a counterrevolution against that spirit. But surely it is clear that the Constitution was profoundly counterrevolutionary. The American Revolution has, in recent years, been depicted by "revisionist" historians as solely a struggle for independence against Great Britain on behalf of rather abstract principles of constitutional law. But legal principles are seldom passionately held and fought for unless instinctively bound up with conflicts in politico-economic reality. The Americans were not anti-British; on the contrary, the need to declare independence was acknowledged very late and almost reluctantly. The Americans were struggling not primarily for independence but for political-economic liberty against the mercantilism of the British Empire. The struggle was waged against taxes, prohibitions, and regulations—a whole failure of repression that the Americans, upheld by an ideology of liberty, had fought and torn asunder. It was only when independence was clearly necessary to achieve their goals did the American Revolution take final form. In other words, the American Revolution was in essence not so much against Britain as against British Big Government—and specifically against an all-powerful central government and a supreme executive.

In short, the American Revolution was liberal, democratic, and quasi-anarchistic; for decentralization, free markets, and individual liberty; for natural rights of life, liberty, and property; against monarchy, mercantilism, and especially against strong central government. From the very beginning of that Revolution and even before, wealthy financial oligarchs in New York and Philadelphia, beginning with Benjamin Franklin, had toyed with the idea of a strong central government in America that would grant them mercantilist powers over the people. In the last phase of the war, Robert Morris, the "grandfather of the Constitution," came within an inch of imposing a nationalist-mercantilist regime upon a revolutionary nation fighting for its existence.

The Articles of Confederation were themselves a concession to nationalism as against the original Continental Congress, but basically they had kept the Congress chained to a leash, and so nationalist power was checked. But with the postwar breakup of the liberal Adams-Lee Junto, the aftermath of wartime destruction, and the opportunity provided by the depression of the mid-1780s, the nationalists fished in troubled waters and succeeded in imposing a counterrevolution.

It has also been charged by recent historians that there was really no continuity between the contending forces during the Revolution (radicals versus conservatives) and the opposing camps in the struggle over the Constitution. But, in the first place, the continuity of *ideas* is striking: from the very beginning, it was the dream of the Right, once remaining with the British government became impossible, to remold America into a form as close as possible to the powerful government of Great Britain. In leadership personnel, the sticking point is that the Right in 1776, the ones most reluctant to break with England (the Morrises, the Dickinsonses, the Jays, the Schulyers—in short, the Philadelphia and New York oligarchy along with the Pendletons and Washingtons in Virginia) were the leaders of the reaction throughout the period and the leaders in the drive for a Constitution. The leaders of the Right in 1776 were also the leaders of the Right in 1789.

The difference between the two periods—and the significant break in continuity—was the shift of large numbers of radical leaders during the war into the conservative ranks a decade later. Indeed, one of the prior reasons for the defeat of the Antifederalists, though they commanded a majority of the public, was the decimation that had taken place in radical and liberal leadership during the 1780s. A whole galaxy of ex-radicals, ex-decentralists, and ex-libertarians, found in their old age that they could comfortably live in the new Establishment. The list of such defections is impressive, including John Adams, Sam Adams, John Hancock, Benjamin Rush, Thomas Paine, Alexander McDougall, Isaac Sears, and Christopher Gadsden. Perhaps an explanation of many of the defectors (Sam Adams, Sears, McDougall, Gadsden, and Paine) was the rightward shift of the big-city artisans who provided these men with their political power base.

Conversely, the Left in 1788 was very apt to have been on the Left in the early years of the Revolution. Among those faithful to the liberal cause: Luther Martin, James Warren, Elbridge Gerry, George Clinton, Abraham Yates, generally the Clintonians in New York, the Constitutionalist Party in Pennsylvania fighting against the counterinsurgency of the conservative Republican Party (except for defections like Paine), Richard Henry Lee, Patrick Henry, and Thomas Person of the old radical Regulator movement in North Carolina. An important test of this hypothesis would be to find individuals or groups who were on the Right in 1776 but had shifted sharply leftward by 1788. Prominent men in that category are undoubtedly rare indeed.

If, then, the Constitution was a counterrevolution, what *kind* of a reactionary movement was it? Contrary to the famous "Beard Thesis," it was not at all a struggle between a sound-money "creditor class" against a small-farmer "debtor class" in favor of inflation and paper money. These were categories that Beard impermissibly smuggled from his experience of the monetary struggles of the late nineteenth century. It is impermissible to speak of debtor and creditor "classes," for these are categories that shift from month-to-month and even day-to-day. Consequently, while it is true that paper money is likely to be favored by debtors, the aggressive debtors were far more likely to be wealthy merchants and great planters than rural farmers far removed from the seats of financial and political power. Wealthy mercantilists have higher credit ratings, can do more with borrowed money, and have much stronger political connections that allow them to secure favorable legislation. In truth, most groups, especially most of the wealthy, favored paper money; the difference came largely in the *ways* in which that money could be emitted and in whether legal-tender laws would accompany them. The oppressive form of debt, against which, for example, the Shaysites rebelled, was not private debt but *public* debt, i.e., against the fastening of a Revolutionary War debt owned by the wealthier classes upon the masses and small farmers who would be taxed to pay for it.

The Constitutional counterrevolution, then, was not a struggle of sound-money men against inflationists or creditors against debtors. Jackson Turner Main's brilliant demonstration that it was a conflict of commercial versus non-commercial factions can be subsumed under a broader truth. It was, as Patrick Henry grasped, a struggle of power and privilege, and to a lesser extent, of aristocracy against democracy. Those familiar categories can also be subsumed in the Liberty versus Power dichotomy, for while aristocracy was the most determined to acquire special privileges, they could not have won without the lures of apparent privileges offered to the urban artisans.

Contrary to Forrest McDonald, the Antifederalists have received a poor historical press, and even the most supposedly extreme Antifederalist historian dedicated his book on the formation of the Constitution to James Madison. He concluded his book as follows:

> Today, Americans continue to debate, as they have ever since the eighteenth century, about the division of power between the states and the central government, and about the role the latter should play in the economy and social life of the nation. Such debate had validity in an earlier and simpler age, but it is now little more than a romantic exercise. Although the Constitution itself remains what it was, the realities of political life in the twentieth century have created an all-powerful national government in fact.[4]

And Staughton Lynd, though utilizing the commercial/non-commercial view of the struggle, and sympathetic to the individualist-libertarianism of the Antifederalists, concludes that Federalism was right by turning to "'positive, planful government'" to "'promote, guide, and discipline' all economic enterprise towards national goals." All this was justified, and even an aggressive internationalist policy was needed "to protect American economic independence" and secure "national economic development."[5]

---

[4]Jensen, *The Making of the American Constitution*, p. 151. Forrest McDonald, "The Anti-Federalists, 1781–1789," *Wisconsin Magazine of History* (Spring 1963): 214.

[5]Staughton Lynd, "Reviewed Works: *The Antifederalists: Critics of the Constitution,*

Professor Cecilia Keyna has derided the Antifederalists as "men of little faith," i.e., little faith in political power.[6] Some recent historians have termed the Federalists "radicals" and liberal reformers, and the Antifederalists "conservatives" because the Federalists favored a sharp change in the *status quo*, while the Antifederalists did not. But to base the concept of radicals versus conservatives solely on the formal fact of change, regardless of context, is to (a) blur the critical difference between revolution and counterrevolution and (b) to arrive at such conceptual absurdities as designating Francisco Franco's rebellion in the Spanish Civil War of the 1930s as "radical," while the Spanish Loyalists were "conservative." But the point is that this "little faith" was precisely in the tradition of the American Revolution Bernard Bailyn writes of the revolutionary thinkers:

> Most commonly the discussion of power centered on its essential characteristic of aggressiveness: its endlessly propulsive tendency to expand itself beyond legitimate boundaries. ... The image most commonly used was that of the act of trespassing. Power, it was said over and over again, has "an encroaching nature"; ... power is "grasping" and "tenacious" in its nature; "what it seizes it will retain." Sometimes power "is like the ocean, not easily admitting limits to be fixed in it." Sometimes it is "like a cancer, it eats faster and faster every hour." ... It is everywhere in public life, and everywhere it is threatening, pushing, and grasping; and too often in the end it destroys its benign—necessarily benign—victim.
>
> What gave transcendent importance to the aggressiveness of power was the fact that its natural prey, its necessary victim, was liberty, or law, or right. The public world these writers saw was divided into distinct, contrasting, and innately antagonistic spheres: the sphere of power and the sphere of liberty or right. The one was brutal, ceaselessly active, and heedless; the other was delicate, passive, and sensitive. The one must be

1781–1788 by Jackson T. Main" and "*Alexander Hamilton: The National Adventure, 1788–1804* by Broadus Mitchell" (Spring 1964), pp. 222–23.

[6]Cecilia M. Kenyon, "Men of Little Faith: The Anti-Federalists on the Nature of Representative Government," *The William and Mary Quarterly* (January 1955): 3–43.

resisted, the other defended, and the two must never be confused.[7]

The Federalists, on the other hand, in their faith in quasi-monarchical power, especially with themselves in the driver's seat, are strongly reminiscent of the Tories—another indication of continuity in the ideological struggle and of the Federalist movement as a reaction against the spirit of the American Revolution. Forrest McDonald is the latest historian to treat the adoption of the Constitution as a counterrevolution in restoring Toryism. However, in contrast to earlier historians of a similar view, McDonald extravagantly eulogizes this process. Apparently for McDonald, the American Revolution was the first step down the inevitable road to Bolshevism, a fate from which America was saved only by the "miracle ... of all ages to come" of the Federalists, "giants" "who spoke in the name of the nation." Happily for McDonald, the giants triumphed instead of those "who, in 1787 and 1788, spoke in the name of the people and of popular 'rights.'"[8]

Overall, it should be evident that the Constitution was a counterrevolutionary reaction to the libertarianism and decentralization embodied in the American Revolution. The Antifederalists, supporting states' rights and critical of a strong national government, were decisively beaten by the Federalists, who wanted such a polity under the guise of democracy in order to enhance their own interests and institute a British-style mercantilism over the country. Most historians have taken the side of the Federalists because they support a strong national government that has the power to tax and regulate, call forth armies and invade other countries, and cripple the power of the states. The enactment of the Constitution in 1788 drastically changed the course of American history from its natural decentralized and libertarian direction to an omnipresent leviathan that fulfilled all of the Antifederalists' fears.

---

[7]Bernard Bailyn, *Pamphleteers of the American Revolution, 1750–1776* (Cambridge, MA: Belknap Press of Harvard University Press, 1965), pp. 38–39. [Editor's remarks] Bailyn later reprinted this statement in his famous *The Ideological Origins of the American Revolution* (Cambridge, MA: Harvard University Press, 1967), pp. 56–58, a book that Rothbard heavily used when revising his *Conceived in Liberty* series but came out after the original draft of volume five was written.

[8]McDonald, *E Pluribus Unum*, p. 371.

With the ratification of the Constitution and the Bill of Rights, the new government was now a fact and the Antifederalists would never again agitate for another constitutional convention to weaken American national power and return to a more decentralized and restrained polity. From now on American liberals, relying on the Bill of Rights and the Tenth Amendment, would go forth and do battle for Liberty and against Power *within* the framework of the American Constitution as states'-righters and Constitutionalists. Their battle would be a long and gallant one, but ultimately doomed to fail, for by accepting the Constitution, the liberals would only play with dice loaded implacably against them. The Constitution, with its inherently broad powers and elastic clauses, would increasingly support an ever larger and more powerful central government. In the long run, the liberals, though they could and did run a gallant race, were doomed to lose— and lose indeed they did. In a sense, the supposedly unrealistic radicals who would totally reject the Constitution and try to rend it asunder (in different ways and from very different perspectives, e.g., the Whiskey Rebels, William Lloyd Garrison, John Brown, and the secessionists of the South) would be far more perceptive about the realities and the potentials of the American constitutional system than those liberals working within it.[9]

---

[9][Editor's footnote] For Rothbard's analysis of these individuals and events, see Murray Rothbard, "Psychoanalysis as a Weapon," *Mises Daily* (2006 [1980]); "The Whiskey Rebellion: A Model for Our Time?" *The Free Market* (September 1994): 1, 8; "America's Two Just Wars: 1775 and 1861," in *The Costs of War: America's Pyrrhic Victories*, ed. John Denson (Auburn, AL: Mises Institute, 1999), pp. 119–33; "Report on George B. DeHuszar and Thomas Hulbert Stevenson, *A History of the American Republic*, 2 vols." in *Strictly Confidential: The Private Volker Fund Memos of Murray N. Rothbard*, ed. David Gordon (Auburn, AL: Mises Institute, 2010), pp. 125–31.

Bibliography

Note: Only the works cited in the manuscript are listed here.

Abernethy, Thomas P. *Western Lands and the American Revolution.* New York: Russell and Russell, 1959.

Bailyn, Bernard. *Pamphleteers of the American Revolution, 1750–1776.* Cambridge, MA: Belknap Press of Harvard University Press, 1965.

Beard, Charles A. *An Economic Interpretation of the Constitution of the United States.* New York: Macmillan, 1961.

Bemis, Samuel F. *Pinckney's Treaty: America's Advantage from Europe's Distress.* New Haven, CT: Yale University Press, 1960.

Benton, William A. "Pennsylvania Revolutionary Officers and the Federal Constitution." *Pennsylvania History* (October 1964).

Brant, Irving. *James Madison: Father of the Constitution, 1787–1800.* New York: The Bobbs-Merrill Company, 1950.

Brunhouse, Robert L. *The Counter Revolution in Pennsylvania, 1776–1790.* Harrisburg: The Historical Society of Pennsylvania, 1942.

Burnett, Edmund C. *The Continental Congress.* New York: W.W. Norton and Co., 1964.

Dalberg-Acton, J.E.E. *Essays on Freedom and Power.* Boston: Beacon Press, 1948.

Dauer, Manning J. *The Adams Federalists.* Boston: Johns Hopkins Press, 1953.

Dorfman, Joseph. "Review of Ferguson, *The Power of the Purse.*" *The William and Mary Quarterly* (April 1961).

——. *The Economic Mind in American Civilization, 1606–1865.* New York: The Viking Press, 1946. Vol. 1.

Elliot, Jonathan ed. *The Debates in the Several State Conventions, on the Adoption of the Federal Constitution.* Philadelphia: J.B. Lippincott Company, 1836. Vols. 2 and 3.

Farrand, Max. *The Records of the Federal Convention of 1787.* New Haven, CT: Yale University Press, 1911. Vols. 1 and 2.

Ferguson, James. "Review of Forrest McDonald, *E Pluribus Unum.*" *The William and Mary Quarterly* (January 1966).

——. *The Power of the Purse.* Chapel Hill: University of North Carolina Press, 1961.

Fischer, David H. "The Myth of the Essex Junto." *The William and Mary Quarterly* (April 1964).

Ford, Paul L. ed. *Essays on the Constitution of the United States.* Brooklyn, New York: Historical Printing Club, 1892.

Hagan, William T. *American Indians.* Chicago: University of Chicago Press, 1961.

Hammond, Bray. *Banks and Politics in America.* Princeton, NJ: Princeton University Press, 1957.

Jensen, Merrill. *The Making of the American Constitution.* Princeton, NJ: D. Van Nostrand Co., 1964.

——. *The New Nation.* New York: Knopf, 1950.

Kenyon, Cecilia M. "Men of Little Faith: The Anti-Federalists on the Nature of Representative Government." *The William and Mary Quarterly* (January 1955).

Lynd, Staughton. "Abraham Yates' History of the Movement for the U.S. Constitution." *The William and Mary Quarterly* (April 1963).

———. *Anti-Federalism in Dutchess County, New York*. Chicago: Loyola University Press, 1962.

———. "Reviewed Works: *The Antifederalists: Critics of the Constitution, 1781–1788* by Jackson T. Main; *Alexander Hamilton: The National Adventure, 1788–1804* by Broadus Mitchell" (Spring 1964).

———. "The Abolitionist Critique of the United States Constitution." In Martin Duberman, ed., *The Antislavery Vanguard*. Princeton, NJ: Princeton University Press, 1965.

———. "The Revolution and the Common Man: Farm Tenants and Artisans in New York Politics, 1777–1788." Unpublished Ph.D. dissertation, Columbia University, 1962.

McDonald, Forrest. "The Anti-Federalists, 1781–1789." *Wisconsin Magazine of History* (Spring 1963).

———. *E Pluribus Unum*. Boston: Houghton Mifflin, 1979 [1965].

———. *We the People: The Economic Origins of the Constitution*. Chicago: University of Chicago Press, 1958.

McMaster, John and Frederick Stone, eds. *Pennsylvania and the Federal Constitution, 1787–1788*. Lancaster: The Historical Society of Pennsylvania, 1888.

Main, Jackson T. "Sectional Politics in Virginia, 1781–1787." *The William and Mary Quarterly* (January 1955).

———. *The Antifederalists: Critics of the Constitution, 1781–1788*. Chapel Hill: University of North Carolina Press, 2004 [1961].

Malone, Dumas. *Jefferson and the Rights of Man*. Boston: Little, Brown and Co., 1951.

Miller, Harry E. *Banking Theories in the United States Before 1860*. Cambridge, MA: Harvard University Press, 1927.

Miller, John C. *Alexander Hamilton and the Growth of the New Nation*. New York: Harper & Row, 1959.

———. *Sam Adams: Pioneer in Propaganda*. Stanford, CA: Stanford University Press, 1936.

Morris, Richard B. "Insurrection in Massachusetts." In Daniel Aaron, ed., *America in Crisis*. New York: Knopf, 1952.

Nettels, Curtis P. *The Emergence of a National Economy, 1775–1815*. New York: Holt, Rinehart and Winston, 1962.

Nevins, Allan. *The American States During and After the Revolution, 1775–1789*. New York: Macmillan, 1924.

Patterson, Bennet B. *The Forgotten Ninth Amendment*. Indianapolis, IN: Bobs-Merrill, 1955.

Pittman, R. C. "Jasper Yeates's Notes on the Pennsylvania Ratifying Convention, 1787." *The William and Mary Quarterly* (April 1965).

Rossiter, Clinton, ed. *The Federalist Papers*. New York: New American Library, 1961.

Rutland, Robert A. *George Mason: Reluctant Statesman*. New York: Holt, Rinehart and Winston, 1961.

———. *The Birth of the Bill of Rights, 1776–1791*. Chapel Hill: University of North Carolina Press, 1955.

Sakolski, A. M. *The Great American Land Bubble*. New York: Harper & Brothers Publishers, 1932.

Spaulding, E. W. *New York in the Critical Period, 1783–1789*. New York: Columbia University Press, 1932.

Taylor, Robert J. *Western Massachusetts in the Revolution.* Providence, RI: Brown University Press, 1954.

U.S. Reports: Griswold v. Connecticut, 381 U.S. 479 (1965).

Van de Water, Frederic F. *The Reluctant Republic: Vermont, 1724–1791.* Cornwall, NY: Cornwall Press, 1941.

Ver Steeg, Clarence L. "The American Revolution Considered as an Economic Movement." *Huntington Library Quarterly* (August 1957).

White, Leonard D. *The Federalists: A Study in Administrative History.* New York: The Macmillan Company, 1956.

Williams, William A. *The Contours of American History.* Cleveland, OH: World Publishing Company, 1961.

Williamson, Chilton. *Vermont in Quandary, 1763–1825.* Montpelier: Vermont Historical Society, 1949.

Index of Names

Compiled by Patrick Newman

Index of Subjects

Compiled by Patrick Newman

330